THE BOLSHEVIK REVOLUTION AND RUSSIAN CIVIL WAR

**Other Titles in the Greenwood Press Guides
to Historic Events of the Twentieth Century**
Randall M. Miller, Series Editor

The Persian Gulf Crisis
Steve A. Yetiv

World War I
Neil M. Heyman

The Civil Rights Movement
Peter B. Levy

The Breakup of Yugoslavia and the
War in Bosnia
Carole Rogel

Islamic Fundamentalism
Lawrence Davidson

Frontiers in Space Exploration
Roger D. Launius

The Collapse of Communism in the
Soviet Union
William E. Watson

Origins and Development of the
Arab-Israeli Conflict
Ann M. Lesch and Dan Tschirgi

The Rise of Fascism in Europe
George P. Blum

The Cold War
Katherine A. S. Sibley

The War in Vietnam
Anthony O. Edmonds

World War II
Loyd E. Lee

The Unification of Germany, 1989–1990
Richard A. Leiby

The Environmental Crisis
Miguel A. Santos

Castro and the Cuban Revolution
Thomas M. Leonard

The End of Apartheid in South Africa
Lindsay Michie Eades

The Korean Conflict
Burton I. Kaufman

The Watergate Crisis
Michael A. Genovese

The Chinese Revolution
Edward J. Lazzerini

The Women's Liberation Movement
in America
Kathleen Berkeley

The 1960s Cultural Revolution
John McWilliams

Anatomy of the Cuban Missile Crisis
James Nathan

The Great Depression and the New Deal
Robert F. Himmelberg

THE BOLSHEVIK REVOLUTION AND RUSSIAN CIVIL WAR

Rex A. Wade

Greenwood Press Guides to
Historic Events of the Twentieth Century
Randall M. Miller, Series Editor

Greenwood Press
Westport, Connecticut • London

Library of Congress Cataloging-in-Publication Data

Wade, Rex A.
  The Bolshevik revolution and Russian Civil War / Rex A. Wade.
    p.   cm.—(Greenwood guides to historic events of the twentieth century,
  ISSN 1092–177X)
  Includes bibliographical references and index.
  ISBN 0–313–29974–9 (alk. paper)
    1. Soviet Union—History—Revolution, 1917–1921.   I. Title.   II. Greenwood
  Press guides to historic events of the twentieth century.
  DK265.W23   2001
  947.084′1—dc21   00–035322

British Library Cataloguing in Publication Data is available.

Library of Congress Catalog Card Number: 00–035322
ISBN: 0–313–29974–9
ISSN: 1092–177X

First published in 2001

Greenwood Press, 88 Post Road West, Westport, CT 06881
An imprint of Greenwood Publishing Group, Inc.
www.greenwood.com

Printed in the United States of America

∞™

The paper used in this book complies with the
Permanent Paper Standard issued by the National
Information Standards Organization (Z39.48–1984).

10 9 8 7 6 5 4 3 2 1

Front cover photograph: Student Militia volunteers and soldiers fire on suspected police snipers.

Back cover photograph: May Day Celebration, Petrograd, 1917.

Copyright Acknowledgments

Contents

A photo essay follows page 84

Series Foreword

As the twenty-first century opens, it is time to take stock of the political, social, economic, intellectual, and cultural forces and factors that made the twentieth century the most dramatic period of change in history. To that end, the Greenwood Press Guides to Historic Events of the Twentieth Century presents interpretive histories of the most significant events of the century. Each book in the series combines narrative history and analysis with primary documents and biographical sketches, with an eye to providing both a reference guide to the principal persons, ideas, and experiences defining each historic event, and a reliable, readable overview of that event. Each book provides analyses and discussions, grounded in both primary and secondary sources, of the causes and consequences, in thought and action, that give meaning to the historic event under review. By assuming a historical perspective, drawing on the latest and best writing on each subject, and offering fresh insights, each book promises to explain how and why a particular event defined the twentieth century. No consensus about the meaning of the twentieth century emerges from the series, but, collectively, the books identify the most salient concerns of the century. In so doing, the series reminds us of the many ways those historic events continue to affect our lives.

Each book follows a similar format designed to encourage readers to consult it as both a reference and a history in its own right. Each volume opens with a chronology of the historic event, followed by a narrative overview, which also serves to introduce and examine briefly the main themes and issues related to that event. The next set of chapters is composed of topical essays, each analyzing closely an issue or problem of interpretation introduced in the opening chapter. A concluding chapter suggesting the long-term implications and meanings of the historic event brings the strands of the preceding chapters together while placing the event in the larger historical context. Each book also includes a section of short biographies of the principal persons related to the event, followed by a section introducing and reprinting key historical documents illustrative of and pertinent to the event. A glossary of selected terms adds to the utility of each book. An annotated bibliography—of significant books, films, and CD-ROMs—and an index conclude each volume.

The editors made no attempt to impose any theoretical model or historical perspective on the individual authors. Rather, in developing the series, an advisory board of noted historians and informed high school history teachers and public and school librarians identified the topics needful of exploration and the scholars eminently qualified to examine those events with intelligence and sensitivity. The common commitment throughout the series is to provide accurate, informative, and readable books, free of jargon and up to date in evidence and analysis.

Each book stands as a complete historical analysis and reference guide to a particular historic event. Each book also has many uses, from understanding contemporary perspectives on critical historical issues, to providing biographical treatments of key figures related to each event, to offering excerpts and complete texts of essential documents about the event, to suggesting and describing books and media materials for further study and presentation of the event, and more. The combination of historical narrative and individual topical chapters addressing significant issues and problems encourages students and teachers to approach each historic event from multiple perspectives and with a critical eye. The arrangement and content of each book thus invite students and teachers, through classroom discussions and position papers, to debate the character and significance of great historic events and to discover for themselves how and why history matters.

The series emphasizes the main currents that have shaped the modern world. Much of that focus necessarily looks at the West, especially Europe and the United States. The political, commercial, and cultural expansion of the West wrought largely, though not wholly, the most fundamental changes of the century. Taken together, however, books in the series reveal the interactions between Western and non-Western peoples and society, and also the tensions between modern and traditional cultures. They also point to the ways in which nonwestern peoples have adapted Western ideas and technology and, in turn, influenced Western life and thought. Several books examine such increasingly powerful global forces as the rise of Islamic fundamentalism, the emergence of modern Japan, the Communist revolution in China, and the collapse of communism in eastern Europe and the former Soviet Union. American interests and experiences receive special attention in the series, not only in deference to the primary readership of the books, but also in recognition that the United States emerged as the dominant political, economic, social, and cultural force during the twentieth century. By looking at the century through the lens of American events and experiences, it is possible to see why the age has come to be known as "The American Century."

Assessing the history of the twentieth century is a formidable prospect. It has been a period of remarkable transformation. The world broadened and narrowed at the same time. Frontiers shifted from the interiors of Africa and Latin America to the moon and beyond; communication spread from mass circulation newspapers and magazines to radio, television, and the Internet; skyscrapers reached upward and suburbs stretched outward; energy switched from steam, to electric, to atomic power. Many changes did not lead to a complete abandonment of established patterns and practices so much as a synthesis of old and new, as, for example, the increased use of (even reliance on) the telephone in the age of the computer. The automobile and the truck, the airplane, and telecommunications closed distances, and people in unprecedented numbers migrated from rural to urban, industrial, and ever more ethnically diverse areas. Tractors and chemical fertilizers made it possible for fewer people to grow more, but the environmental and demographic costs of an exploding global population threatened to outstrip natural resources and human innovation. Disparities in wealth increased, with developed nations prospering and underdeveloped nations starving. Amid the crumbling of former European colonial empires, Western technology, goods, and culture increasingly enveloped the globe, seeping into, and undermining, non-Western cultures—a process that contributed to a surge of religious fundamentalism and ethno-nationalism in the Middle East, Asia, and Africa. As people became more alike, they also became more aware of their differences. Ethnic and religious rivalries grew in intensity everywhere as the century closed.

The political changes during the twentieth century were no less profound than the social, economic, and cultural ones. Many of the books in the series focus on political events, broadly defined, but no books are confined to politics alone. Political ideas and events have social effects, just as they spring from a complex interplay of non-political forces in culture, society, and economy. Thus, for example, the modern civil rights and women's rights movements were at once social and political events in cause and consequence. Likewise, the Cold War created the geopolitical framework for dealing with competing ideologies and nations abroad and served as the touchstone for political and cultural identities at home. The books treating political events do so within their social, cultural, and economic contexts.

Several books in the series examine particular wars in depth. Wars are defining moments for people and eras. During the twentieth century war became more widespread and terrible than ever before, encouraging new efforts to end war through strategies and organizations of international cooperation and disarmament while also fueling new ideologies and instruments of mass persuasion that fostered distrust and festered old national rivalries. Two world wars during the century redrew the political map, slaughtered or uprooted two generations of people, and introduced and hastened the development of new technologies and weapons of mass destruction. The First World War spelled the end of the old European order and spurred communist revolution in Russia and fascism in Italy, Germany, and elsewhere. The Second World War killed fascism and inspired the final push for freedom from European colonial rule in Asia and Africa. It also led to the Cold War that suffocated much of the world for almost half a century. Large wars begat small ones, and brutal totalitarian regimes cropped up across the globe. After (and in some ways because of) the fall of communism in eastern Europe and the former Soviet Union, wars of competing cultures, national interests, and political systems persisted in the struggle to make a new world order. Continuing, too, has been the belief that military technology can achieve political ends, whether in the superior American firepower that failed to "win" in Vietnam or in the American "smart bombs" and other military wizardry that "won" in the Persian Gulf.

Another theme evident in the series is that throughout the century nationalism continued to drive events. Whether in the Balkans in 1914 triggering World War I or in the Balkans in the 1990s threatening the post–Cold War peace—or in many other places—nationalist ambitions and forces would not die. The persistence of nationalism is yet another reminder of the many ways that the past becomes prologue.

We thus offer the series as a modern guide to and interpretation of the historic events of the twentieth century and as an invitation to consider how and why those events defined not only the past and present, but also charted the political, social, intellectual, cultural, and economic routes into this century.

Randall M. Miller
Saint Joseph's University, Philadelphia

Chronology of Events

All dates are according to the Russian calendar, which was thirteen days behind the Western calendar until February 1/14, 1918.

1894	Nicholas II ascends throne.
1904–1905	Russo-Japanese War.
1905	
January 9	Bloody Sunday sparks Revolution of 1905.
October 18	October Manifesto promises legislature, civil rights.
1906	
April	First Duma meets.
1907	
June	Stolypin dissolves second Duma and restricts electoral franchise.
1914	
August	Outbreak of World War I, beginning series of Russian defeats.
1916	Growing popular discontent, among both educated elite and the masses.
1917	
February 9–22	Rising tide of strikes in Petrograd.

February 23–26   Women's demonstrations (February 23) expand to include most of the population of Petrograd by February 25; troops reluctant to act against demonstrators; government barricades street and orders troops to fire on demonstrators (February 26).

February 27   Garrison mutiny; Petrograd Soviet formed; Temporary Committee of the State Duma formed and announces assumption of authority.

March 1   Order No. 1.

March 2   Provisional Government formed; abdication of Nicholas II.

March 14   Soviet "Appeal to the People of the World" for a "peace without annexations or indemnities."

March 20   Tsereteli arrives in Petrograd from Siberian exile.

Provisional Government abolishes all discriminations based on nationality or religion.

March 21–22   Tsereteli and Revolutionary Defensists establish leadership of Petrograd Soviet.

April 3   Lenin arrives in Petrograd from Switzerland.

April 4   Lenin issues "April Theses."

April 18–21   April Crisis.

May 2–5   Government crisis and reorganization to include Soviet leaders in the government: "coalition government."

June 3–5   First All-Russia Congress of Soviets of Workers' and Soldiers' Deputies.

June 10   Ukrainian Central Rada issues First Universal.

June 18   Russian military offensive begins.

June 18   Soviet-sponsored demonstration in Petrograd turns into massive antiwar and antigovernment demonstration.

July 1   Provisional Government delegation and Central Rada reach agreement on limited self-government for Ukraine.

July 2   Kadet ministers resign over Ukrainian issue—new government crisis begins.

July 3–5   July Days; Lenin and other Bolshevik leaders forced to go into hiding.

July 5   German counteroffensive and collapse of Russian offensive.

July 8   Kerensky becomes Minister-President.

July 18	General Kornilov appointed Supreme Commander of army.
July 20	Provisional Government extends right to vote to women.
July 21–23	New government crisis, leading to second coalition government.
August 27–31	Kornilov Affair; government collapses again.
August 31	Bolshevik resolution passes in Petrograd Soviet for first time.
September 1	"Directory," a five-man government headed by Kerensky, established.
September 5	Bolshevik resolution passes in Moscow Soviet.
September 14–22	Democratic Conference to find a new base of support for Provisional Government; debates forming an all-socialist government, but fails to reach agreement.
September 25	Trotsky elected chairman of Petrograd Soviet, Bolshevik-led radical bloc takes control.
September 25	Third coalition government formed under Kerensky.
October 10–16	Bolshevik leadership debates seizing power.
October 21–23	MRC challenges military authorities over control of Petrograd garrison.
October 22	"Day of the Petrograd Soviet" with rallies for Soviet Power.
October 24	Kerensky moves to close Bolshevik newspapers, sparking the October Revolution.
October 24–25	Struggle for control of key points in Petrograd between pro-Soviet and progovernment forces—the former prevail.
October 25	Provisional Government declared deposed; Kerensky flees to front seeking troops; Second Congress of Soviets opens in evening.
October 26	Second session of Second Congress of Soviets passes decrees on land, on peace, and on formation of a new government—Council of People's Commissars.
October 27	Decree establishing censorship of press.
October 29	Vikzhel appeals for broad socialist government and forces negotiations.
October 26–November 2	First wave of spread of Soviet power across country, culminating in victory in Moscow on November 2.

November 7	Third Universal proclaims Rada the government of Ukraine.
November 10	Abolition of ranks and titles.
November 12	Elections to Constituent Assembly begin.
November 20	Bolsheviks take over army general staff headquarters.
November 28	Arrest of Kadet Party leaders ordered.
December 2	Formal armistice with Germany and Austria-Hungary, but informal armistices already begun between troops.
December 7	Cheka established.
Mid-December	Further spread of Soviet power in south and at front.
December 12	Left SRs join the government.
December 16, 18	Decrees on divorce, marriage, civil registration.

1918

January 4	Soviet government officially accepts Finnish independence.
January 5–6	Constituent Assembly opens and is closed by force.
January 9	Ukrainian Rada issues "Fourth Universal" declaring independence.
January 15	Red Army officially founded.
January 20	Decree separating church and state, including church and education.
February 1/14	Russia adopts Western calendar, skips thirteen days (February 1 becomes February 14).
February–March	Cossack and Volunteer Army opposition in south Russia collapses.
March 3	Treaty of Brest-Litovsk signed, formally ending World War I for Russia.
March 8	Bolsheviks' name formally changed to Russian Communist Party.
March 12	Seat of government moved from Petrograd to Moscow.
March 16	Trotsky appointed People's Commissar of War.
March–May	German troops occupy Ukraine and parts of southern and western regions.
May 13	Decree on food procurement.
May 14–28	Revolt of Czechoslovak Legion and beginning of hostilities with Bolsheviks.

June 8	Komuch (Committee of Members of the Constituent Assembly) government founded at Samara.
June 28	Decree on nationalization of industry.
July 2	Allies formally decide to intervene in Russia.
July 16	Nicholas II and his family executed at Ekaterinburg.
August	Denikin's army makes important gains in south.
August 4	Decree authorizing food requisitioning detachments.
August 6	Czechs and Komuch forces capture Kazan, their furthest advance.
September 4–5	Bolsheviks proclaim intensified Red Terror.
September 10	Red Army retakes Kazan, begins to push Czechs and Komuch army back.
September 8–23	Anti-Bolshevik groups in Siberia meet and agree to create a unified government, the Directory, centered at Omsk.
November 11	Armistice ends World War I on the Western Front.
November 17–18	Directory overthrown and Kolchak proclaimed "Supreme Leader" of Russia.
November–December	Intensified fighting begins in south, Ukraine, and west as German troops withdraw.

1919

January–February	Red Army retakes most of Ukraine and some areas in west.
March	Kolchak begins his major offensive from Siberia, makes early gains.
March 2–7	First Congress and founding of the Communist International (Comintern).
April 26	Kolchak's offensive stopped before reaching the Volga River.
May 19	Denikin begins offensive from south.
June 9	Red counteroffensive against Kolchak begins, pushes steadily eastward.
October 11	General Iudenich launches attack on Petrograd from Estonia; stopped by October 22.
October 14	Denikin takes Orel, about 235 miles south of Moscow, his furthest reach.
October 20	Red Army retakes Orel, begins general offensive against Denikin.

November 14	Kolchak's capital, Omsk, taken by Red Army.
November–December	Red Army drives south, taking most of Ukraine and south Russia.
December 16	Trotsky's proposal for labor armies.
1920	
February 7	Kolchak executed by pro-Soviet authorities in Irkutsk.
March	Denikin's defeated army retreats to Crimean Peninsula.
April 24	Poland attacks, beginning Russo-Polish War; makes early gains.
June–July	Red Army counterattacks, reconquers Ukraine and drives toward Warsaw.
August 15	Polish counteroffensive stops Reds before Warsaw and drives them back.
October 12	Armistice with Poland.
October–November	Red offensive against General Wrangel (successor to Denikin) drives Whites from Crimea, destroys last White army; remainder evacuated by sea.
Mid-1920–mid-1921	Height of the peasant revolt and "Green" armies in Tambov and surrounding provinces.
Late 1920–early 1921	Red Army reconquers most remaining territories that had declared independence, except Poland, Finland, and Baltic states, which remain independent.
1921	
March 1–18	Kronstadt rebellion.
March 8–16	Tenth Party Congress; Lenin introduces the New Economic Policy and a resolution "On Unity," designed to clamp down on debate within the party.
March 18	Treaty of Riga ends war with Poland.
1922	
December 30	Declaration of Union and Treaty of Union lay foundation for the Union of Soviet Socialist Republics, completed by the approval of the constitution in January 1924.

Introduction

The Bolshevik Revolution, encompassing the Russian Revolution of 1917 and the civil war of 1918–21, remains one of the most important events of modern history. It reshaped the political, social, and economic structure of one of the world's "great powers"—Russia/the Soviet Union—a reshaping that continues to influence today's post-Soviet successor states: Russia, Ukraine, and others. It also had an enormous international impact, for the Bolsheviks saw their revolution as the beginning of an international revolution and transformation of human political, economic, social, and cultural patterns. It inspired Communist movements in Europe, America, and across the globe, and offered the Soviet political and economic system as an alternative to both the Western market democracies and the traditional societies of Asia and Africa. Moreover, the Bolshevik Revolution has the dubious distinction of leading the way in forming the modern one-party dictatorships that became such a widespread feature of the twentieth century. It clearly was one of the (some would say *the*) most important events of the past century.

Despite the importance of the Bolshevik Revolution and the Russian civil war, and the tremendous amount written about them, reliable brief histories have been rare. This book attempts to provide such a history in a new account that brings together both my own long study of the revolution and the fruit of recent scholarship. Chapter 1 provides an overview of the Russian Revolution and civil war, exploring the reasons for the revolution, its hopes and failures in 1917, the reasons for the rise of the Bolsheviks and the radical left, the nature of the October/Bolshevik Revolution, and the course and nature of the multifaceted civil war.

Chapter 2 explores the aspirations of Russian society, what the Russian people expected from their revolution, and how they organized to fulfill their aspirations. The revolution began as a popular uprising, and popular self-assertiveness remained a central feature. The reasons for the outcome of the revolution cannot be fully comprehended without understanding popular aspirations and how they interacted with the ambitions of political leaders. Traditional histories of the revolution largely ignored the people, focusing instead on political leaders, parties, and ideologies. In recent years, historians have turned to exploring the people and their activities, allowing a richer and more nuanced picture of the revolution to emerge, one which gives appropriate attention to the people as well as to the political leaders, to the social as well as the political history of the revolution. This chapter also brings in people, such as women and front soldiers, who all too often are omitted from the story of the revolution.

The importance of examining social as well as political issues becomes more apparent in chapter 3, which studies the rise of the Bolsheviks and radical left, examines the nature of the October Revolution, and explores how Lenin turned a revolution in the name of "All Power to the Soviets" into a Bolshevik Revolution and dictatorship. It begins by looking at the reasons for and circumstances of the rapid rise in popular support for the radical political parties, the Bolsheviks in particular, in the late summer and early fall of 1917, and especially the importance of the demand for "All Power to the Soviets." It then turns to the nature of the October Revolution, emphasizing its complexity and the degree to which it was part of a genuinely popular struggle for "All Power to the Soviets" and only later a "Bolshevik Revolution." This allows a clearing away of the old myth of the carefully planned and executed seizure of power under Vladimir Lenin's direction, which was the official interpretation in the former Soviet Union and, in a different form, found in most early Western histories, and which is still widely reflected in journalistic and popular writing. The chapter concludes by tracing Lenin's evasion of efforts to force him to share political power, the beginning of the establishment of a dictatorial and repressive regime, and how, by destroying the grounds for electoral politics, Lenin and the Bolsheviks plunged Russia into civil war.

Chapter 4 studies the several overlapping ingredients of the civil war(s). It begins by tracing the military civil war and the reasons for the Bolshevik victory. It then examines the economic civil war, and in particular the Bolshevik struggles with the workers and peasants as the regime attempted simultaneously to construct a socialist society and mobilize the economic resources for warfare. Finally, it looks at the Red Terror and at the cultural and international dimensions of civil war.

Chapter 5 turns to the role of the minority nationalities (more than half of the population) during the revolution and civil war. The February Revolution allowed an explosion of nationalist expression, which quickly produced movements calling for the restructuring of Russia into a federal state with extensive national-territorial autonomy. This led to conflict between the nationalities and the central government. With the Bolshevik Revolution and the dismissal of the Constituent Assembly, many nationalities considered the old political ties broken and declared their independence. The struggle of the nationalities against both Bolsheviks and anti-Bolshevik Russians was an important part of the civil war. The Bolshevik solution—the creation of the Soviet Union as formally a federal state along nationality lines, but under the control of a single, centralized Communist Party—both dampened nationalism (temporarily) and set the foundations for a new nationalist eruption in 1990–91 that helped destroy the Soviet Union and created an array of independent states (Ukraine, Belarus, Latvia, Armenia, Uzbekistan, and others) on the territory of the former Russian Empire and Soviet Union.

Finally, Chapter 6 tries to look at some of the consequences of the Bolshevik victory. It explores how both Russia and the world have been very different places because of that victory. The collapse of the Soviet Union has made it easier to do this. Previously, writing about the revolution raised questions of implicit or explicit judgements on an existing government and ideology, but that is no longer the case, and thus it is easier to put the revolution in better historical perspective, with fewer political overtones, and to assess its legacy more dispassionately. True, there are still both believers in Russian communism and fervid anticommunists writing their accounts (which, curiously, often have much in common, especially in their interpretation of the October Revolution), but they play less of a role and have less credibility now. The significance of the revolution, however, remains. To take only one example, the renewed struggle in Russia today for democratic government, national identity, and over the social and economic structure of society reaffirms the continuing importance of the revolution and civil war, when those issues were first fought out. Understanding the Bolshevik Revolution sheds light on the current problems and controversies. The outcome of those struggles, now as then, is important for Russia, for its neighbors, and for the world.

Writing about Russia introduces special issues of spelling and dating. Russian is written in a different alphabet—Cyrillic—than English, and thus all Russian names and words must be transliterated into the Latin alphabet. Unfortunately, various transliteration systems are used. The text of this book, as most modern scholarly works, uses a simplified form of the Library of Congress system: the "soft sign" is omitted (Lvov rather than L'vov), and "sky" rather than "skii" is used for name endings (Kerensky and Trotsky rather than Kerenskii and Trotskii). I have tried to standardize spelling in the documents to the extent possible, but sometimes that could not be done because of copyright, and thus minor variations occur. For first names, I have generally used the English version of names with common equivalents, especially for well-known people: Nicholas and Alexandra (who communicated in English), Alexander Kerensky, Leon Trotsky, and Paul Miliukov—rather than strict transliteration of the Russian spelling (Nikolai, Aleksandr, Lev, Pavel), but the Russian form for names without a common English equivalent (Lavr) or for less well known people. In some instances, I have used the Russian convention of two initials instead of a first name. Similarly, cities and places are given in the manner most familiar to contemporary readers; thus, they are usually given in their Russian variant rather than in the various nationality language forms (Kharkov rather than Kharkiv, Kiev rather than Kyiv). I also use the name familiar today rather than the official Russian names of 1917 for some cities (Tallinn rather than Revel, Helsinki instead of Helsingfors). While producing some inconsistencies in usage, I think that this common sense approach to names and terms will make it easier for the reader unfamiliar with Russian and already confronted by numerous new names and terms.

All dates are in the Russian calendar of that specific time. Until February 1/14, 1918, the Russian (Julian) calendar was thirteen days behind the Western (Gregorian) calendar. Thus, the February Revolution and the October Revolution (Russian calendar in use in 1917) are called the "March Revolution" and the "November Revolution" (Western calendar) in some books. To get the Western date, simply add thirteen days. This discrepancy ended when the Soviet government brought the Russian calendar into line with the Western calendar by changing February 1, 1918 to February 14, 1918 by jumping forward thirteen days.

My narrative and interpretations of the revolution and civil war have taken form over many years of research, reading, listening, conversing, and teaching. I owe intellectual debts to many more people than can be named and in more ways than I could possibly recall, having had the good fortune to interact with most of the leading scholars in the field. If I have inadvertently borrowed, unconsciously and without acknowledgment, too directly from any of them, I do apologize and hope that they accept it as testimony to their own scholarship and persuasiveness. Special thanks are due to Michael Hickey and Semion Lyandres, who read the manuscript, and to Mollie Fletcher-Klocek, who prepared the maps.

Finally, but by no means least, this book is dedicated, with love and appreciation, to Vola Johnson Wade Hotvedt.

THE REVOLUTION AND CIVIL WAR EXPLAINED

I

Historical Overview

The Russian Revolution was a multifaceted upheaval that not only transformed Russia, but affected the entire world. It was a series of concurrent and overlapping revolutions: a political revolution that replaced the tsarist autocracy with a short-lived effort in the direction of democratic government and then with a Communist dictatorship; a social revolution that uprooted the old social order and temporarily gave unprecedented power to the lower classes; an economic revolution that destroyed the traditional landowning and private entrepreneurial system and replaced it with an experiment in socialism and the command economy of the Soviet Union; a cultural revolution that aimed at nothing less than the remaking of mankind and its basic values; a revolt of the national minorities in the name of autonomy, federalism, or independence. All of these revolutions culminated in what might be called the "Bolshevik Revolution," by which a political party on the radical left of Russian politics managed to take over the Russian Revolution of 1917 and transform it, after three years of brutal civil war, into an experiment with a new type of society and dictatorship. The impact this has had—and still has—on our world defies easy summary or exaggeration.

Why was Russia revolutionary in 1917 and after? The answer lies in the coming together of specific Russian tensions and sources of discontent with a revolutionary movement committed to the transformation of Russia and the world. At the beginning of the twentieth century, Russia found itself in a peculiar situation. Although one of the "great powers," it lagged behind in many of the key elements of modern power, such as industrialization, while large segments of its population were impoverished and extremely discontented. Russia was one of the poorest countries in Europe on a per capita basis, and also was a diverse multinational empire, not a modern nation-state. Sprawling across Europe and Asia, from Poland in the west to the Pacific Ocean in the east, it contained more than one hundred different ethnicities, including about twenty major nationalities. Russians made up less than half of the population (44.3 percent by the census of 1897 declared Russian to be their native tongue, which was the yardstick used). East Slavs (Russians, along with the closely related Ukrainians and Belorussians) composed about two-thirds of the total population; a wide variety of peoples made up the other third.

Political discontent was widespread, especially among educated Russians, who resented a political system that denied them civil and political rights. Russia was the last major power of Europe in which the monarch was an autocrat, unlimited by laws or institutions. The emperor ruled through a large bureaucracy that kept tight control over society, especially the formation and functioning of organizations for any purpose. Censorship restricted open political discourse, forcing most of it into illegal, often revolutionary, channels. Rather than create a more modern political system in which the populace became citizens instead of subjects, with at least a modest stake in political life and the future of the state, Nicholas II clung to an outdated autocratic view of God-given ruler and loyal subjects. Shortly after coming to the throne in 1894, Nicholas dismissed calls for an elected representative assembly, even a very limited one, as "senseless dreams." His wife, Alexandra, constantly encouraged him to defend his autocratic authority: "show more power and decision," "be Peter the Great, John [Ivan] the Terrible, Emperor Paul—crush them all under you."[1] Nonetheless, not even Alexandra's constant urging that he be firm and assert himself could make Nicholas an effective ruler. Mild-mannered, of limited ability, disliking governance, indecisive but stubbornly committed to maintaining his autocratic rights, he led Russia into two unsuccessful wars and two revolutions in just over two decades of rule. Although personally kind and a loving father and husband, he became known to his subjects as "Nicholas the Bloody."

The society over which Nicholas ruled was changing, putting enormous strains on the population and making continuation of the old political system doubtful. Recognizing that industrialization was essential if Russia was to retain its great power status in a world where industrial might and military power were increasingly linked, the government undertook to spur industrial development. As a result, Russia experienced an industrial revolution during the last three decades before the revolution, averaging an industrial growth rate of more than 5 percent between 1885 and 1914, with even faster growth rates of about 8 percent in the 1890s. Industrialization sparked a social transformation with enormous political implications. It created a new, deeply discontented, industrial working class of enormous revolutionary potential. The factories demanded long hours (twelve or more daily) at low pay, amid unsafe conditions, a harsh and degrading system of industrial discipline, and a total absence of employment security or care if ill or injured. Housing was overcrowded, unsanitary, and lacked privacy. Families often shared single rooms with other families or single workers. The conditions of industry not only left workers poor, but robbed them of personal dignity. At the same time, the government blocked most efforts to organize to improve their lot, thereby stimulating a belief that improvement in their economic condition required a change of political regimes. This paved the way for their attraction to the revolutionary movements. Moreover, the industrial workers were concentrated in a relatively small number of industrial centers, especially the "two capitals," St. Petersburg (Petrograd) and Moscow.* This enabled them to have a political impact, especially in a revolutionary situation, far beyond their percentage in the population (Russia remained overwhelmingly a rural society, about 80 percent).

The social and economic changes in Russia also produced a new educated "middle" class of professionals and industrial managers—doctors, lawyers, teachers, engineers, entrepreneurs, managers, and other white-collar professionals and employees. Along with some of the old nobility, they made up an educated society that provided the basis for a liberal political movement focused on changing the political system through reform. This educated society also produced the important, specifically Russian at the time, phenomenon of the "intelligentsia." This primarily intellectual element had evolved out of small circles of mid–nineteenth-century nobles discussing public issues to become the most politically involved portion of educated society. The intelligentsia was generally characterized by opposition to the existing order in Russia and a strong desire to change it. Out of its radical wing emerged the revolutionary parties, and from the more moderate wing came the political reformers and liberal parties.

At the opening of the twentieth century, Russia was a rapidly changing society. In addition to industrialization, urbanization, and the growth of new social classes, the era saw a rapid expansion of education and literacy, new directions in art and literature, the emergence of a feminist movement, na-

---

*The Russian capital was moved to the new city of St. Petersburg in the eighteenth century. In 1914, it was renamed Petrograd. In 1918, the capital moved back to Moscow. In 1924 Petrograd was renamed Leningrad, and after 1991 reverted to the original name, St. Petersburg.

tionalist stirrings among some of the half of the population who were not Russians, a broader contact with the Western world, and many other changes. In this changing world, the old political structure seemed increasingly out of tune and, more important, unable to deal effectively with the needs and problems of society.

Not surprisingly, numerous political movements came forward to offer alternative visions and leadership. Because of the autocracy, these movements were mostly illegal and revolutionary before 1905. The earliest revolutionary movements emerged in the mid–nineteenth century, calling for the overthrow of the government and a social-economic revolution to distribute the land among the peasants. Some turned to terrorism, assassinating government officials, including the emperor Alexander II in 1881. By the early twentieth century, the revolutionary movements evolved into the parties that played the key role in the revolution: the Socialist Revolutionaries (SRs) and the Social Democrats (SDs), the latter soon dividing into two major parties, the Bolsheviks and the Mensheviks. At the same time a liberal movement emerged, producing in 1905 the main liberal party, the Constitutional Democrats (Kadets).

The SRs organized in 1901 as a party stressing a broad class struggle of all toilers (peasants and urban workers) against exploiters (landowners, factory owners, bureaucrats, and middle-class elements), but with a special focus on land for the peasants. Although influenced by Western ideas, including Marxist ideas of class struggle, they believed that Russia could follow its own path of development by drawing on the communal and egalitarian features of Russian peasant society. Soon dubbed "the peasants' party," they became the largest party in Russia in 1917. Under the banner of "Land and Liberty," they called for the overthrow of the autocracy, a broad class struggle, and the distribution of private estate land among the peasantry.

Other Russian radicals turned toward Marxism, by then the dominant revolutionary philosophy in Europe. They saw industrialization as taking Russia down the same path as Western Europe and focused their attention on the new industrial working class as the vehicle for revolution. This led in 1903 to the formation of the Russian Social Democratic Labor Party, or "SDs," which immediately split. The key role in the split was played by Vladimir Ulianov, soon to be known to the world by his revolutionary name, Lenin. A man who by turns could be charming and humorous or cold and ruthless, he devoted his life to a revolutionary seizure of power and remaking of society, both in Russia and throughout the world. In 1902, he published the fundamentals of his political ideas for organizing a revolutionary party (and, by extension, of the Soviet state that followed), *What Is to Be Done*. It became one of the most influential books of the twentieth century.

In it, Lenin argued that the workers were unable to acquire for themselves the necessary consciousness for a successful revolution. That required a small party of professional revolutionaries from the intelligentsia that would provide leadership for the revolution in the name of the proletariat—the industrial workers. This would be a disciplined, tightly organized cadre of revolutionaries, united by theory and subordinated to central leadership. "No revolutionary movement can endure without a stable organization of leaders maintaining continuity . . . [and] such an organization must consist chiefly of people professionally engaged in revolutionary activity."[2] After 1903, Lenin formed the Bolshevik Party in the image of his ideas.* His Social Democratic opponents from the 1903 split coalesced as the Mensheviks, a somewhat more moderate but still revolutionary party that placed greater emphasis on worker participation and democracy. Smaller revolutionary parties emerged as well, but the SR, Bolshevik, and Menshevik parties were the largest and most important.

Alongside the emergence of the revolutionary socialist parties, a liberal and reformist political movement also developed in the early twentieth century. Drawing upon the ideas of West European liberalism and the emergence of a larger urban middle class, liberalism belatedly took hold in Russia. It emphasized constitutionalism, parliamentary government, the rule of law, and civil rights, within either a constitutional monarchy or a republic. It also stressed the importance of major social and economic reform programs, but rejected both socialism and sweeping revolution. Liberalism took its main political form in 1905 as the Constitutional Democratic Party (Kadets), the main liberal party down through the revolution of 1917 and civil war.

In 1905, popular discontents, fueled by the unpopular and unsuccessful Russo-Japanese War of 1904–1905, exploded into revolution. The Revolution of 1905 began when police and tsarist troops in St. Petersburg fired upon unarmed working-class demonstrators attempting to petition Nicholas II for redress of grievances. Hundreds of men, women, and children were killed. "Bloody Sunday" ignited riots and demonstrations across Russia that the government could not contain, as virtually all sectors of society turned against it. The year 1905 unfolded as a series of uncoordinated, overlapping revolutions by the peasantry, industrial workers, educated society

---

*The party name was changed to Russian Communist Party in March 1918. The term Bolshevik was used until that date, with Bolshevik and Communist used interchangeably through the 1920s, but with Communist gradually supplanting Bolshevik. In the documents given in this book, the Bolsheviks often refer to themselves by their official (to 1918) name—Social Democrats. Both the Bolsheviks and Mensheviks claimed this name, so Bolshevik was commonly used to distinguish them, as it is in this book.

and the middle classes, and even mutinies in the army. These lacked the leadership necessary to topple the regime, however. Finally, at the urging of advisors, Nicholas issued the "October Manifesto," promising expanded civil rights and an elected legislature. This was sufficient to appease part of the opposition and allow the government to suppress the more radical revolutionaries, workers, and peasants by force.

The Revolution of 1905 left the political situation unsettled. Nicholas retained extensive authority and the political balance of power between him and the new legislature, the Duma, remained uncertain. When the first Duma elections returned a liberal majority led by the Kadet Party, the latter pushed for immediate reform of the government structure to include "ministerial responsibility"—responsibility of the government to a majority in the Duma. When the Duma opened in April 1906, its leaders clashed with Nicholas's government over a wide range of issues. In July, Nicholas dissolved the Duma and called new elections. The second Duma proved even more radical, with the socialist parties increasing their vote. The government, under the leadership of Peter Stolypin, again dissolved the Duma. Before new elections, however, Stolypin revised the electoral system so as to disenfranchise effectively most of the population and guarantee a conservative majority.

While Stolypin's rigging of the Duma elections gave Nicholas's government a cooperative third Duma, it increased dramatically the likelihood of a new revolution. Nicholas and his advisors were determined to retain as much of the old system as possible and were unlikely to resolve the deep-seated roots of popular discontent. The complaints of the industrial workers and urban lower classes were not addressed. After 1912, increasingly numerous and violent strikes spread across the country, many of them linked to the view that the overthrow of the monarchy was essential to attaining the goal of bettering workers' conditions. A closer link was forged between the revolutionary socialist parties and the industrial workers. At Stolypin's urging, the government made more of an attempt to improve the situation of the peasants, but did so by trying to transform the agricultural landholding and production systems of the peasants by breaking up old communal systems in favor of new individual farms, rather than through the peasants' own demand for land distribution. This, it was hoped, would create a more productive agriculture and, through a class of prosperous small farmers, a conservative political base. Whether the reforms could have worked as intended remains unknown, for they would have required several decades to work out and the regime had only a few years yet to survive. Indeed, however rational from an economic perspective, in the short run the "Stolypin reforms," resisted by most peasants, added new turmoil to the countryside. The years before the outbreak of war in 1914 saw a revival of peasant revolts. Nor were the educated middle classes satisfied with the new political system. The period after 1905 saw a lessening of censorship and government control of private institutions, the legalization of political parties, and other positive steps. The educated classes, however, continued to be dissatisfied with what they saw as minor concessions by the government and a system that was still more autocratic than constitutional or representative (Nicholas II still thought of himself as an autocrat, not as a constitutional monarch). Overall, workers, peasants, and educated classes all remained aggrieved, thus paving the way for a new revolution when circumstances were again right, as they would be in 1917.

Despite its internal problems, Russia played an active role in the international affairs and crises of the age. Expansionist ambitions led it first to consolidate its conquests in Central Asia and then into the disastrous Russo-Japanese War of 1904–1905. At the same time, Russia was deeply involved in the alliance system that developed in Europe in the late nineteenth century and in the complex political affairs of the Balkans. The latter, and especially Russia's patronage of Serbia, contributed directly to the outbreak of World War I in 1914, a war for which Russia was militarily, economically, and politically unprepared and which led, once more, to revolution.

The war that erupted across Europe in 1914 put enormous strains upon Russian society and government, and profoundly influenced the coming of the revolution of 1917, its outcome, and the regime that followed. Russia was poorly prepared for the war and suffered massive losses. Nearly 15 million men were called to active service during the war, and by the end of 1916, about 5,700,000 were casualties: dead, wounded, or captured. Public opinion, after an initial rallying to the defense of the country, turned against the regime, which was seen as having mismanaged the war and as responsible for the terrible losses. The war, moreover, led to serious economic dislocations and worsened the situation of the lower classes. By 1915 protests emerged among all social classes, intensifying in 1916. Among the lower classes, antiwar and antiregime sentiment grew ever stronger. In January and February 1917, a huge strike movement engulfed the capital, Petrograd, and strikes broke out elsewhere as workers protested both their economic situation and the war. The army, comprised mostly of peasants, was demoralized as a result of the heavy losses and the sense of futility. The educated classes mostly remained supportive of the war itself, but increasingly critical of the government. By the opening of 1917, most of educated society believed that the government needed fundamental reform, perhaps even the forced removal of Nicholas and his wife, Alexandra, whose interference was widely seen as a major cause of mismanagement and incompetence in the government. Alexandra's patronage of the disreputable "holy man," Rasputin, and the latter's public scandals and personal intervention into government affairs, alienated even the most conservative supporters of the monarchy and tarnished Nicholas's image. Symbolic of the demise of the royal family's prestige was the popular reference to Alexandra as "the German woman," a reference to her birth, at a time of intense anti-German sentiment.

By 1917, the conditions for revolution were present: incompetent government, a discredited and obstinate monarch, alienation of educated society, deteriorating economic conditions, a revival of social-economic tensions and industrial strikes, an extreme war-weariness, resentful soldiers, and a revival of activity by revolutionary parties. The sense that something had to break soon was widespread. Meanwhile, Nicholas, on whom any attempt to head off revolution through political reform depended, waved away all warnings of approaching disaster. On February 24, 1917, even as revolution was beginning in the capital, he wrote to Alexandra: "My brain is resting here [at army front headquarters]—no ministers, no troublesome questions demanding thought."[3]

1917—THE RUSSIAN REVOLUTION

The February Revolution developed out of a wave of industrial strikes in Petrograd in January and February 1917. It gathered force when, on February 23, "Women's Day," women workers at a few factories, angered by the food shortages on top of their already difficult economic situation, as well as by general discontents over issues such as the war, marched out from their factories demanding bread. They called on men at nearby factories to join them. The next two days, more and more factories joined the demonstrations, which grew to include most of the industrial workforce. By February 25 they were joined by students and broad sections of the urban lower and middle classes, as virtually the entire population of Petrograd joined the antigovernment demonstrations. Soldiers called out to help break up demonstrations acted with reluctance. When the government ordered troops to fire into the crowds on February 26, this broke the fragile bonds of discipline among the soldiers, who were mostly recent draftees who shared the same grievances as the demonstrators. Dismayed by this shooting, one detachment of the Volynskii Guard Regiment, when ordered to form up again on the morning of February 27, revolted. This quickly spread to other regiments. By midday, the government lost control of the means of armed coercion and collapsed.

To this point, the revolution had been mainly a popular revolt with little leadership. What leadership there was came from lower-level activists at the factory level and from isolated individuals who emerged as organizers of factory demonstrations and leaders in attacks on police stations and other symbols of authority. The revolutionary parties, whose main leaders were in exile, had provided little direction during the February demonstrations. Now, however, leadership was necessary to consolidate the revolution that had taken place in the streets. Two groups stepped forward to play this role. One was a group of Duma leaders who had watched the events of the preceding days, concerned about their implications for the war effort, but also realizing that this might offer the opportunity to force Nicholas to reform the government. During the evening of February 27, they proclaimed the formation of a "Temporary Committee of the State Duma," which would take governmental responsibility in Petrograd. They opened negotiations with the army high command to secure its support in forcing Nicholas to make concessions. The involvement of these respected public figures proved vital in the following days. At the same time, a multiparty group of socialist intellectuals met at the Duma building and led workers and soldiers in the formation of the Petrograd Soviet of Workers' and Soldiers' Deputies. This was a more avowedly revolutionary body, committed to making the street revolt into a sweeping social and economic, as well as political, revolution. Indeed, some wanted to proclaim a radical revolutionary government immediately, but most urged caution. The Duma Committee and the Petrograd Soviet leaders immediately, if warily, began to cooperate to consolidate the February Revolution and form a new government. On March 1 came news of support for the revolution in Moscow and other cities. On March 2, the Duma and Soviet negotiators announced formation of a "Provisional Government" that would govern Russia until a new governmental system could be created by a Constituent Assembly, which was to be elected by universal franchise. The same day, Nicholas II, yielding to the reality of events in Petrograd and elsewhere and to the pressures from his army commanders, abdicated.

The new government was drawn primarily from the liberal political leadership of the country. Its head, Minister-President, was Prince G. E. Lvov, a well-known liberal. Politically, it was dominated by the Kadet Party, the main liberal party. An offer to the Petrograd Soviet to have well-known socialist Duma members join was turned down, but one, Alexander Kerensky, joined anyway. He soon became the government's most prominent member and replaced Lvov as Minister-President in July. The Petrograd Soviet leaders promised to support the new government in so far as it pursued policies of which they approved. This political situation, however, was very unstable. The existence of the Petrograd Soviet alongside the Provisional Government robbed the latter of much of its actual authority, giving rise to what quickly was dubbed "dual-authority" (*dvoevlastie*). In this, the government had the generally recognized official authority and responsibility, but not the effective power, while the Soviet had the actual power, but not responsibility for governing. This was because the Soviet commanded the primary loyalty of the industrial workers and garrison soldiers, the main bases of power in Petrograd, and could call on this support in a conflict with the government. Moreover, a similar situation developed in the cities across the country. News of the revolution in Petrograd sparked mostly peaceful revolutions in the cities and towns of Russia. New city governments, drawn primarily from liberal educated society, replaced the old government authorities. Alongside them, local soviets of workers' and soldiers' deputies sprang up, replicating the dual authority in Petrograd.

During March and April, the contours of politics became clearer as a fundamental political realignment took place. This cut across party lines and reflected the emergence of political blocs that were in many ways more important than traditional parties. This realignment had four aspects. First, the revolution swept away the old right wing of Russian politics as represented by the monarchist and truly conservative political parties. It thereby shifted the liberal parties over to being the new conservatives of the post-February political world and the effective right wing of the new political spectrum. This left the socialist parties alone on the left wing of the new political system. Second, at the same time, both the left (socialists) and the right (nonsocialists) split into two subfactions, with centrist and more extreme wings. Third, a broad centrist combination soon emerged, composed of the "right-center" from the liberals and the "left-center" of moderate socialists. The cooperation of these two centrist groups produced the broad liberal-moderate socialist political coalition—primarily Mensheviks and SRs and the left wing of the Kadets and nonparty liberals—that dominated Russian politics from February to October. Fourth, a radical left bloc of Bolsheviks, Left SRs, and others completed the realignment. Moreover, a similar political realignment took place in the major provincial cities, making it a national phenomenon.

Although the Provisional Government formed on March 2 seemed to represent the triumph of liberal, reform-oriented Russia over autocratic Russia, public opinion soon revealed that it was the revolutionary socialist parties that had real popular support. Indeed, as early as March 13, Alexander Guchkov, the minister of war and a moderate conservative, frankly told a conference of high-ranking army commanders that "We [the government] do not have authority, but only the appearance of authority; the real power rests with the Soviet of Workers' and Soldiers' Deputies."[4] The political future of the revolution, therefore, hinged on the outcome of struggles for influence among the socialist parties and within the Soviet. Two political leaders returning from exile with fundamentally different programs of revolutionary action, Irakli Tsereteli and Vladimir Lenin, drove the realignment on the Left and the evolution of Soviet policies.

Tsereteli returned from Siberian exile on March 20 and headed a group that forged the Menshevik-SR led bloc of "moderate socialists" under the banner of "Revolutionary Defensism." This bloc dominated the Petrograd Soviet until September, and most provincial soviets until then or later. The key to the Revolutionary Defensist bloc's identity and success was the war issue. They developed a program calling for vigorous efforts to end the war by negotiations on the basis of a "peace without annexations or indemnities," defense of the country and the revolution until then, and cooperation with the government to achieve this. From May onwards they supported "coalition government," i.e., a government based on a centrist bloc of socialist and nonsocialist parties that united "all the vital forces of the country" in a government of moderate socialists and liberals.

The radical left was ill-defined, disorganized, and lacking strong leadership until the return of major political leaders, mostly from abroad. These included V. I. Lenin of the Bolsheviks, as well as some prominent Mensheviks and SRs, who quickly formed left wings of those parties in opposition to the dominant right and center wings. Lenin in particular galvanized the radical left. On his return to Russia (from exile in Switzerland) on April 3, he delivered the speech that became the "April Theses," one of the most important documents of the revolution. In it, he denounced all cooperation with the Provisional Government or even with the moderate socialist leaders of the Soviet, and called for rapid movement toward a radical revolution. Led by the Bolsheviks, the radicals pressed for more rapid and more sweeping social and economic reforms, demanded more vigorous efforts to end the war, criticized the policies of the coalition government and Soviet leadership, and increasingly called for the Provisional Government's replacement by a socialist government based on the soviets. The Bolsheviks were the most strident, but the left SRs, left Mensheviks, anarchists, and others were a key part of the radical left bloc. Initially, the radical left's extremism was out of keeping with the mood of optimism following the fall of the autocracy. However, their opposition stance positioned these parties and groups to become the beneficiary of any failures of the government and Soviet leadership to solve the many problems facing the country.

The first crisis of the new political system, the "April Crisis," arose over the war. Paul Miliukov, the Kadet leader and new foreign minister, took the position that the revolution did not change Russia's foreign policy interests, which required that Russia continue the war in close alliance with its allies (primarily Britain, France, Italy, and soon the United States). The socialists in the Soviet, however, immediately attacked this policy, demanding that Russia find a way to end the war. Tsereteli's Revolutionary Defensism provided a seemingly viable and very popular program for doing so. Under the slogan of "peace without annexation or indemnities, self-determination of people," it called for continued defense of the country *and the revolution* while actively seeking a negotiated general peace. Miliukov's attempts to defend a policy of war to victory led to massive street demonstrations, with armed clashes between rival demonstrators on April 20–21, raising the specter of civil war. The "April Crisis," as it was immediately dubbed, clearly showed the preponderant power of the Soviet and the need to restructure the government to reflect that. This took place on May 5, when Miliukov and some other liberals were replaced by several of the leading members of the Soviet in what was termed a "coalition government," that is, one that included the socialist parties as well as nonsocialists, primarily liberals.

The formation of the coalition government reinforced the expectations of the population that the revolution would fulfill their aspirations. The role of popular aspirations is extremely important to the history of the revolution. Summarized briefly, the population put forth a wide range of often conflicting demands. The industrial workers who had begun the revolution demanded increased wages, an eight-hour day, better working conditions, dignity as individuals, an end to the war, and other aspirations. Soldiers demanded and implemented fundamental changes in the conditions of military service, and then became the most ardent opponents of continuing the war. The educated middle classes looked forward to expanded civil rights and a society based on the rule of law. Women demanded the right to vote and better access to education. National minorities demanded expanded use of their language, respect for cultural practices, and political autonomy within a federal state. Youth groups called for equitable wages and better educational opportunities. Hundreds of groups—soldiers' wives, wounded soldiers, medical assistants, apartment residents' associations, and others—expected the government to address their needs. Russia became a vast meeting house filled with thousands of committees, associations, clubs, soviets, and other organizations, all advancing the aspirations and needs of their members in the newly free atmosphere of revolutionary Russia. The nature of the February Revolution as a popular uprising unleashed a great wave of self-assertiveness that profoundly affected the later course of the revolution.

The new Revolutionary Defensist (moderate socialists) and liberal political coalition that controlled the Provisional Government after April found it impossible to meet the many aspirations of the population, and the general optimism of spring gave way to a summer of discontents. First and especially pressing, the coalition not only failed to find a way to end the war, but decided to launch a military offensive in June in the hope that this would lend weight to Russian diplomacy in favor of a negotiated peace. Unpopular from the beginning, the offensive soon turned into a devastating defeat. By that time, unfulfilled aspirations, opposition to the war, worsening economic conditions, and a foreboding sense of pending social conflict amplified the demand for "All Power to the Soviets," especially among the urban workers and garrison soldiers. On the surface this meant simply that an all-socialist government based on the Petrograd Soviet or Congress of Soviets should replace the Provisional Government. Beyond that, however, was an underlying demand for a government that unequivocally advanced the interests of the worker, peasant, and soldier masses against the "bourgeoisie" and privileged society, one that would rapidly carry out radical social and economic reforms and end the war. These yearnings came together in the simple slogan of "All Power to the Soviets."

The demand for Soviet power and the underlying frustrations of the workers and soldiers burst loose with the tumultuous disorders usually called the "July Days" or the "July Uprising." Some units of the Petrograd garrison—which consisted primarily of troops training as replacements for the front—had become increasingly discontented with the policies of the government and bitterly opposed the offensive. Their discontent coincided with growing restiveness in nearby factories. The two sets of discontents interacted with each other and exploded the evening of July 3. Soldiers and workers, encouraged by anarchist, Left SR, and Bolshevik factory activists, now took the lead in the agitation. In the early evening, workers from several factories and soldiers of the First Machine Gun Regiment took to the streets chanting "All Power to the Soviets" and other radical slogans. By midnight, tens of thousands of workers and soldiers had assembled at Soviet headquarters, where they angrily demanded the transfer of all power to the Soviet. The Revolutionary Defensist leadership refused and the demonstrations temporarily broke up between 3 and 4 A.M. on July 4.

The Bolshevik Party leadership had not planned or authorized the demonstrations, contrary to an enduring myth that they did so as part of a calculated seizure of power. However, lower-level Bolshevik activists had been prominent among those radicals whipping up popular discontent and the demand for Soviet power. Finally, on the night of July 3, faced with the fact of massive demonstrations and demands from their supporters for action, the Bolsheviks' Military Organization (created for work among the garrison soldiers) announced that it was ready to support and lead the demonstra-

European Russia, 1917

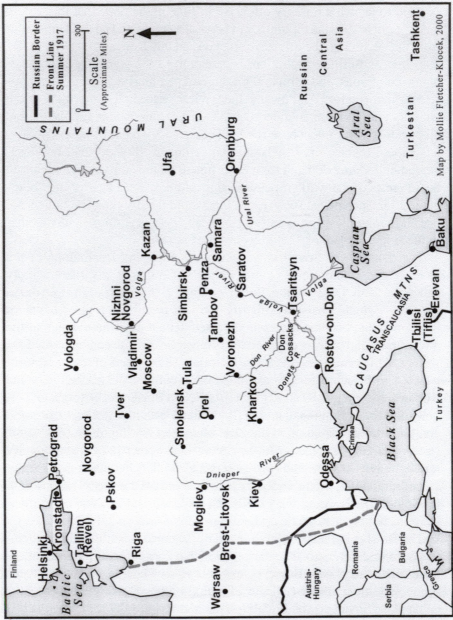

N

URAL MOUNTAINS

Russian Border
Front Line
Summer 1917

Scale
(Approximate Miles)
0   300

Finland

Baltic Sea

Helsinki
Kronstadt
Tallinn (Revel)
Riga

Petrograd
Novgorod
Pskov

Vologda

Nizhni Novgorod

Kazan

Ufa

Orenburg

Ural River

Volga

Tver
Vladimir
Moscow

Simbirsk

Samara

Warsaw
Brest-Litovsk
Mogilev
Smolensk
Tula
Orel

Penza
Tambov
Voronezh

Saratov

River Volga

Volga

Kiev
Kharkov

Don River
Donets R.
Don Cossacks

Tsaritsyn

Rostov-on-Don

Odessa

Dnieper River

Crimea

Black Sea

CAUCASUS MTNS
TRANSCAUCASIA

Caspian Sea

Baku

Tbilisi (Tiflis)
Erevan

Austria-Hungary

Romania

Bulgaria

Serbia

Greece

Turkey

Aral Sea

Russian Central Asia

Turkestan

Tashkent

tions for Soviet power. Early the next morning, the Bolshevik Central Committee (without Lenin, who was vacationing in Finland), announced a similar willingness to lead "a peaceful demonstration" in support of an all-socialist government based on the Soviet. They had hardly done so, however, when the demonstrations floundered. The unwillingness of the Petrograd Soviet's Revolutionary Defensist leaders to take power, news that troops from the front were arriving to support the Soviet leaders and government, and a sensational release of documents purporting (falsely) to show that the Bolsheviks were German agents, combined to deflate the demonstrations. By July 5, they were over. There was a temporary reaction against the Bolsheviks and radical left. The government ordered the arrest of Lenin and some others, who fled into hiding, where Lenin stayed until the outbreak of the October Revolution.

A peculiar situation developed after the July Days, in which the newspaper headlines and political leaders spoke of a conservative reaction, even a possible military dictator, while the events of daily life printed on the inside pages revealed a steady radicalization of the population. The latter was revealed both in news articles about the radical left bloc's capture of one worker or soldier committee and organization after another in elections, and in the general popular discontent revealed in other stories. The question of land distribution remained a major source of dissatisfaction among both peasants and soldiers, and rural violence continued. A general economic disintegration coupled with inflation made workers fear the loss of gains made thus far and fueled industrial conflict. Economic crisis brought hardship to everyone, especially the urban masses, as necessary goods became unavailable or prohibitively expensive. Fears grew about adequate food provisions for the cities and the army. On August 10, there was only enough bread reserve in Petrograd for two days, among other signs of shortages. Separatist movements in some of the national minority regions gained momentum. There was a dramatic increase in crime, ranging from simple theft to armed robbery and murder, as well as violence and public disorders of all kinds. *Rabochaia gazeta*, the Menshevik newspaper, wrote as early as June 22 of the appearance of "new, grievous and even terrifying signs of the beginning of a breakdown." It went on to cite reports of "lynchings, savage arbitrary dealings with those holding different views, the wanton tearing down of placards bearing slogans of confidence in the Government, . . . drunken pogroms, [and] mass rapes of women and girls." Society seemed to be disintegrating and life increasingly insecure. The government and the Revolutionary Defensist leaders of the Soviet appeared unable to meet people's basic needs, much less fulfill their aspirations for improvements.

In addition to these problems, the government was terribly unstable, undergoing constant reorganization. The first cabinet of the Provisional Government had resigned on May 2, to be replaced on May 5 by a new one, still under Prince Lvov. On July 2, this government resigned, and it took until July 23 to complete formation of a new one under Alexander Kerensky's leadership. Talk of this government's replacement immediately filled the newspapers. Some conservatives began to look for a military man, "the Napoleon of the Russian Revolution," to accomplish a "restoration of order." Attention increasingly settled on General Lavr Kornilov, the newly appointed commander of the armies. Kornilov and Kerensky shared an apprehension about the growing signs of disintegration and the growing popularity of the radical left, and both agreed on the need for "order." They meant different things by that, however, and did not really trust each other. Kerensky wished to enhance the authority of the Provisional Government and reduce the influence of the Petrograd Soviet, but did not want to upset in a major way the political balance of which he was the living embodiment. Kornilov, convinced of the need for a "firm government" and with an exaggerated belief that "German spies," Bolsheviks, and other undesirable elements were too influential in Petrograd, appears to have had in mind a much more sweeping political change than did Kerensky. Finally, Kerensky became convinced that Kornilov was planning a coup d'etat against him, and hastily dismissed Kornilov as army commander on August 27. Kornilov, outraged, flung a small military force against Petrograd. His attack quickly collapsed when the soldiers were told by Soviet delegates that they were being used for counterrevolution. Kornilov and the drive for "order" collapsed, with enormous repercussions. The government also collapsed, ushering in nearly a month of renewed government crisis.

The Kornilov affair, with its threat of counterrevolution, crystallized all the discontents and fears of the mass of the population into an even more insistent demand for Soviet power. The main beneficiaries of this were the radical parties, especially the Bolsheviks, who had been gaining influence and support in August. The Kornilov fiasco catapulted a Bolshevik-led radical left coalition into control of the Petrograd Soviet, the main bastion of revolutionary authority, and also into the leadership of the Moscow and many other city soviets. It is worth stressing that the Bolsheviks and their allies, primarily the Left SRs, won control of these soviets through elections, as moderate deputies either became radicalized and switched parties or were replaced by their factory and army electors with more radical spokesmen. This popular support was genuine and essential to the Bolshevik seizure of power in October, something often lost sight of because of the later Bolshevik dictatorship.

With the Bolsheviks and their allies in power in the Petrograd and some other soviets, the question naturally arose as to what they would do. They had been the most vocal advocates of Soviet power and presumably would attempt to implement that. The question, widely debated, was when and how. The Bolshevik leaders were not in agreement on how to proceed. Lenin, in hiding in Finland, now advocated an immediate armed seizure of power. He bombarded the Bolshevik leadership in Petrograd with a series of letters. On September 12, he wrote that "the Bolsheviks, having obtained a majority in the Soviet of Workers' and Soldiers' Deputies of both capitals, can and *must* take power in their own hands." Moreover, he argued, "the present task must be an *armed uprising*. . . . History will not forgive us if we do not assume power now."[5] Most Bolshevik leaders opposed this, focusing instead on the forthcoming Second All-Russia Congress of Soviets, where the Bolsheviks and other parties supporting Soviet power would have a majority. The Congress could then declare the transfer of governmental power to itself.

The October Revolution began, in fact, not in response to Lenin's demand for a seizure of power or any Bolshevik plan, but because of an action by Kerensky. The government, apprehensive over the rising demand for Soviet power and Bolshevik behavior in drumming up support for it, decided on a minor strike against the Bolsheviks. During the predawn hours of October 24, the government sent military cadets to close down two Bolshevik newspapers. The alarmed newspapermen ran to Soviet headquarters, where Soviet leaders declared that counterrevolution had again reared its head and called on soldiers and armed workers to defend the Soviet and the revolution and guarantee the opening of the Congress of Soviets the next day. Their posture was basically defensive. Throughout the day, progovernment and pro-Soviet forces engaged in a series of confused and uncoordinated confrontations for control of key buildings and the bridges over the rivers. The pro-Soviet forces had the greater numbers, morale and determination—nobody wanted to die for the Provisional Government—and by midnight they controlled most of the city, with almost no shooting.

At this point, the character of events changed. Lenin, who had been hiding the past few days on the edge of the city and unable to have much influence on events, on hearing rumors of the events in the city, made his way to the Soviet headquarters at the Smolny Institute shortly after midnight. Lenin now pressed the Soviet leaders to offensive action. Around mid-morning on October 25, he wrote a proclamation declaring the Provisional Government overthrown, which was quickly printed and distributed through the city. Lenin had, against all odds and logic, achieved his goal of an armed seizure of power before the Congress, but he got it because of Kerensky's ill-considered action, not because the Bolsheviks planned or began an armed seizure of power.

During the evening of October 25, attention shifted to the Congress of Soviets. The Congress, as expected, had a majority in favor of Soviet power. The Bolsheviks, although the largest party, had to rely on the Left SRs and others to form a majority. At this point, Lenin received another unpredictable stroke of luck. Shortly after the Congress opened, the right SRs and Mensheviks denounced the Bolsheviks and walked out. This left the Bolsheviks with an absolute majority and in full control of the Congress, which proceeded to declare the Provisional Government overthrown and all power to rest in its own hands.

The Bolsheviks moved quickly to consolidate power. At the second session of the Congress of Soviets on October 26, they passed a Decree on Land that distributed land to the peasants and a Decree on Peace announcing their willingness to enter into immediate peace negotiations. These were important in consolidating their mass support, especially among the soldiers. A third decree announced the new government, termed the Council of People's Commissars, headed by Lenin. Over the next few days and weeks, Lenin and the Bolsheviks struggled to consolidate power and ward off threats to their government, including demands to share power with other socialist parties. An attempt by Kerensky to gather troops at the front and retake power also failed. At the same time, a number of city soviets—Moscow, most importantly—and some front army committees took power locally and declared their acceptance of the new government, giving it a tenuous control of the Russian heartland as "Soviet power" spread across the country in erratic fashion (some areas refused to recognize the new government).

By about November 2—a week after the October Revolution—the Bolsheviks and their allies had triumphed in Moscow, evaded demands to share power, and turned the popular demand for "All Power to the Soviets" into a Bolshevik government. This had not been the expectation of most advocates of Soviet power, who assumed a broad coalition of socialist parties, nor had it been the well-planned Bolshevik seizure of power of Soviet and Western myth. The story of a planned Bolshevik seizure of power under Lenin's direction was a myth of later Soviet writers to glorify Lenin, which was also adopted by Western writers to explain an event they did not understand. The October Revolution was in fact something quite different and more complex. It represented the coming together of the popular demand for a more radical government based on the soviets, the rising popularity of the Bolsheviks and other radicals because of their support for Soviet power, their control of key soviets and popular institutions, some lucky breaks for Lenin on October 24 and 25, and Lenin's determination to turn this to his advantage to take and hold power. The question now was whether they could hold it. Answering that propelled the Bolsheviks down the path of dictatorship and pushed Russia into civil war.

MAKING THE REVOLUTION BOLSHEVIK AND THE PATH TO CIVIL WAR

Having unexpectedly found themselves the new government, the Bolsheviks moved to consolidate power and turn the revolution for "All Power to the Soviets" into a Bolshevik Revolution. This first involved political control: creating a new government structure, developing a means of applying repressive measures against political opponents (including press censorship and creation of a political police, the Cheka), and wrestling with what to do about the forthcoming Constituent Assembly. Throughout 1917, all parties, including the Bolsheviks, had demanded the quick convocation of a democratically elected Constituent Assembly that would have the moral authority to settle the political future of Russia. The Bolsheviks continually attacked the Provisional Government's delays. Elections were finally scheduled for November, by which time the Bolsheviks had taken power. After hesitation, Lenin allowed the elections to take place. As expected, the Bolsheviks received a minority—about a quarter—of the vote, while the SRs got about half. The Bolsheviks were faced with relinquishing power, which Lenin and Trotsky were unwilling to do. Therefore, they allowed the Constituent Assembly to meet on January 5, 1918, but after one session closed it by force on January 6.

Dispersing the Constituent Assembly made civil war unavoidable. The Bolsheviks' opponents, deprived of all possibility of voting them from power, had no recourse but to take to the fields with arms. The civil war was a complex event, really a series of civil wars going on simultaneously. Militarily, the first main phase came in the summer of 1918. The main fighting was in the Volga River-Ural Mountains region, between the newly formed Red Army and an SR-based government that set itself up there claiming to be the legitimate heir of the Constituent Assembly, in which the Red Army prevailed. There was also fighting in south Russia and elsewhere. During the fall of 1918, the moderate political elements in the various anti-Bolshevik Russian governments were replaced by more conservative, military-led movements, known as the "Whites." By late 1918, two main White forces had emerged. One was in Siberia under Admiral Alexander Kolchak, and the other was in south Russia under General Anton Denikin. Smaller anti-Bolshevik forces, as well as secessionist nationality-based armies, existed elsewhere. In March 1919, Kolchak launched an offensive out of Siberia, but after initial gains was thrown back. Denikin began his offensive from the south in May and scored greater successes, but by November the Red Army stopped his offensive about 235 miles short of Moscow. By the end of 1919, the White armies had been decisively defeated. In April 1920, Poland invaded Soviet Russia in an attempt to seize territory, but was repulsed. The same year, the Red Army began the conquest of some of the nationality areas that had declared independence and fielded their own armies, such as Ukraine and the Caucasus Mountains republics of Georgia, Armenia, and Azerbaijan. During 1920, major peasant rebellions and "green" armies appeared, as the peasants, now freed from the fear of a White victory and return of landlords, turned against the Bolsheviks because of the latter's brutal requisitioning policies during the civil war. It took the Red Army two years to subdue them.

The civil war was much more than a military war. The Bolsheviks seized power not just to rule Russia, but to initiate a global revolution and to usher in a new world of remade mankind. The two parts were closely intertwined and derived from their Marxist ideology. Traditional Marxism had envisioned a worldwide socialist revolution, beginning in the most advanced industrial states and spreading to less developed areas such as Russia. Lenin and Trotsky, however, had both theorized, somewhat differently, that the world revolution might begin in Russia, whose revolt would spark revolution in the advanced industrial countries, who in turn would come to the aid of economically backward Russia. This belief had many ramifications. It led the Bolshevik leaders to expect an international revolution momentarily, a hope that sustained them through the darkest days of the civil war. To give form to this international revolution, they organized the Communist International (Comintern), centered in Moscow and Bolshevik-led, to work for world revolution. This belief in coming world revolution also set the theoretical framework for their continual denunciations of other European governments, calling for their overthrow, and for an unwavering hostility to the Western countries that set the tone for international relations for most of the rest of the century. Allied intervention in the Russian civil war in 1918–19 (too small to affect its outcome) did not create this outlook, which derived directly from Bolshevik ideology, but seemed to the Soviet leaders to confirm their view of the world as divided into warring camps.

The Bolshevik Revolution was a cultural and social as well as a political revolution, and the Bolshevik rise had been based in significant part on their advocacy of radical and swift social revolution and the vision of a new and better society. Not surprisingly, therefore, amid the many problems of the civil war era, the Bolshevik leadership moved quickly to carry out a fundamental restructuring of society, supported in most instances by the Left SRs and other radicals. The Bolshevik government immediately issued sweeping social and economic decrees, and continued to do so during the civil war years. During the first weeks after the October Revolution, the Bolsheviks introduced the eight-hour day in industry and gave workers a significant role in running of factories. They extended the great egalitarian revolution that had begun with the February Revolution, confirming the abolition of privileges and restrictions based on religion, nationality, or class, and abolishing all titles and ranks. Marriage and divorce were made civil procedures. Plans for universal education, social insurance, and other socially transforming actions were announced. Some Bolshevik leaders argued that a cultural and social revolution was the goal, with the political revolution only the means to that end. Bolshevik theorists put forth a wide range of ideas about completely altering family relations, child-rearing, and the status of women. The regime encouraged artists and others who wanted to sweep away the old "bourgeois" forms of art, education, marriage, and family and to replace them with some as yet undefined "proletarian" culture. Many expressed these ideas in civil war terms, as a war, a struggle to the death, between old and new, "proletarian" and "bourgeois," socialist and capitalist, worlds. The period 1918–21 was, indeed, an era of civil wars—political, military, economic, cultural, and even to a degree international.

By 1921, Lenin and the Soviet leaders stood militarily successful against their domestic and foreign foes. They ruled, however, over a country with a shattered economy and a population seething with discontent and traumatized by years of war and civil war. Precise figures for the losses of life during the terrible years from 1914 to 1923 do not exist. Overall population loss, however (not counting those who broke away with the newly independent Polish, Finnish, and Baltic states) was perhaps as high as 25–30 million. This includes about 10 million during the civil war, mostly from disease rather than direct fighting (which accounted for 2–2.5 million, roughly divided between Reds and Whites, but including some from nationality and other armies). About 5 million died in the great famine of 1921–23, which adversely affected another 35 million people. Millions more died from other war-related causes. Deaths, even with such horrendous figures, were only part of the story. Millions were permanently maimed, crippled, or left with impaired health from disease, hunger, and wounds. The social dislocations were terrible as well. There were perhaps as many as 7 million homeless children roaming the cities and countryside at the end of the civil war. Untold millions of women were widowed or abandoned, and most of them consequently further impoverished (along with their children). All major cities lost more than a quarter of their populations, and Petrograd more than half. Two to three million, mostly from the best-educated sectors of society, had fled abroad, permanently as it turned out. Large portions of the remaining middle and upper classes lost their jobs, homes, and status (large numbers of women from those classes were forced to resort to prostitution). The sufferings of this period were so terrible that they are difficult to fully comprehend. All of these agonies and travail are the more tragic when compared to the high hopes of the first days of the revolution, when the future had seemed bright and limitless.

Beyond these horrendous population losses and social dislocations, other serious problems and dislocations confronted the regime. The industrial economy stood at about 13 percent, and agriculture about half of prewar levels. Hopes for international revolution were fading. Many of the social and cultural expectations of revolutionaries and the regime lay shattered. The regime confronted a sullen and discontented population. Faced with these problems, which were thrown into sharp relief by the widespread peasant revolts and the uprising of the Kronstadt sailors in March 1921, Lenin led the Communist Party in a startling about-face. At the Tenth Party Congress in March–April 1921, he unveiled two new initiatives. First, he laid the basis for the New Economic Policy, or NEP, by which the Bolsheviks loosened their control of the economy, promising the peasants the end of requisitioning in return for a fixed 10-percent tax. NEP also provided for increased private entrepreneurial activity, while retaining control of major industry and an ideological commitment to central planning. This allowed the devastated economy to recover (it reached prewar levels in 1925–26) and set the stage for the debates over future economic directions that dominated the 1920s and contributed to the rise of Joseph Stalin to power after Lenin's death in January 1924. The second initiative Lenin unveiled at the Tenth Party Congress was a resolution "On Unity," that provided for tighter control within the Communist Party by the leadership. Shortly thereafter, the remaining legal political parties, such as Mensheviks and SRs, were outlawed, turning Russia into a one-party state. At the same time, the Red Army completed the reconquest of most of the nationality areas that had broken away or become autonomous during the civil war, which were soon incorporated into the newly formed Union of Soviet Socialist Republics. The Bolshevik Revolution was completed, and the Soviet Union was born. Indeed, the latter's formation symbolized for the Bolshevik leaders, their domestic supporters and foreign admirers, amid all the ruins of 1921–22, their commitment to the vision of the birth of a new society, a new era of human history, that they believed they were bringing into being by their actions. It proved, in truth, to be a new society, but not the one they expected.

NOTES

1. *The Nicky-Sunny Letters: Correspondence of the Tsar and the Tsaritsa, 1914–1917* (Gulf-Breeze, FL: Academic International Press, 1970), 145, 454.

2. V. I. Lenin, *Collected Works*, vol. 5 (Moscow: Progress Publishers, 1964), 453.

3. *The Nicky-Sunny Letters*, 315.

4. Quoted in Rex A. Wade, *The Russian Search for Peace, February–October 1917* (Stanford, CA: Stanford University Press, 1969), 14.

5. Lenin, *Collected Works*, vol. 26, 19–21. Emphasis in the original. Lenin typically wrote with much underlining of words and phrases.

2

The People and Their Revolution: The Aspirations of Russian Society

The origins of the February Revolution in popular demonstrations unleashed a remarkable outburst of popular self-assertiveness that became one of the main features of the revolution. Freed from the censorship and control system of tsarist Russia, people could express their aspirations and organize for their fulfillment in ways never before possible. A teenaged girl later recalled a Moscow in which "everywhere there were meetings, on every corner someone was talking. Everyone ate lots of sunflower seeds the whole time, so all the pavement was covered with sunflower seeds and husks. Everyone was talking, talking, talking and there was always a meeting."[1] Organizations of every kind and for every purpose sprang up overnight. Amid all the committees, congresses, meetings, speeches, posters, resolutions, newspaper editorials, and other clutter of untrammeled free expression, one can perceive the process by which the various parts of society began to articulate their aspirations and to organize to fulfill them. Through these organizations, they put forth their vision of what the revolution meant and ought to be. Everyone measured the revolution, the political parties, and leaders by the extent to which they fulfilled their expectations. They moved political support from parties that failed to do so to ones whose programs seemed to fit better with their goals. Therefore, knowing those aspirations and the organizations created to fulfill them is essential to comprehending the revolution's development, as well as to understanding how ordinary people saw the revolution.

In the optimistic first weeks of the revolution, it seemed that all problems could be solved and all aspirations met. After the overthrow of Nicholas II, everything seemed possible and the future appeared limitless. Such optimism was ill-founded, for in fact the varied aspirations of society could not easily be satisfied. None of the problems causing the revolution were resolved by the February Revolution except the removal of Nicholas and his government. Russia still faced serious political, economic, and social issues, as well as the ongoing war. Solutions were complicated by the fact that Russia was an enormously diverse society, divided by wealth, occupation, education, nationality, religion, legal status, region, and more. Moreover, individuals had multiple identities and aspirations. A worker in a Moscow factory, for example, could well have continuing concerns about land distribution in the village from which he or she had migrated, plus identities based on work, gender, religion, nationality, and politics. Nonetheless, identifiable important groupings with shared grievances and aspirations did exist. Moreover, mobilization to fulfill those aspirations took place primarily along certain group lines. In order to understand that process, we will take some of the more important social groupings, outline their aspirations, explore how they worked to achieve those goals in the new world of revolutionary turmoil, and assess their impact on the revolution's outcome.

THE URBAN WORKERS

Central to the history of the revolution, key players in all stages of its development, were the urban, especially industrial, workers. Although workers made up only about 10 percent of the population, the workers' aspirations and actions were exceptionally important because of their concentration in the major cities, their organization by the industrial process, the attention political parties devoted to them, and the role they played in the February and October Revolutions and the civil war. The workers' aspirations might be divided into two broad groupings: (1) economic and workplace issues, and (2) broader political and social questions. The two were linked, as political developments affected the ability to achieve economic objectives.

Wages were an important part of workers' aspirations. Wages had always hovered at the poverty line, and inflation during the war worsened the situation. Operating in the newly free society and through their newly created organizations, the workers successfully pressed for immediate wage increases. These early wage gains soon were negated by inflation, prompting renewed wage demands in the summer and fall. The ongoing conflict over wages fueled industrial and political conflict throughout 1917. Workers also sought to improve the unsafe, harsh, and degrading working conditions. Workers demanded safety improvements, meal breaks, sick leave, reformed hiring and firing procedures, and other improvements in the workplace and conditions of labor. The workers moved immediately to get rid of unpopular and abusive managers and foremen, in some cases putting a particularly odious one in a wheelbarrow and dumping him outside the factory gate or in a particularly unpleasant place. Such actions promised real improvement in working conditions, while providing a psychological boost to workers, who demanded to be treated with a reasonable degree of dignity and respect. That insistence to be treated with respect and dignity was one of the broad themes running through the actions of many social groups in the course of the revolution. At the same time, such actions contained an element of revenge against bosses for past mistreatment.

The workers also expressed their views on broader political issues. The war was very unpopular among them, and a demand for its swift end quickly found favor. Resolutions passed at factory meetings called for the convening of the Constituent Assembly, a democratic republic, universal and direct suffrage, and land distribution for the peasants. More broadly, workers were keenly aware that the Russian government played a major role in social and economic relationships and were determined that the new one would be as favorable to their interests as the old one had been hostile. They distrusted the Provisional Government because of the role of upper-class elements in it. This attitude reflected not only social hostility and the influence of the socialist parties, but the extent to which many workers invested real legitimacy and authority in the soviets, Petrograd and other, which workers considered "their" institutions. By summer, resolutions calling for a government based on the soviets, for "Soviet power," were common.

Workers moved quickly to create institutions to advance their interests. The Petrograd and other city soviets were especially important as institutions through which the workers could and did pursue their aspirations. The soviets had enormous popular support because they were class-based organs that pursued unabashedly class objectives. The soviets also were the primary institutions where working-class activism interacted with the socialist political parties. Here, parties put forth their respective programs for approval and competed for worker support, while workers influenced the political process by supporting this or that party. The allegiance of the workers (and soldiers) to the soviets, in turn, made the latter the most powerful political institutions in Russia.

Factory committees and trade unions were also important organizations through which workers struggled to fulfill their aspirations. The factory committees emerged during the February Revolution as the most direct way for workers to organize to advance and defend their interests. Elected by the workers in their shops and factories, they became the focal point for efforts to implement the eight-hour day, reform the internal working of the factory, and achieve other worker demands. A key function of the factory committees was "workers' supervision" (sometimes called "workers' control"), the demand for a larger voice in the running of the factories. The failure of the moderate socialists to support wholeheartedly workers' supervision became a major source of friction with the workers and a reason for the latter's turn toward the radical socialists such as the Bolsheviks. Management bitterly resented the factory committees, and this became another source of industrial conflict. The trade unions emerged more slowly than the factory committees, but more than two thousand were created in 1917. They illustrate both the urge to organize and the unions' importance to workers. By late spring, they undertook industry-wide wage contract bargaining.

Volunteer workers' armed bands, the workers' militias, and (later) Red Guards, were another important form of workers' organization. They first emerged at factories during the February Revolution. They signaled a willingness by at least the more assertive elements to pursue their aspirations by force if necessary. Sometimes they worked with the factory committees to put pressure on management, providing muscle to worker demands. They also saw themselves as having a political purpose to "protect the revolution" and advance the interests of the working class against its enemies. Not surprisingly, they tended to be in the forefront of radical sentiment among workers. Although nonparty in origin, they increasingly allied with the most radical parties, especially the Bolsheviks but also the Left SRs, and played a central role in the October Revolution and afterwards in defending the new Soviet regime.

In addition, the industrial workers formed a host of cultural, educational, economic cooperative, and other organizations to meet their varied needs and aspirations. Many of the factory committees and unions set up workers' clubs, which organized concerts, theatrical performances, and lectures on cultural and political issues. They also provided libraries and a wide range of classes, from basic literacy to the political issues of the day. The workers' organizations also turned their attention to the health and welfare of the workers and their families, organizing excursions out of the city and summer camps for children. This was important, given the squalor and unhealthy conditions in which many lived: on June 29, 1917, Petrograd city officials stated bluntly that "it is simply impossible to describe what is now to be observed in the quarters of the city poor . . . The population swims in mud and filth, insects are everywhere, and so on."[2] The workers were determined to use their new-found freedom and power to obtain a better life for themselves and their families.

One of the key issues of the history of the revolution is the nature of the relationship between the workers and the socialist parties, the role of these workers' organizations in that relationship, and the question of leadership.

Was the relationship one of top-down leadership by socialist parties? Such a view has long been embodied in both official Soviet and some Western histories. Or did the workers themselves have a major role in providing leadership and choosing among political parties, as most recent Western historians have argued?

The leadership for the worker organizations came from two basic sources: the workers themselves, and the socialist intelligentsia. During the long process of strikes and demonstrations stretching from the Revolution of 1905 to the February Revolution, leaders had developed among the industrial workers. They were drawn mostly from the better educated, more assertive, more politically aware, more highly skilled, and longer experienced workers. These worker-activists now took up the leadership of the new organizations, laid out strategies for gaining immediate economic objectives, and provided linkage to the political parties. As the revolution progressed, a dual development occurred among these worker-leaders: they were forced to identify more strongly with one or another political party as parties took on a more important role in public life, and at the same time they became increasingly radical because the Provisional Government and moderate socialists failed to satisfy worker aspirations. The worker-leaders established a critical link between the mass of workers and the political parties, and both influenced and were influenced by the socialist parties.

The other source of leadership was the socialist intelligentsia organized in the socialist parties. They saw this revolution as their opportunity to lead in the creation of the new emerging society and to impose their long-held vision of a socialist society. The socialist parties had long labored to influence the workers and to build party organizations in the factories. Eager to take leadership of the worker organizations, they had to compete for influence and support within them. In particular, they had to win over the worker-activists who provided leadership at the factory level. The workers and socialist intellectuals had a complex relationship. The socialist parties' newspapers, speeches, and debates informed the workers and helped shape their view of events and even of themselves as a class. The workers, especially the worker-activists, took ideas from the ideological smorgasbord the parties made available to them, according to how well they explained reality and pointed toward fulfillment of their aspirations. By their votes, workers chose which parties would represent them, which would prosper, and which would fail. At the same time, the intelligentsia's leadership was critical, especially in larger issues such as government formation and implementation of policies. The relationship of workers and political parties was extremely complex and by no means a one-way street, much less simple manipulation or even just one of leaders and followers.

The workers saw the revolution as the beginning of fundamental changes in their lives and in the social and political structure of Russia. They were determined to have their aspirations fulfilled. Initially, the programs of the moderate socialists appealed to the workers and it appeared that worker objectives could be met within the framework of the post-February political system. As 1917 progressed, however, that seemed less and less likely. Unsolved problems and deteriorating conditions in the summer pushed the workers toward the radical socialists and prepared the ground for a new, radical stage of the revolution. That happened because the workers saw the Bolsheviks, Left SRs, and other radicals espousing positions that they believed supported their own aspirations, not because they were some kind of inert, passive lump molded by outside political agitators. In 1917, Russia was a marketplace of competing ideas, explanations of reality, and proposals for actions, and the workers turned increasingly to those offered by the radicals. Moreover, both workers and radical socialist intellectuals realized the importance of the political arena and control of the government for social and economic policies. Hence the appeal of the call for "All Power to the Soviets" and the growing popularity of the Bolsheviks, paving the way for the October Revolution.

THE SOLDIERS AND SAILORS

The soldiers and sailors were, along with the industrial workers, perhaps the other group whose aspirations bore most directly on the fate of the revolution. The Petrograd garrison had played a key role in the February Revolution and took seriously a vision of themselves as revolutionary guardians. Armed and organized by the miliary structure, the 180,000–man Petrograd garrison was a potent element in the political life of the capital. Moreover, almost all cities and towns of European Russia had garrisons, often very large ones, that influenced local politics. The impact on politics of the 7 million front-line soldiers was slower and less direct, but their aspirations and actions nonetheless also had a profound influence on the revolution. The sailors of the Baltic Fleet, especially those of the Kronstadt naval fortress just offshore from Petrograd, played a very active role and were core supporters of radicalism throughout the revolution.

The response of the soldiers (and sailors—most comments apply to them, as well) focused on three sets of aspirations: service conditions, peace, and general social, economic, and political issues. First and immediately, the soldiers insisted on a change in the nature of military service. After the revolt on February 27, the Petrograd soldiers resisted efforts to get them to return to their barracks and to resubmit to their officers and traditional military discipline. Theirs had been in part a revolt against the harsh disciplinary and hierarchical system of the old army. Calls for election of officers and for formation of unit committees were already circulating among them, while forcible disarming of officers was widespread. On the evening of March 1, soldiers literally took over the meeting of the Soviet, which had just been renamed the Petrograd Soviet of Workers' and Soldiers' Deputies. Under the leadership of a multiparty group of soldier socialist intellectuals, they fashioned the main points of the soldiers' demands into a coherent document and named it Order No. 1. This was quickly printed and spread throughout the city and then disseminated through the entire army, setting in motion a vast upheaval in military relationships which in turn had enormous implications for political power in the following months and for the fate of the Russian army.

Three major changes especially emerged from Order No. 1. First, it ordered the immediate formation of committees of elected representatives from the lower ranks. This quickly resulted in a network of committees throughout the entire army and navy paralleling the military command structure, from the smallest unit through regiments and armies to whole fronts, from ship committees to fleet committees. These committees gave soldiers a vehicle for challenging officer authority, changing the military system, and looking after their own interests. Second, it fundamentally altered the personal relationship between officers and men. The order forbad the use of coarse and derogatory language by officers toward soldiers and the use of honorific titles for officers. Both were standard in the Russian army. Other changes in permitted behavior by officers and soldiers reflected the soldiers' determination to assert their personal dignity and their political and civil rights. These provisions reflected the deep social tension between the educated classes—noble and non-noble—who made up most of the officer corps and the peasant and urban lower classes who made up the rank and file soldiers. As one officer wrote, "Between us and them is an impassable gulf . . . [and] in their eyes we are all *barins* [lords] . . . In their eyes what has occurred is not a political but a social revolution, which in their opinion they have won and we have lost."[3] Socialist agitation reinforced this perception. Third, Order No. 1 solidified the loyalty of the soldiers to the Soviet, setting a pattern of primary loyalty to the Soviet and only conditional support for the government. Social-political affinities would have brought the soldiers under Soviet influence in time, but Order No. 1 hastened the process. As a result, the soviets now held, in fact if not theory, the preponderance of armed coercion in Petrograd and soon in the country.

Once the service conditions were altered, soldiers could then express their feelings about the war and their desire for peace. They desperately wanted an end to the slaughter that had taken so many of their comrades and threatened them as well. Yet, they strongly supported the need to maintain the front and to defend Russia and the revolution. The soldiers at the front initially were hesitant to speak of peace, but as that became a major political issue in late March and early April, the soldiers took up the question also. The result was a quick and solid swing of the soldiers' committees to support of the Soviet's peace policy as embodied in the Revolutionary Defensist program of Irakli Tsereteli and the moderate socialists (defense of the country while actively seeking a negotiated peace). Soldier resolutions soon began to include demands for an end to the war, usually through the Revolutionary Defensist slogan of "peace without annexations or indemnities." Having begun to talk of the end of the war, the soldiers quickly translated that into a peculiar approach to all military orders and potential military actions. They accepted, at least in principle, the need to maintain the front and defend the country, but were reluctant to translate that into active fighting. "What the devil do we need another hill for, when we can make peace at the bottom," exclaimed agitated soldiers.[4] For the soldiers, Revolutionary Defensism implied a passive defense, and when the Soviet leaders later tried to interpret it to include offensive actions, the soldiers felt betrayed and abandoned them for the Left SRs and Bolsheviks.

The soldiers, like the workers, developed organizations to help them achieve their aspirations and to represent them in confrontations with their superiors, the officers. The most important of these were the soldiers' committees, which undertook a number of functions. At all unit levels they became the primary political policy body for the unit, interpreting events for the soldiers, passing resolutions, and even carrying on educational activities. They provided a channel of information for the soldiers and transmitted Soviet resolutions to the men and the soldiers' sentiments to the Petrograd or local soviet. They mediated disputes between officers and men, including the removal of unpopular officers. On certain issues they cooperated with commanders to keep the units battle-ready, but in other cases, they became the active agents through which soldiers challenged the authority of their officers and resisted military action. Ship, base, and fleet committees played similar roles for the sailors. The other important institutions for expression of the soldiers' aspirations were the urban soviets, since most cities and many towns had army garrisons. These soviets provided a means for unifying the garrison units into citywide organizations, and through them the soldiers were able to play a much more active political role than they could through the unit committees.

The February Revolution transformed the formerly submissive soldiers and sailors into a self-conscious political force with their own aspirations and organizations. The committee system, based on the military's own hierarchical structure, augmented by the urban soviets, provided the vehicle for the soldiers and sailors to assert their aspirations and become a powerful institutional force in the revolution and the new political power structure. The soldiers originally elected mostly moderate socialist leaders, mainly SRs, for these organizations, and supported Revolutionary Defensism. With the passage of time and the failure of the government to find a way out of the war, however, and especially after the unpopular June offensive, both front and garrison committees elected more radical, especially Left SR and Bolshevik, leadership.

THE PEASANTS

News of the revolution trickled into the peasant villages during March and inaugurated a massive rural revolution. The peasants identified revolution with obtaining land. Land was the first principle. Second was the closely related goal of gaining greater control over their lives and creating a new economic, political, and even moral relationship in the countryside modeled on the peasant view of the world. The February Revolution and the collapse of traditional authority that followed it created an opportunity for the peasants to fulfill these ancient aspirations. The peasants quickly grasped the fact that, with the weakness of the state and of landowners, they could now act with little fear of retribution. The thousands of scattered villages moved to implement a sweeping agrarian revolution. The peasants would judge the new government and political parties by the way they did or did not promote peasant aspirations, especially land distribution.

While waiting for the government to pass a land distribution law, the peasants carried out a revolution in the village. Acting through their own chosen village committees and buttressed by periodic meetings of the village assembly, the peasants took control of local life, diminishing or ending the role of representatives of the government and nonpeasant elements (policemen, teachers, priests, merchants, nobles, and others). These committees discussed and acted on such issues as land distribution, rents, wages for rural laborers, relations with landlords, access to woods and meadows, and public order. They also met and determined the course of action in the more violent deeds undertaken by the villagers collectively, such as land seizure or estate destruction. Within the villages, the peasants implemented their view that the land by moral right belonged to those who worked it and that in the right order of things each family would have use of only what it could work by its own labor. Expropriated landowners were, in fact, often left a share of land to work themselves.

This peasant self-assertion and self-organizing quickly brought it into conflict with the government's priorities and its efforts to create a new administrative structure in the countryside through appointment of rural commissars at the various levels of administration. The government's immediate concern was the food supply for the army and the cities. It considered land distribution and other agrarian reform issues important, but they took second place in its priorities to the food issue. For the peasants, in contrast, land and related local issues were not only paramount, but pressing. Moreover, seasonal time pressures for planting and harvesting gave peasant demands urgency. Conflict was inevitable and swift in coming.

The Provisional Government inherited a shortfall in food delivery from the old regime and moved quickly to set up a food procurement system, establishing a hierarchy of central, provincial, and district food supply committees. The peasants generally distrusted these primarily town committees. They saw them—correctly—as dominated by landowners, townsmen, merchants, and government officials, and recognized that these committees' primary purpose differed from their own interests. Angered by government policies, low grain prices, high costs and shortage of manufactured goods, plus being concerned over the relatively poor spring harvest in 1917, the peasants resisted parting with their grain. This led to conflicts between peasants and the government's food-supply agents. In some cases, the latter tried to use military units to force the peasants to deliver grain, but these were rarely successful and only fueled resentments. At one village, for example, when the supply officials and soldiers arrived, the church bells were rung and the peasants—men, women, and children—assembled and shouted that the grain would be taken "only over our dead bodies." The officials left without grain.

Throughout all these controversies, the peasants kept their attention focused on their main concern—the land and its redistribution. The peasantry believed that the purpose of revolution was to take land owned by private landlords, the state, the church, and other outsiders and distribute it among those who tilled it, i.e., themselves. The rhetoric of the socialist parties supported these attitudes. The Provisional Government, however, found it difficult to develop a satisfactory land distribution policy. The political parties were divided, even within themselves, on the issue of what kind of land distribution to have. This made it easy to delay action, citing the authority of the Constituent Assembly on so important a matter. The government repeatedly assured the peasants that there would be a general land distribution and created commissions to study how to do it, but in the end failed to develop, much less implement, land redistribution.

Although most peasants waited reasonably patiently for the land distribution, the government's inaction spurred them to begin direct, self-initi-
ated measures to take control of the land and redistribute it among
themselves (a process completed by early 1918). Land seizure was the key
action by peasants, but it often led to confiscation of tools, implements,
draft animals, and even buildings, as these were seen as directly tied to use
of the land. In some instances, the peasants burned estate houses and property records, which reflected a hard practicality about driving the nobles
away and securing their own claim to the land. There was a long-held peasant belief, reflected in various sayings, that if the bird's nest (the manor
house) is destroyed, the bird (landowner) will have to fly away. Now, more
than ever, this seemed a realistic hope. At the same time, the destruction of
estate owners' furniture, art, books, pianos, ornamental gardens, fountains,
and other evidence of a privileged and alien lifestyle provided the symbolic
destruction of the elite oppressor. In land seizures, the peasants usually
acted as a unit, with the entire village participating under the direction of its
village committee or assembly.

The peasants had many other ways to harass estate owners and even independent peasant farmers. Farm employees were driven off. Searches were
mounted by villagers on various pretexts. They encroached on private land
by putting their livestock on private pastures, cutting timber, and beginning
to use the land, ignoring landowners' protests. Each success, of course, encouraged further encroachment. Such actions drove home to the landowner
how powerless he was (or she was—peasants seem to have been opportu-
nistic in taking advantage of women landowners or wives whose husbands
were away in the army). Landowners' appeals to local authorities for help
were usually unsuccessful, if indeed the latter had not been involved in the
infraction. Higher government officials were more sympathetic, but powerless to prevent these actions. Physical violence against persons and deaths
were relatively rare in 1917, although there were spectacular exceptions.
Later, during the civil war, they became more common.

The peasant revolution, while focused on land and relations within the
village, was not divorced from the larger world. Their aspirations in this
realm were very similar to the bulk of the population—peace, the Constituent Assembly, social reforms. The socialist parties, especially the SRs, the
"peasants' party," attempted to guide them on larger political issues, with
some success. The scattered nature of the peasantry across the vast countryside, however, made it difficult to organize them into an effective political
force in the conditions of 1917, and even more so in 1918–20. Successful
physical mobilization of large numbers to bring force to bear at key places
was more important than numbers and voting, and in this the peasants were

at a disadvantage compared to workers or soldiers, although dominant over landowners.

The great peasant rebellion gained momentum steadily in 1917. The peasants took advantage of government weakness to acquire control of the land and of their own lives. By late summer, if not earlier, the government essentially lost control of the countryside. The peasants set up their own local authority largely excluding outsiders. The process of land and property seizure accelerated in the fall, especially after the October Revolution sanctioned it, and was largely completed by early 1918. The Provisional Government lacked the administrative apparatus and the means of physical coercion necessary to oppose unlawful seizures or to stem the tide of peasant revolt. Indeed, the central and local political leaders in 1917 could never really agree on measures for order in the countryside. Failure to implement land reforms not only pushed the peasants to take matters into their own hands, but set the stage for the Bolshevik land decree sanctioning peasant land seizure. The latter, in turn, brought the Bolsheviks the acquiescence of the peasants during the key stages of the civil war, as well as reinforcing peasant control of the land and countryside, at least for the time being.

WOMEN AND YOUTH

In addition to these three large social groups whose actions profoundly affected the outcome of the revolution, there were many others. The non-Russian nationalities played a special role and are discussed in chapter 5. Among other groups, women represent a particularly illuminating example of how one segment of the population responded to the revolution. The war and revolutionary upheaval presented women with new opportunities and perhaps even greater problems and stresses. Women responded in many different ways to war and revolution because they shared many of the same political, social, economic, ethnic, and other attributes and interests that affected men. Non-gender identities were very important as mobilizing factors for most women in 1917, and therefore it is difficult to generalize about women's aspirations in the way one can about workers, soldiers, or peasants. Nonetheless, the revolution did affect them as women and some reacted to it in certain gender-specific ways. The drafting of so many men into the army, for example, opened up new job and civic participation opportunities. While some benefitted from this, many women were forced to take over basic bread-winning and other unwelcome responsibilities for which they were poorly prepared. War and revolution left many such women living in greater financial hardship and physically and emotionally exhausted. Urban women also bore the brunt of housing and food shortages, inflation, and declining public services, while rural women had to take over the farm work formerly done by men. For such women, class and economic issues were more important than gender-based issues.

Russian feminists were one of the most successful groups in grasping the opportunities opened up by the revolution. A feminist movement which focused on the vote and educational and professional opportunities existed before 1914, although hobbled by the general tsarist control over organizations. Invigorated by the February Revolution and the freedoms it brought, and drawing especially upon politically liberal educated women of the middle and upper classes, feminists immediately expanded their organizational activities and lobbied for the vote and other rights. When the initial declaration by the Provisional Government about "universal" elections to the Constituent Assembly did not specifically include women, feminist organizations reacted promptly. The League for Women's Equal Rights organized a great demonstration on March 19, 1917, in which about forty thousand women marched to the government to demand the vote. Despite opposition by many men from all political persuasions, on July 20 the Provisional Government gave women the right to vote, the first of any of the European major powers to do so.

The feminist movement was the achievement primarily of middle- and upper-class women from the liberal political parties; socialist women rejected feminism. The socialist parties had long argued that women's interests were more strongly defined by class than by gender and that they had more in common with men of their own class than with women of other classes. Although the socialist parties' programs called for universal suffrage, equal rights, and programs to provide maternity leave and other specific needs of women in the workplace, the emphasis was on class goals. Most issues of special interest to women, they argued, would be resolved through a sweeping revolution that would transform fundamental legal, economic, and social structures, including property ownership, marriage, family life, living arrangements, the economic relations between men and women, and other facts of women's lives. In general, the socialist parties subordinated gender issues to class politics.

Women of all classes and outlooks played a greater role in political and public affairs in 1917 than ever before. All the major parties had prominent women members who engaged in a wide range of political roles: public orators, agitators, party organizers, union activists, writers, delegates to city councils and soviets, and other activities. Countess Sofia Panina, a liberal and Kadet Party member, broke gender barriers by becoming Deputy Minister of Education in the Provisional Government, the highest government office held by a woman to that time (none held such offices in tsarist Russia). After the October Revolution, Alexandra Kollontai went a step further by becoming People's Commissar (Minister) for Social Welfare in the Bolshevik government. Women gained the right to vote in both general and special elections (such as for factory committees and soviet deputies), which forced all parties to pay greater attention to their concerns. Russian society remained patriarchal and men filled almost all the leadership positions at all levels, while women usually played support roles or focused on issues traditionally considered "women's" (such as education, family, and health). Nonetheless, the newly expanded public role of 1917, along with the right to vote, marked major and permanent advances for women.

The new spirit of public activism and organization affected young people also. They founded clubs and political associations to meet their educational needs, for social and civic activities, and, in the case of working class youth (many of them in their teens), to protect their interests within factories, where they campaigned for less discriminatory pay scales. In Petrograd, a youth organization, Labor and Light, that was oriented toward economic issues, enrolled huge numbers in the spring. Some youth organizations were created by or in cooperation with political parties. Youth groups were subject to the same political dynamics as other groups and moved left politically as the year wore on. In the fall, the politically moderate Labor and Light gave way to a more radical organization, the Socialist League of Young Workers, which aligned itself with the Bolsheviks and laid the basis for the extensive Communist Party youth organizations of the Soviet era.

Freed from the controls imposed by the tsarist government, the population of the Russian empire engaged in a lively public debate and created a remarkable range of organizations to express their aspirations and advance their interests. Thousands of committees, professional associations, unions, apartment residents' associations, cultural and literacy clubs, political movements, nationality-based organizations, and others organized and demanded acknowledgment of their interests. Civic identity and activism were complex, because people had multiple identities and interests based on occupation, income, nationality, religion, gender, political affiliation, and other characteristics. These complexities did not, however, prevent large segments of society from perceiving events from the perspective of broad class or other interests, and from mobilizing and creating organizations to promote such interests. Indeed, despite the multitude of organizations and interest groups, it is clear that most of the population also divided into large social groupings such as those discussed in this chapter, with shared general aspirations which they organized to fulfill. At the same time, all group identities existed alongside and usually within a very important general tendency to divide the society into two broad sociopolitical categories that were seen as inherently antagonistic. These were variously expressed as *nizy* (lower classes) versus *verkhi* (upper classes), "democratic" versus "privileged," soldiers versus officers, "workers" against "bourgeoisie" or "capitalists." These distinctions were widely used during the revolution and civil war in the press, speeches, and resolutions, reflecting a way people saw the larger society and their own interests within it. They not only represented real social-economic divisions, but also took on important political implications as the revolution became an intense struggle for control of government, with full awareness that government did not merely represent the "public interest," but advanced the interests of some groups over others. The Bolsheviks' success in speaking to these popular aspirations and in mobilizing the support of the more important groups and organizations—and in fostering the perception that other political forces were hostile to these aspirations—was essential to the Bolshevik victory in the revolution and civil war.

NOTES

1. Irina Sergeevna Tidmarsh, in Anna Horsbrugh-Potter, ed., *Memories of Revolution* (London and New York: Routledge, 1993), 63.

2. *Vestnik gorodskogo samoupravleniia* (Petrograd), June 29, 1917.

3. Quoted in Allan K Wildman, *The End of the Russian Imperial Army. The Old Army and the Soldiers' Revolt (March–April 1917)* (Princeton, NJ: Princeton University Press, 1980), 245.

4. Quoted in Wildman, *The End of the Russian Imperial Army. The Old Army*, 222.

3

From "All Power to the Soviets" to Bolshevik Revolution

A key issue of the history of the Russian Revolution is the nature of the event variously described as the October Revolution, the Bolshevik Revolution, the Bolshevik seizure of power, the Bolshevik coup d'etat, or, to use the term officially sanctioned in the former Soviet Union, "The Great October Socialist Revolution." Ironically, none of these fully reflect the true nature of the event as it was seen at the time, as primarily an attempt to transfer power to the soviets of workers' and soldiers' deputies under the slogan of "All Power to the Soviets." We will explore the nature of this revolution by examining what really happened and by looking at how what began as a demand for "All Power to the Soviets"—Soviet power—led to the October Revolution and then was transformed into a Bolshevik Revolution, and seeing where the notion of a "seizure of power" fits in. Central to this is understanding how the two most important political trends of 1917—the frustrated popular aspirations leading to a growing demand for "Soviet power" and the rise of the Bolshevik party and the radical left—came together to cause the October/Bolshevik Revolution. Both trends developed in significant part because the Provisional Government failed to meet the aspirations of Russian society discussed in the previous chapter.

ASPIRATIONS, DISCONTENTS, AND THE DEMAND FOR SOVIET POWER

The demand for Soviet power arose out of the failure of the Provisional Government to fulfill the popular aspirations described in the previous chapters and the worsening conditions in Russia in mid-1917. By late summer, it became obvious that the basic aspirations of most groups either were not being met or that early gains were jeopardized. First of all, and perhaps most important, the moderate socialists' program for ending World War I through a general negotiated peace failed by midsummer. This left them and the Provisional Government without a viable plan for getting Russia out of the war (all political groups, including the Bolsheviks, at this time rejected a separate peace with Germany). Peace, however, was an increasingly impatient demand of the great majority of the population. The radicals—Bolshe- viks, Left SRs, Menshevik-Internationalists and Anarchists—criticized the government mercilessly over this failure, demanding peace quickly. Meanwhile, the war continued to put enormous stress on the economy, bringing it to the verge of collapse.

Growing political radicalism fed on the worsening economic situation. An important factor in the mood of fall 1917 was the sharp increase in prices coupled with growing scarcity of food and other supplies. The situation in Petrograd not only was especially bad, but also, given the city's political importance and volatility, especially critical. Bread had been rationed since spring, and in mid-October incoming bread supplies fell dramatically below daily demands. Although most attention focused on bread—the staple of lower-class diets—delivery of other foodstuffs also lagged dangerously behind previous consumption levels. A government conference on October 15 painted a bleak picture of a city with only three to four days of food reserves and little prospect for improvement. Once again, long lines snaked out from food shops while prices rose rapidly, increasing about fourfold from July to October. The problem existed in other cities as well. A survey of the food situation by the Ministry of Food Supply on October 12 registered for Novgorod the bleak entry: "starvation is appearing."[1] The threat of starvation was real, especially for the lower classes, who were least able to take advantage of the flourishing black market with its high prices. "Every discussion in a public place in Russia now concerns food," noted the traveling journalist Morgan Phillips Price on October 8 at the conclusion of a trip along the Volga River. "It is the essence of politics."[2] The food crisis led to riots in some places, reinforcing the general popular perception that the Provisional Government had failed and that radical change was imperative.

The industrial economy also continued to deteriorate, and that in turn helped drive other discontents. Whatever economic gains workers had made in the spring had long since been wiped out by skyrocketing prices, management resistance to new salary increases, and wage losses due to factory closings and shortened hours. Strikes became even more bitter and politically polarizing. The collapsing railroads moved less and less food and materials, compounding all other problems. On October 9, the director of the Putilov factory, Petrograd's and the country's largest factory, reported that it had run completely out of coal and that as a result, thirteen shops were completely closed and six would operate at partial capacity. Factory closings and shortened work hours threatened the workers' very survival and fed suspicions that owners were deliberately using them to throttle the revolution. For workers, therefore, preserving factories, employment, and their economic and organizational gains became the focus of a desperate struggle against employers and the Provisional Government (which they believed supported the employers). Workers pressed their representatives toward more vigorous action to keep the factories working. As the situation worsened, workers turned to more radical leadership and policies, fueling the leftward shift of politics.

Other problems heightened the sense of a society falling apart and in need of drastic measures. Crime and public disorder continued to increase. The newspapers were full of reports of robberies, assaults, and other violence. Lynch law emerged to deal with thieves and criminal activity. In Petrograd, for example, the American journalist John Reed saw "a crowd of several hundred people beat and trample to death a soldier caught stealing."[3] Travel became unreliable and more dangerous because of breakdowns on the railroads and the appearance of thieves and riotous soldiers—often deserters—on trains. Hundreds of thousands of soldiers from the front and garrisons roamed the country in the fall, pillaging, disrupting trains and towns, spreading rumors and violence, and offering fresh evidence of a social and political breakdown. On a different level, the stock market collapsed in September, impoverishing portions of the middle classes and creating financial chaos. The government found itself less and less able to collect taxes and thus fund its obligations, including salaries for its workers, stipends to soldiers and war-widows, and payments that war industries needed to keep working. In the borderlands, nationality groups increased demands for autonomy or even independence, which undermined the authority of the Provisional Government and increased the sense of a state collapsing. The peasants continued to press their claim to the land, and the ongoing peasant unrest and violence agitated the cities and army as well as the countryside, for many workers and most soldiers were peasants or still had relatives in the villages.

All of these problems and discontents stimulated belief in government incompetence at all levels and fed into the growing demand for Soviet power. There was a growing sense among the urban workers and garrison soldiers especially—the two elements most able to bring direct force to bear on government, central and local—that a fundamental political revolution was necessary. This was summed up in the slogan of "All Power to the Soviets." While this somewhat ill-defined slogan had different meanings for different people, at its core it meant the Soviet in some way taking power and replacing the current "coalition" government (one including nonsocialists) with a new multiparty, but socialist-only, government. The issue by mid- October was not *whether* a socialist government, but *when* and *how*, whether to support a transfer of power at the forthcoming Second Congress of Soviets or wait until the Constituent Assembly. Either would provide a socialist government, with the radicals urging the former course and the moderate socialists the latter. In the mood of crisis that existed, the earlier solution seemed ever more preferable to growing numbers of workers and soldiers. Steps were needed *now*. Bolshevik, Left SR, and other leftist political rhetoric supported workers' and soldiers' demands and provided an explanation of why their perceptions were correct. Just how broadly based this government would be remained a source of disagreement, but the general meaning was clear: an all-socialist, more radical government that would implement more radical social and economic policies, end the war, and rule in "our" (lower class) interests.

THE RISE OF THE BOLSHEVIKS AND THE RADICAL LEFT

As popular discontent and demand for action grew, the radical political parties, and especially the Bolsheviks, grew rapidly in popular support. The Bolsheviks had begun 1917 as the least influential of the three major socialist parties. Lenin's initial position after his return from Switzerland, as laid down in the April Theses, placed the party in unwavering opposition to the Provisional Government and to the moderate socialist/Revolutionary Defensist leadership of the Petrograd Soviet. "No support for the Provisional Government; the utter falsity of all its promises should be made clear."[4] This was out of keeping with the optimism of the first weeks of the revolution and temporarily marginalized the party. By positioning themselves as the opposition, however, the Bolsheviks were able to reap the political benefits of the failures of the Provisional Government and Revolutionary Defensism.

The Bolsheviks' appeal was not merely negative, for they also drew support for the policies they advocated. They promised quick action on the problems facing Russia: immediate peace, rapid and complete land distribution, workers' supervision in industry, and various other social-economic changes. They supported the demands of nationality groups for autonomy and championed the claims of specific groups in a way that the parties responsible for government or even Soviet actions could not. Moreover, they provided clear and believable, if often simplistic or even erroneous, explanations for the complex problems and uncertainties of the times. Their explanation that the problems of society grew out of hostile actions of "capitalists," "bourgeoisie," and other privileged elements was more easily grasped than was the working of complex and often impersonal economic forces. The lesson to be drawn, of course, was that the problems of society could not be solved as long as the capitalists and bourgeoisie held any share of power. These ideas neatly coincided with the call for "All Power to the Soviets," which both the Bolsheviks and growing numbers of the population embraced, but which the Revolutionary Defensist leaders stubbornly rejected. The Bolsheviks capitalized on the growing correspondence of their views with that of the workers and soldiers by waging an energetic propaganda campaign in the press and by orators, in which they drove home their criticism of the government and Revolutionary Defensism and highlighted their own prescription for radical change. Their politics of sweeping change, of a revolutionary restructuring of society, aligned them with popular aspirations as the disgruntled population turned toward more radical solutions to the mounting problems of Russia.

The party's success also grew in part out of its organization. The Bolshevik Party in 1917 was a unique combination of centralization and decentralization. A small Central Committee served as its top decision-making body. Below it were city and provincial committees and then on down were the district committees in large cities and the smaller regional organizations countrywide. At the bottom, at the grass-roots level, stood the party committees in factories and army units. The Bolsheviks also had a special Military Organization to work among the soldiers. Not being distracted by the responsibilities of government that affected other parties, the Bolsheviks were able to devote more energy and personnel to party organizational work and to gaining new supporters. Moreover, the party leadership was more cohesive than the other major parties. The Mensheviks and SRs suffered from numerous deep splits that tore them apart, whereas the Bolshevik divisions were less significant. The party had its own divisions and internal debates, but compared to other parties the Bolsheviks were more united in policy and leadership. They had a recognized leader—Lenin—to a degree that the other parties did not, and one, moreover, with an unusually focused drive for power combined with a vision of new society and a belief that only he and his party had the correct understanding of how Russia must be ruled and remade.

The Bolsheviks were not the only party on the radical left opposing the government, advocating sweeping changes, and reaping the political benefits therefrom. Next in importance were the Left SRs, a left tendency within the SR party that became an identifiable opposition to the dominant Revolutionary Defensism (which included the right and center SRs). The Left SRs gained influence in the late summer and fall, especially among the soldiers. A left Menshevism emerged as the Menshevik-Internationalists and was an important force in a number of provincial cities. Anarchists were influential in many factories and army barracks, especially in Petrograd. The rise of the Bolsheviks was in fact part of the broader phenomenon of the growth of this radical left. Radical victories in soviets and in workers' and soldiers' organizations in late summer and early fall usually rested on a left-bloc coalition of Bolsheviks, Left SRs, Menshevik-Internationalists, and other smaller groups such as the anarchists, among whom Bolsheviks were usually but not always the predominant group. Many so-called "Bolshevik resolutions" were in fact joint left-bloc resolutions, and this left bloc provided the majority in many local soviets and other organizations often described as "Bolshevik" by later accounts and even by some contemporaries. What unified this left bloc was agreement on several key issues: opposition to the Revolutionary Defensist leadership of the Soviet, opposition to coalition government with the liberals, a call for some form of Soviet power or all-socialist government, and insistence on quicker action to end the war and implement social and economic reforms.

By August, the radical left's criticism of the failure of the moderates, its advocacy of radical reform, and its calls for Soviet power, began to translate into institutional power. Factories and army units reelected deputies to soviets and workers' and soldiers' institutions, and in the process generally chose more radical representatives. As a result, a combination of Bolsheviks, Left SRs, and Menshevik-Internationalists took control of one after another of the Petrograd city district soviets in the summer, dominated the Petrograd trade unions and the factory committees, and gained control of some provincial city soviets and soldiers' committees. The process accelerated in September, after the counterrevolutionary scare of the Kornilov Affair gave the left a gigantic boost. Especially important was the capture of the main bastion of revolutionary authority, the Petrograd Soviet. On August 31, a Bolshevik-sponsored resolution passed in the Petrograd Soviet for the first time. In response, the Revolutionary Defensists put their leadership to a vote of confidence on September 9 and lost. On September 25 the Soviet elected a new radical left leadership of Bolsheviks and Left SRs. Leon Trotsky, who joined the Bolshevik party in July and swiftly became one its most prominent leaders, became chairman of the Soviet. Simultaneously, the Bolsheviks and radical left took over the Moscow Soviet of Workers' Deputies, thereby giving them leadership of the two most important soviets.

Victories in other cities accompanied this as the radical left bloc—and sometimes the Bolsheviks alone—won reelection campaigns in factories and barracks and took control of soviet after soviet. General elections to city and district government councils also revealed the shifting political loyalties. The Bolsheviks and radicals made gains nationwide, and in Moscow, Bolsheviks won a majority in voting for city district government councils in September. These electoral successes allowed the October Revolution to take place; without them that revolution is difficult to imagine. Indeed, the October Revolution would begin as a defense of the Petrograd Soviet and the idea of Soviet power.

THE BOLSHEVIK DEBATE OVER GOVERNMENT POWER

With the Bolsheviks and their allies in power in the Petrograd and other soviets, and given their support for the idea of "All Power to the Soviets," the question quite naturally arose, "What are the Bolsheviks planning to do?" Would they make a bid to take control of the government? If so, when and how? By mid-October everyone debated these issues: in the press, on street corners, in food lines, in private apartments, at factories and army barracks, in political circles, even in the government. What, especially, were the Bolsheviks planning for the upcoming Second All-Russia Congress of Soviets, originally scheduled for October 20, but then postponed to the twenty-fifth? (The first All-Russia Congress of Soviets, composed of delegates from soviets around the country and dominated by the moderate socialists, was held in June.)

These questions tormented Lenin, as well. From his Finnish hiding place— an order for his arrest dating from the July Days still existed—Lenin feared that the Bolsheviks would do too little, too late. He already had turned away from any idea of cooperation with the moderate socialists in some kind of shared Soviet power. Lenin's hostility toward the moderate socialists and his view of them as betrayers of Marxism made cooperation within the generally understood meanings of Soviet power unacceptable. Ignoring the debates going on in Petrograd about what kind of broad socialist government to form, Lenin in mid-September shifted to a strident call for an immediate armed seizure of power by the Bolsheviks. For him, Soviet power meant a new type of government dominated by the Bolsheviks. From Finland, he wrote to the Bolshevik Central Committee that "The Bolsheviks, having obtained a majority in the Soviets of Workers's and Soldiers' Deputies in both capitals [Petrograd and Moscow], can and *must* take state power into their own hands. . . . The majority of the people are *on our side*."[5] Limited in his ability to impose his will on the party from his Finnish hiding place, he sent message after message insisting that the time was ripe for a seizure of power and that the party must organize and prepare for it. Lenin realized that the fall of 1917 offered a unique opportunity for a radical restructuring of political power and for a man such as himself. Not only was the situation in Russia ripe for revolution, he believed, but also in Germany and elsewhere in Europe. Like other Russian socialists in 1917, Lenin saw the Russian Revolution as the beginning of a broader, sweeping world revolution. He saw it as a fundamental turning point in both Russian and world history: "history will not forgive us," he wrote, if the Bolsheviks miss this opportunity to take power.[6] The seizure of power by the Bolsheviks was now his obsession.

Lenin's call divided the party leadership. A minority supported Lenin's call to arms. Another group, led by Grigorii Zinoviev and Lev Kamenev, two of Lenin's oldest and closest associates and among the most authoritative party leaders, urged caution. They argued that the party was growing stronger day by day and that it would be foolish to risk that in an ill-conceived adventure that the government might yet have the strength to suppress. Moreover, they had a different vision of the future revolutionary government, favoring a broad coalition of socialists in a democratic left government. A third position emerged in between Lenin's demand for a violent seizure of power by the Bolsheviks and the caution of Zinoviev and Kamenev. Increasingly identified with Leon Trotsky and probably representing a majority of the party's leadership, this group looked to the forthcoming Second All-Russia Congress of Soviets as the vehicle for the transfer of power. The Bolsheviks and other parties supporting Soviet power would have a majority at the Congress, and the Congress could then declare the transfer of power to itself. Although this would be a revolutionary move, they believed that Kerensky's government would be helpless to resist. Despite Lenin's demands, therefore, the party's political efforts focused on the forthcoming Congress of Soviets and the selection of deputies to the Congress who would support a transfer of power. From September 27 onward, the main Bolshevik newspaper carried across its front page the headline: "Prepare for the Congress of Soviets on October 20! Convene Regional Congresses Immediately." Nor were the Bolsheviks alone in this focus: the Left SR newspaper carried a similar slogan, as well as regularly cautioning against any kind of "coming out" before the Congress.

Lenin did not share the Petrograd party leaders' focus on the Congress of Soviets. Frustrated and fearing that an irretrievable opportunity was slipping by, Lenin took the chance of moving from Finland to Petrograd. On October 10 he met, for the first time since July, with the Central Committee of the party. After an all-night debate, it seemingly gave in to Lenin's passionate demands for a seizure of power. It passed a resolution stating "the Central Committee recognizes that . . . [follows a long list of international and domestic developments] all this places armed uprising on the order of the day."[7] This resolution later became central to the myth of a carefully planned seizure of power carried out under Lenin's direction. It was, in fact, something different and more complex than that. First of all, it did *not* set any timetable or plan for a seizure of power. Rather, it was a formal reversion of Bolshevik Party policy to the idea that an armed uprising was a revolutionary necessity, after the interlude since July in which they had held that a peaceful development of the revolution was possible. The resolution thus represented a shift in formal policy, but did not commit the party to a seizure of power *before* the Congress of Soviets or at any other specific time, nor did it start actual preparations for a seizure of power. It was a general statement of policy for a turbulent and seemingly favorable period in the revolution, not a plan for the immediate seizure of power. At the most, it was a statement of intent to overthrow the Provisional Government and replace it with a Soviet-based government when the time was right and a suitable opportunity arose, whenever that might be. This was hardly a new idea by October. The idea of replacing the Provisional Government by a Soviet-based government had been widely discussed since midsummer.

The resolution of October 10 did, however, do two things. First, it set off a vigorous debate within the Bolshevik Party about the exact meaning of the resolution for their future course of action, and it revealed the divisions in the party. A few interpreted it in a narrow sense, in Lenin's meaning, as a decision to launch an armed seizure of power as soon as possible. "The sooner the better," argued one delegate to a party leadership meeting on October 15. Most, however, interpreted it in the broader sense of meaning that a seizure of power would be carried out at some time, in some way, probably via the Congress of Soviets or in reaction to some government provocation. As Mikhail Kalinin, another major party leader, stated at the same meeting, "when this uprising will be possible—perhaps in a year—is uncertain."[8] Moreover, party leaders acknowledged that little or nothing had been done to organize the soldier and worker supporters who would presumably carry it out, and nothing done to prepare Bolsheviks in key centers such as Moscow or to insure control of railroads and communications. Indeed, they had organized no central planning or directing center. Others reported that while the workers and soldiers would come out to defend the Soviet and the revolution against counterrevolution, they would not come out for a Bolshevik action. As the date for the Congress of Soviets neared, the top Bolshevik leadership was divided. In part by default and in part because that seemed to reflect the opinion of most party leaders, attention focused on the Congress of Soviets as the time, place, and vehicle for the transfer of power, for making the new revolution called for in the Bolshevik resolution of October 10 as well as in hundreds of local workers' and soldiers' resolutions. The Bolsheviks' Left SR allies also were aiming at the Congress to take power and form an all-socialist government.

THE OCTOBER REVOLUTION

Lenin now became the recipient of a series of unforeseeable lucky breaks that made possible the violent seizure of power that he wanted, gave rise to the durable myth of a well-planned Bolshevik revolution, and helped shape the nature of the political system that ruled the Soviet Union most of the rest of the century. First, on October 12, the moderate socialists decided to postpone the opening of the Congress of Soviets from the twentieth to the twenty-fifth because an inadequate number of delegates had arrived. This was momentous, for the Bolsheviks were unprepared for and could not have attempted any seizure of power before the twentieth, even if they wished. The five extra days changed everything, allowing time for the further buildup of tensions in Petrograd, for a major struggle for control of the garrison, and for mobilization efforts by the Red Guard. Most of all, they gave time for Kerensky's fateful decision to strike at the leftists on the 24th, which precipitated the armed seizure of power before the Congress met. Without those events between October 20 and 25, the October Revolution as we know it could not have occurred.

The mobilization of supporters during this period was especially important. A declaration of the transfer of power at the Congress of Soviets, however much expected, would after all be an insurrectionary action. The Bolsheviks and Left SRs could assume that Kerensky's government would try to resist. Therefore, they worked to insure that the Congress of Soviets could successfully take power upon itself and launched a series of measures designed to weaken the government and deprive it of its remaining legitimacy. Central to this was taking away the government's last bits of authority over the garrison of Petrograd, thus destroying any ability of the government to use its soldiers against the seizure of power by the Congress of Soviets. They did this through the newly formed Military Revolutionary Committee of the Petrograd Soviet (MRC). The MRC organized meetings to rally the support of the soldiers for the Soviet and to obtain pledges from army regiments that they would obey only orders signed by the MRC. This insured that the soldiers would support the Congress of Soviets' declaration of power, or at least not oppose it. On October 21 the MRC declared to the military authorities in Petrograd that "henceforth orders not signed by us are invalid." The next day, October 22, which had earlier been declared the "Day of the Petrograd Soviet," turned into a series of rallies in favor of Soviet power. These intensified tensions in the city. At the same time, the Soviet leaders repeatedly called on workers and soldiers to be ready to defend the revolution and the Congress of Soviets against counterrevolution. Seen in this light, as preparation to defend a transfer of power at the Congress of Soviets, the actions by the government, the Bolshevik and Left SR leaders, and other political figures and local activists have a logic that they do not have if one holds to the old myth of careful planning for a Bolshevik seizure of power *before* the Congress.

The government watched these developments with anxiety and took what it considered adequate steps to counter them. Kerensky declared that he had sufficient power to suppress any attempted overthrow. At this point, Lenin's second piece of luck fell into place: Kerensky decided to act against the Bolsheviks. As most of Petrograd slept in the pre-dawn morning hours of October 24, a small detachment of military cadets and militiamen sent by the Provisional Government raided the press where two Bolshevik newspapers were published. The alarmed press workers ran with the stunning news to the Smolny Institute, headquarters of the Petrograd Soviet, the MRC, and the Bolshevik Party. Officials at Smolny quickly branded the press closure a counterrevolutionary move and summoned the leaders of the MRC, Petrograd Soviet, and the Bolshevik and Left SR parties. These (not including Lenin, who remained in hiding) assembled at Smolny to find that in addition to the account of the printers, reports were coming in from various places around the city of suspicious troop movements. The MRC then declared the appearance of counterrevolution and appealed for support: "Counterrevolutionary conspirators went on the offensive during the night. A treasonous blow against the Petrograd Soviet of Workers' and Soldiers' Deputies is being planned. . . . The campaign of the counterrevolutionary conspirators is directed against the Congress of Soviets on the eve of its opening, against the Constituent Assembly, against the people."[9] It sent "Directive No. 1" to army regimental commissars and committees: "You are ordered to bring your regiment to fighting readiness."[10] Unbeknownst to anyone, including the Bolshevik leaders, the October Revolution had begun. Kerensky's simple but ill-conceived act provided the very "counterrevolutionary" action against which the left had been warning, precipitating the October Revolution and unexpectedly handing Lenin his seizure of power before the Congress of Soviets.

Despite some radical leaders who wanted to respond to Kerensky's action with an immediate insurrection, most of those present at Soviet headquarters on the morning of October 24 focused on defensive measures to guarantee that the Second Congress of Soviets would meet the next day. Through the twenty-fourth, the Soviet leaders called on workers and soldiers to defend the Congress and the revolution, while Kerensky's government tried to find reliable military support for the growing confrontation. Their efforts met very different responses. Kerensky found little support within the city or from nearby garrisons. In fact, few soldiers were eager to fight for either side, and those who were willing overwhelmingly supported the Soviet. Some radicalized army units and the workers' Red Guards took to the streets to defend Soviet power. In confused, largely uncoordinated, struggles that involved mostly push and shove, bluff and counterbluff, Red Guards and pro-Soviet soldiers gradually took control of bridges and key buildings. There were few people on the streets and little shooting, in contrast to the earlier major demonstrations of 1917. Few were willing to die for either side and what enthusiasm and hard support existed rested on the side of the Soviet. By nightfall, pro-Soviet forces controlled most of the city.

Throughout October 24, the focus of Bolshevik and Soviet leaders remained on the Congress of Soviets and defensive measures, but this changed shortly after midnight, around 2 A.M. the morning of the twenty-fifth. They now shifted to an offensive drive to seize power because of two things coming together. One was a growing realization that the government was much weaker than thought and that the city was coming under the physical control of soldiers and Red Guards rallying to the defense of the Soviet. The second was the arrival of Lenin at Soviet headquarters. Lenin had been in hiding on the city outskirts, but no longer able to stand being out of touch with the events happening in the city, he left his hiding place to go to Smolny (Soviet and Bolshevik Party headquarters). Wearing a wig, a cap and a bandage on his face, near midnight he set off accompanied by a lone bodyguard. On the way, they were intercepted by a patrol of military cadets, but mistaken for a pair of drunks and not recognized, allowed to pass. Then, when they arrived at Smolny, the Red Guard at the door initially refused them entry for lack of proper credentials![11] Lenin's arrival, coinciding with the dawning realization of the success of pro-Soviet forces, dramatically changed the situation. Lenin had not been part of the cautious defensive reaction of October 24, and he was the one leader who had consistently urged an armed seizure of power before the Congress of Soviets met. Under his pressure and the reality of their growing strength, the Soviet leaders shifted from a defensive posture to the offensive about 2 A.M. the morning of the 25th. The MRC began to work out plans for arresting the Provisional Government and taking control of remaining key installations. By the time a cold, gray, windy day dawned on October 25, pro-Soviet forces had extended their control to almost all of the city except the Winter Palace. There, the members of the Provisional Government still sat behind a small band of increasingly dispirited defenders, surrounded by a large but disorganized force of Red Guards and pro-Soviet soldiers.

Lenin took advantage of this to achieve his goal of proclaiming the overthrow of the Provisional Government *before* the Congress of Soviets met. By mid-morning of the twenty-fifth, the situation had progressed to the point where, at about the same time, Lenin proclaimed the transfer of power while Kerensky fled to seek support from outside the city. About 10 A.M., Lenin finished a hastily written proclamation of the overthrow of the Provisional Government and handed it over for immediate printing and distribution. When Kerensky sped out of the city shortly later that morning in his search for military support, he might well have passed the first distribution of the leaflets proclaiming his overthrow. Meanwhile, at the Winter Palace, the besieging forces waited, unsure of what resistance they might meet, while groups of "defenders" now and then marched away out of it. Finally, in the evening, the pro-Soviet forces—Red Guards and soldiers—began to filter into the palace. There was no "storming" of the palace, a nonevent invented by later artists and filmmakers. About 2 A.M. on October 26, some of the attackers finally found their way to the room where the government ministers sat awaiting arrest. By that time, the city was completely in the hands of pro-Soviet forces and the Congress of Soviets already in session.

By the evening of October 25, it appeared that Lenin had obtained his goal of a transfer of power by a violent act of seizure before the Congress of Soviets. It is worth noting, however, that the transfer of power was in the name of the Petrograd Soviet and affirmed by it. It was not a revolution in the name of the Bolshevik Party, and the multiparty Congress of Soviets was still to be the ultimate legitimizing institution. Transforming a seizure of power in the name of Soviet power into a Bolshevik regime would depend on yet a third unforeseeable stroke of luck, this one at the Congress of Soviets.

THE CONGRESS OF SOVIETS

As the armed struggle for control of Petrograd drew toward a close the evening of October 25, the focus of events shifted to the political struggle at the Second All-Russia Congress of Soviets. Events unfolding there that night shaped the nature of the new government in ways no one, not even Lenin, could have foreseen at the time. They gave the Bolsheviks full control of the Congress and the new government, contrary to all expectations, and transformed the debate about just what "Soviet power" meant now that it was a reality. They profoundly influenced the outcome of the revolution and the Soviet regime that followed for the next several decades.

The Second All-Russia Congress of Soviets opened at 10:40 P.M., October 25. The Bolsheviks were the largest party, with about three hundred of the approximately 650–670 seats (figures for the number of delegates and their party distribution are not precise). To obtain a majority, they needed the support of other advocates of Soviet power, especially the eighty to eighty-five Left SRs. These numbers, however, did guarantee that the new leadership would be from the radical left and predominately Bolsheviks. Most participants assumed that the Congress would create a new government composed of a multiparty coalition of socialist leaders, what almost everyone but Lenin took Soviet power to mean. The main question was its exact composition and how radical it would be. The Congress, meeting amid suspense over just what was happening in the city and to the background sound of cannons booming at the nearby Peter-Paul fortress (although with little damage), immediately moved toward creating a broad socialist government in order to avert bloodshed. That miscarried, however, when Menshevik and SR spokesmen rose to denounce the Bolsheviks and walked out. Lenin thus received his third stroke of luck—the Bolsheviks unexpectedly found themselves in an absolute majority and in full control of the Congress, while the idea of a broad socialist government was damaged. Under Bolshevik leadership, the Congress enthusiastically declared the Provisional Government overthrown and that political authority now rested in the Congress of Soviets.

The Bolshevik leaders moved quickly to consolidate power. At the second session of the Congress of Soviets, which opened the evening of October 26, they passed three major resolutions. Lenin, appearing in public for the first time since July, introduced a Decree on Peace. It called for the warring governments to join in a general peace negotiation on the familiar "peace without annexations or indemnities" formula and appealed to the workers of the warring countries to support the peace effort. Whether this appeal would be any more successful in leading to peace than had those of the old Revolutionary Defensists leaders was unclear, but it was important as a dramatic gesture to the war-weary troops and the Petrograd garrison in particular. Lenin then introduced a Decree on Land, which turned over all the land along with buildings, livestock, and other resources to the peasants, sanctioning the peasants' seizure of land in 1917 and legitimizing the new government in their eyes. It also reinforced the support of the soldiers and workers for the new government. Finally, Lenin proposed a new government, the Council of People's Commissars (*Sovnarkom*), headed by himself. The terminology was chosen to emphasize the revolutionary nature of the new government, commissar being the term used for revolutionary officials in 1917, while "People's" stressed that the government supposedly represented the true interests of the people more than had previous regimes.

The new government, because of the walkout of the Mensheviks and SRs, was unexpectedly made up entirely of Bolsheviks. This had not been envisioned in the many debates about a Soviet-based government, all of which had assumed some kind of multiparty socialist government. The walkout of the moderates changed that. The Left SRs insisted that they would join the government only as part of a broad socialist coalition, but with the moderates gone such a coalition was impossible. Therefore, an all-Bolshevik government was formed. Lenin became Chairman of *Sovnarkom* and thus head of the government, with Trotsky as People's Commissar for Foreign Affairs. The new political structure was completed when the Congress of Soviets chose a new Central Executive Committee (CEC) to act in its name between congresses. The Bolsheviks initially took sixty-two seats, the Left SRs twenty-nine, and ten were divided among the Menshevik-Internationalists and minor leftist groups. The Bolsheviks thus dominated the CEC as well. The socialist parties that had withdrawn from the Congress were unrepresented.

CONSOLIDATING THE NEW REGIME

When the Congress of Soviets adjourned in the early morning hours of October 27, the new government was extremely insecure, facing several immediate threats which might unseat it. The first was an attempt by Kerensky to retake the city with troops from the front, supported by an uprising of military cadets in the city. This failed by November 3, amid bloodshed greater than during the October Revolution itself. More threatening was the pressure from political circles to reorganize the government into a broad socialist coalition, the assumption inherent in the slogan of "All Power to the Soviets." The most effective pressure forcing negotiations came from Vikzhel, the All-Russia Executive Committee of the Union of Railway Workers, which was Left SR led. Their ability to control the movement of troops, foodstuffs, and other goods put them in a strong position to demand that all political groups pay attention. On October 29, Vikzhel called for political negotiations, declaring that "The government of the Council of People's Commissars, formed at Petrograd by one party only, cannot expect to be recognized or supported by the country as a whole. It is, therefore, necessary to form a government that will have the confidence of the democracy as a whole and have enough prestige to retain the power until the meeting of the Constituent Assembly."[12] The Bolsheviks agreed to negotiations, uncertain of their ability to hold on to power and with some of their own leaders, such as Kamenev, in favor of such a multiparty government. Lenin opposed such a restructuring, and again fortune smiled on him. The Mensheviks and SRs overplayed their hand, demanding more concessions from the Bolsheviks than their weak position permitted, allowing Lenin to rally the party leadership against reorganization of the government. After a few days, the Vikzhel negotiations dragged to an end without any change of government. One reason the Bolsheviks could allow the negotiation to die was the failure of Kerensky to take the city, but even more important was the apparent spread of acceptance of the new government to other key cities, especially Moscow.

That the new Bolshevik government created by the October Revolution would be accepted by the rest of the country had by no means been certain. During 1917, the authority of the central government over the rest of the country had weakened. The situation was very unlike February, when news of the revolution in Petrograd sparked immediate supporting revolutions across the country. Now every major locality made a decision, often accompanied by fighting, to accept or not accept Soviet power and the new Bolshevik central government. This stretched out over weeks and months as the many local revolutions for Soviet power worked themselves out. The local responses to Petrograd's October Revolution depended upon a host of local conditions: the political coloration of the local soviet, the social composition of the community, the vigor of local political leaders, the presence or absence of a garrison, nationality conflicts, and others. Control of the local soviet was especially important because the soviets, not officials of the Provisional Government or elected city councils, exercised predominant authority locally in most instances. As a result, Soviet power came to the Russian provinces in several waves of revolutionary upheaval between October 1917 and early 1918. Critical, however, was the situation in Moscow and at the front nearest Petrograd. In Moscow, the Bolshevik and radical left parties finally prevailed on November 2, but only after bitter fighting that left several hundred dead (compared to only a handful in Petrograd and most other cities that had armed confrontations). At the same time, the Bolsheviks and Left SRs secured the allegiance of the front soldiers and garrison troops of the Northern Front, the military front nearest Petrograd, as well as the nearby Baltic Sea fleet sailors.

By November 2, a week after the Bolsheviks first declared Soviet power, the government had beaten back its immediate military adversaries and seen the acceptance of Soviet power in Moscow, most cities of central Russia, and the nearest military sectors. This in turn allowed Lenin to let the Vikzhel negotiations die, force into line those Bolshevik leaders who advocated a broader-based government, and evade the attempt to force the Bolsheviks to share power. The new "provisional workers' and soldiers' government," as Lenin initially styled it in the announcement of the new government issued by the Second Congress of Soviets on October 26, could now consider itself less "provisional" and turn its attention to longer term issues, both political and social-economic. The Bolsheviks had successfully turned a popular revolution for Soviet power to their own advantage and unexpectedly found themselves the sole party in the new government.

THE CONSTITUENT ASSEMBLY AND THE PURPOSES OF POWER

Turning the widely popular October Revolution in the name of "Soviet power" into a genuinely Bolshevik revolution involved the Bolsheviks' abandonment of the democratic elements of the revolutions of 1917 in favor of holding on to power by dictatorial force. For Lenin, the problem was the further consolidation of Soviet power and specifically how to ensure that Soviet power meant Bolshevik power. In facing that, he had to answer basic questions about the nature and purposes of political power in the new political order, and with those answers rested the future of democracy or dictatorship in Russia. This initially focused on the intertwined problems of creating a government structure while at the same time dealing with the forthcoming Constituent Assembly and other political parties, especially their erstwhile allies, the Left SRs.

In establishing their authority, the Bolsheviks quickly turned to repressive measures. The first law issued by the new government, on October 27, instituted press censorship in the name of combating counterrevolution—some opposition newspapers already had been closed. At the same time, the new government and its supporters readily used armed force against actual or suspected opponents, who were broadly and vaguely defined. This trend toward repressive measures alarmed the Left SRs and even some Bolsheviks. As soon as the immediate military threat to the regime from Kerensky was defeated, they challenged those policies. A major debate erupted on November 4 in the CEC. Iurii Larin, a recent Bolshevik convert from Menshevism, introduced a resolution repealing the press censorship decree. The Left SRs and some Bolsheviks invoked the absurdity of trying to establish democracy and freedom via censorship. Lenin, Trotsky, and some other Bolsheviks justified censorship and other repressive measures as essential at the current moment. The Bolshevik-dominated CEC defeated the motion. A Left SR spokesman declared the vote "a clear and unambiguous expression [of support for] a system of political terror and for unleashing civil war."[13] Lenin, however, held firm, and the Bolshevik majority with him. The Bolsheviks soon moved toward even more repressive measures. On November 28, the government ordered the arrest of leading Kadets, declaring it "a party of the enemies of the people." The order sparked another debate in the CEC on December 1. In response to protests from their radical left coalition allies, Trotsky responded that "You wax indignant at the naked terror which we are applying against our class enemies, but let me tell you that in one month's time at the most it will assume more frightful forms, modeled on the terror of the great French revolutionaries. Not the fortress [imprisonment] but the guillotine will await our enemies."[14]

The turn toward repression required a special organization for that purpose instead of the assorted forces of Red Guards, volunteer soldiers, and Bolshevik officials. On December 7, the government established the "All-Russia Extraordinary Commission for the Struggle with Counterrevolution and Sabotage," generally known simply as the "Cheka." The Cheka quickly became the main vehicle for political terror and the origins of the political, or secret, police, which under various names became a fundamental part of the later Soviet political system. The rhetoric of Lenin, Trotsky, and some other Bolsheviks of this period was extremely violent. Physical threats against opponents, class or individual, were a regular part of their statements: "Let them shoot on the spot every tenth man guilty of idleness," Lenin exclaimed in December 1917.[15]

The debate over censorship and coercion inevitably raised questions about their implications for the Constituent Assembly. All political parties in 1917, including the Bolsheviks, had declared a democratically elected Constituent Assembly to be the legitimate institution to determine Russia's future. When the new Soviet government was formed in October, it had declared itself "provisional," and many of the early decrees and proclamations stated that they were in force until the Constituent Assembly acted. Lenin and some of the Bolsheviks quickly changed their attitudes, however. They wanted to cancel the elections, but other Bolshevik leaders successfully opposed such a radical step and the elections were allowed to proceed. This created a dilemma for the Bolsheviks, for predictions of their defeat proved well founded. Overall, the Bolsheviks obtained only about a quarter of the votes, the SRs in their various manifestations received just over half, and the remainder was split among the Kadets, nationality candidates, and others. This meant that the SRs would have a sufficient majority to control the opening and initial work of the assembly and that the Bolsheviks would be a minority, and therefore presumably would have to relinquish government power. Lenin, Trotsky, and growing numbers of the Bolshevik leadership, however, were not willing to consider their government provisional or to relinquish power. How was the circle to be squared? How could the Bolsheviks solidify *this* government and avoid handing over power to rivals at the Constituent Assembly?

As it became apparent that the Bolsheviks would not prevail at the Constituent Assembly, Lenin began to search for a way out of the problem, for he was unwilling to relinquish power. Now he and other Bolsheviks began to challenge the legitimacy of the Constituent Assembly and to threaten violence against it. Lenin declared a republic of soviets to be "a higher form of democracy" and that because of "the divergence between the elections . . . and the interests of the working and exploited classes," the only function for the Constituent Assembly would be to endorse the Soviet government and its actions.[16] Some Left SRs joined in this repudiation of the Constituent Assembly. It became clear that Lenin was prepared to ignore the election results. Moreover, the Bolsheviks took measures to guarantee armed control of the city and the ability to enforce a dispersal of the assembly. The Constituent Assembly opened January 5, 1918, with an SR majority, but after one day the Bolshevik government dispersed it by force.

The dispersal of the Constituent Assembly marked the end of any possibility for a democratic outcome of the revolution, and, in effect, the end of the revolution itself and the beginning of civil war. By dispersing the Constituent Assembly, the Bolsheviks announced that they would not be voted from power. If they could not be voted from office, then a political struggle was no longer an option and the only alternative was armed opposition; only by force could they be removed. Civil war was inevitable and would now determine the future of Russia and its peoples. Moreover, by this act the Bolshevik party irrevocably set itself upon the course of dictatorship and authoritarian government. The Bolsheviks' decision to abandon the electoral politics of 1917 and thus to rule by force laid the foundations of the dictatorship and political culture of the future Soviet Union. They built further upon those foundations during the civil war that swiftly followed their suppression of the Constituent Assembly.

NOTES

1. *Ekonomicheskoe polozhenie Rossii nakanune Velikoi Oktiabr'skoi sotsialisticheskoi revoliutsii* (Moscow, 1957), vol. II, 319.

2. Morgan Phillips Price, *Dispatches from the Revolution: Russia 1915–1918* (Durham, NC: Duke University Press, 1998), 75.

3. John Reed, *Ten Days that Shook the World* (New York: Vintage, 1960), 49.

4. Lenin, *Collected Works*, vol. 24 (Moscow: Progress Publishers, 1964), 21–24.

5. Lenin, *Collected Works*, vol. 26, 19. Emphasis Lenin's.

6. Lenin, *Collected Works*, vol. 26, 21.

7. Robert H. McNeal, ed., *Resolutions and Decisions of the Communist Party of the Soviet Union*, vol. I edited by Ralph Carter Elwood (Toronto: University of Toronto Press, 1974), 288–89.

8. The debates at the Petersburg Committee are in *Pervyi legal'nyi Peterburgskii komitet bol'shevikov v 1917 godu: Sbornik materialov iprotokolov zasedanii Peterburgskogo komiteta RSDRP(b) i ego Ispolnitel'noi komissii za 1917 g.* (Moscow-Leningrad; Gosizdat, 1927), 316.

9. *Petrogradskii voenno-revoliutsionnyi komitet: Dokumenty i materialy* (Moscow, 1966), vol. I, 84.

10. *Petrogradskii voenno-revoliutsionnyi komitet*, vol. I, 86.

11. This episode is especially well described in Robert V. Daniels, *Red October: The Bolshevik Revolution of 1917* (New York: Scribners, 1967), 158–61.

12. James Bunyan and H. H. Fisher, eds., *The Bolshevik Revolution, 1917–1918: Documents and Materials* (Stanford, CA: Stanford University Press, 1934), 155–56, slightly modified.

13. The debate and resolutions are in John L. H. Keep, ed., *The Debate on Soviet Power: Minutes of the All-Russian Central Executive Committee of Soviets, Second Convocation, October 1917–January 1918* (Oxford: Oxford University Press, 1979), 69–78.

14. The debate is in Keep, *Debate*, 173–81.

15. In W. Bruce Lincoln, *Passage Through Armageddon. The Russians in War and Revolution, 1914–1918* (New York: Simon and Schuster, 1986), 138.

16. Lenin, *Collected Works*, vol. 26, 379–83.

4

The Civil War(s)

What is usually called the Russian civil war might better be put in the plural, "civil wars." It was in fact a complex, multiphased event, with overlapping military, economic, national, international, and other conflicts. There was the military civil war, which included several protagonists and was itself plural rather than singular. There was the closely connected attempt to create a new Bolshevik-controlled social-economic system, which included strong elements of class warfare and reinforced the military struggle (and embittered it). In addition, civil wars among nationality groups paralleled the Russian event, as did wars between Bolsheviks and nationalist forces. On the cultural front, advocates of a sweeping cultural revolution carried on a war against the old cultural and artistic norms. Moreover, the Bolsheviks saw themselves engaged in an international civil war, a violent international class war, as revolution spread (they hoped) across Europe and then the world.

THE MILITARY CIVIL WAR

Fear of civil war had motivated most Russians and political leaders in 1917 to seek compromises, but as the year wore toward an end, it loomed ever more likely. Not only had social and political polarization increased, but unlike its predecessor, the new Bolshevik government did not fear civil war, and some Bolsheviks even welcomed it. Then, the dispersal of the Constituent Assembly made civil war inevitable. If the Bolsheviks would not relinquish political power through elections, then their opponents had little choice but to take to the field with arms.

Civil war developed slowly during the first half of 1918. Opposition to the Bolshevik government was widespread, but not united. Three major groups emerged, each as suspicious of the other as of the Bolsheviks. First, conservative military officers and liberal and conservative politicians quickly made known their opposition and began making their way to south Russia, especially to the Cossack lands, where they hoped to build a base for opposing the Bolsheviks. There, officers of the old army created the "Volunteer Army," a highly motivated but small force with a large percentage of former junior officers in its ranks. It was one of the most effective fighting forces of the civil war. Second, nationality leaders declared independence and took up arms to defend that claim against Bolshevik efforts to bring their areas under Soviet control. They had little grounds for cooperation with the conservative officers, who, in the name of "Russia one and indivisible," opposed nationalist separatism or even autonomy. Third, some SR Party leaders retreated to their electoral stronghold on the Volga River area southeast of Moscow to establish a rival government. There, in June 1918, they founded Komuch (Committee of Members of the Constituent Assembly), claiming that it was the legitimate Russian government based on the SR majority at the Constituent Assembly. They had only a weak military force, but this democratic opposition represented in many respects the greatest initial threat to the Bolsheviks, and it was here that serious civil war erupted in late spring of 1918. Assorted anti-Bolshevik movements also appeared in other areas.

Meanwhile, in the spring and summer of 1918, the Soviet government began to build a new Red Army under the direction of Trotsky, who became People's Commissar of War. Under his leadership, the Red Army swiftly moved away from the initial revolutionary ideals of a volunteer army, elected officers, democratic structure, and the abolition of the death penalty, on which the Bolsheviks had campaigned in 1917. Trotsky built a more conventional army based on appointed officers, conscripts, a hierarchical structure, and liberal use of the death penalty for military infractions. A major innovation, however, was the creation of military commissars, trusted Communists who watched over the behavior of the often-distrusted officers (many from the old army), countersigned orders, and carried on political education activities among the soldiers. This became a permanent feature of the Red and later Soviet Army. Under Trotsky's energetic leadership (often from his special armored train headquarters), the Red Army developed into an effective fighting force, with a dedicated core drawn especially from urban workers and Bolsheviks, backed by a larger but less reliable body of peasant conscripts. This army would both fight the civil war and carry Soviet power into areas where it had not yet been established. By the end of 1918, it numbered some half-million men, larger than the armies of all its opponents combined, and by the end of 1919 about 2 million.

The Bolsheviks not only built a larger army than their opponents, but they also began the war with distinct geographic and resource advantages. Controlling the compact and heavily populated heartland of Russia and with the advantage of a single command and unified political leadership, the Bolsheviks were in a strong position to fight their opponents. The latter, in contrast, were scattered around the periphery, controlled a much smaller and more heterogenous population, had neither a unified command nor unified political leadership, lacked common goals other than defeating the Bolsheviks, and often mistrusted (and sometimes fought) each other as much as they did the Bolsheviks. Bolshevik territory also included the main industrial resources of the country, whereas their primary opponents controlled little industrial or other economic resources. The Bolsheviks also benefited from controlling the central railway junctures, which allowed them to move troops from one front to another, something their opponents could not do.

The preliminary stage of the civil war came in December 1917–March 1918, as the Soviet government attacked various groups that had refused to accept its authority. Particularly important among these were the Cossack lands and the anti-Bolshevik Volunteer Army in South Russia, the Ukrainian Rada, and some other nationality areas. Using hastily organized detachments composed of Red Guards from Moscow and Petrograd, small groups of soldiers and sailors, plus local supporters, the Soviet government launched the "railway war," moving small detachments along the railway system to secure control of key cities. By February 1918, they had forced the Volunteer Army out of the Don Cossack region and neutralized Cossack opposition. These detachments also moved southwest into Ukraine, where in December 1917 they aided local Bolsheviks in seizing power in Kharkov and declaring a Ukrainian Soviet Republic. They then pushed on to defeat the Ukrainian Rada's forces and take Kiev in early February 1918, thus bringing most of Ukraine temporarily under Soviet authority. Other pro-Soviet detachments took control of areas to the east, especially in the Ural Mountains region and parts of Siberia and Central Asia. By March 1918 (the same month that they signed the peace treaty with Germany),[1] the Bolsheviks seemed to have prevailed militarily against their domestic rivals, as well as significantly expanding the territory where "Soviet power" had been proclaimed.

In the early summer of 1918, things turned against the Bolsheviks and the civil war began in earnest. New centers of political and military opposition emerged and the territory under Bolshevik control shrank dramatically. A key event was the revolt of the Czechoslovak Legion in May–June and the resulting strengthening of Komuch. The Czechoslovak Legion was a special unit formed in 1917 from prisoners of war who were willing to fight on the Allied side for an independent Czechoslovakia (then part of the Austro-Hungarian state). By early 1918, they were moving east across the Trans-Siberian railway to the Pacific Ocean, where they planned to take ship to France to continue the fight (direct travel westward was, of course, impossible because of Germany and Austria-Hungary). Conflict soon broke out between them and local Communist authorities. When Trotsky rashly ordered their disarming in late May, the Czechs rebelled and seized control of key points along the railway. The Allied governments, who had been searching for a way to oppose the new Soviet government after the latter signed the peace treaty with Germany, realized that the Czechs could play a key role by helping the anti-Bolshevik and pro-war Russians. The Czechs could provide much-needed military muscle to the newly formed, SR-led, Komuch government. This made the latter a significant political-military opponent for the Bolsheviks, probably the greatest threat at the time.

About the same time, the Bolsheviks suffered other setbacks. A second major center of opposition emerged in South Russia. The harsh behavior of Communist officials toward the Don Cossack population led to a revolt in that region that drove out the Bolsheviks, while the Volunteer Army under General Anton Denikin established itself in the Kuban region farther south. Thus, a major anti-Bolshevik armed force emerged and survived in south Russia. Smaller anti-Bolshevik movements established themselves in the far north and elsewhere. Meanwhile, German, Austrian, and Turkish armies occupied the Baltic states, Ukraine, Belorussia, and parts of the Caucasus, overthrowing pro-Soviet governments where they existed. The Bolsheviks were now thrown back to the Russian heartland. It was during this tumultuous period that the Bolsheviks executed Nicholas II and his family on June 16, as Komuch troops approached their place of imprisonment, the city of Ekaterinburg. This event, however, had little effect on the civil war.

The Czech revolt also was a key event leading to Allied intervention in the Russian civil war. It overcame President Woodrow Wilson's reluctance to sanction the British and French desire to intervene militarily. Soon thereafter, small contingents of American, British, French, and Japanese troops landed at the far northern, eastern, and southern edges of the Russian empire, where they aided anti-Bolshevik forces. Their main concern was the war with Germany. They hoped that a victory of the anti-Soviet forces would compel Germany to keep more troops in the east and slow their transfer to the western front, and also deny Germany access to the desperately needed raw materials and foodstuffs of Russia. After the end of World War I in November 1918, continued Allied intervention became more ideologically motivated and aimed directly at helping anti-Bolshevik forces defeat the Soviet regime. The goals of Allied intervention, however, were confused and uncertain, and Allied troops were too few and too far away from the Russian center to affect seriously the outcome of the civil war (although Allied assistance probably prolonged it). The main contribution of intervention turned out to be something quite different—the "proof" for Soviet propaganda, throughout the Soviet Union's existence, that the Western powers were poised to invade the Soviet Union and destroy it at the first opportunity.

The fighting of 1918 was inconclusive. By September, the Red Army defeated the Komuch forces along the Volga, but a new anti-Bolshevik government, the Directory, and army emerged at Omsk, in western Siberia. Denikin's army in the south neither prevailed nor was defeated. During the winter of 1918–19, however, the nature of the civil war changed. The collapse of Germany in November 1918 removed the dominant military power in the western areas, from Ukraine north to the Baltic region, creating political and military instability in a vast area. The same month, Admiral Alexander Kolchak and conservative officers overthrew the Directory, replacing it with conservative, military-dominated government. Kolchak was named "Supreme Ruler." This changed the political complexion of the struggle in the east. In south Russia, General Anton Denikin united the Volunteer Army, the Don Cossacks (who had been alienated by the Bolsheviks' anti-Cossack policies), and other anti-Bolshevik forces into the Armed Forces of South Russia (AFSR), and took control of civil as well as military authority in the area under its control. With the emergence of Kolchak and Denikin, the civil war became more clearly a struggle between extremes of left and right, Communists versus conservative military dictators, "Reds" versus "Whites." Still, it was more than that, and other forces emerged. Besides the main Red versus White antagonists, many other armies—nationalist armies fighting for independence, anarchist forces in Ukraine, warlords, and peasant "Green" armies attempting to repel all outsiders—fought the main armies and each other in pursuit of their various goals. This made the period one of civil wars rather than a single civil war, even militarily.

The key military struggle came in 1919, between Reds and Whites. In March 1919, Kolchak launched a major offensive out of Siberia and across the Urals. Faced with vast distances, a small army, poor organization, and peasant revolt behind his lines, his offensive quickly stalled. In May, the Red Army launched a counteroffensive that drove Kolchak steadily east across Siberia through the rest of 1919, until they finally captured and executed him in February 1920. As Kolchak began his retreat, Denikin launched his armies from the south. Much better organized, equipped, and

The Civil War

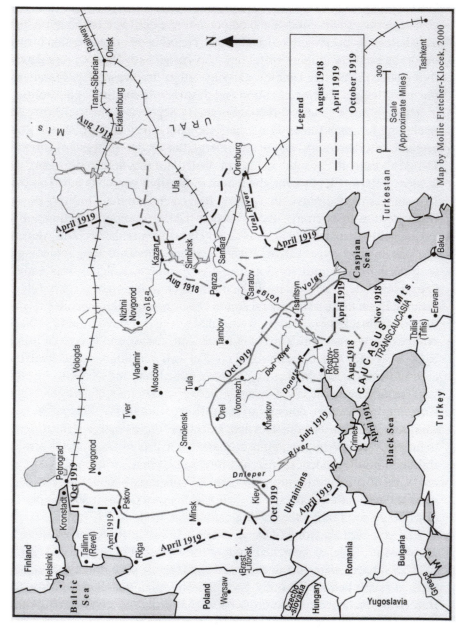

Finland

Helsinki

Baltic Sea

Tallinn (Revel)
April 1919

Kronstadt
Petrograd
Oct 1919

Riga
April 1919

Pskov
Oct 1919

Novgorod

Minsk

Poland

Warsaw

Brest-Litovsk

Czecho-slovakia

Hungary

Romania

Bulgaria

Greece

Yugoslavia

Kiev
Oct 1919

Ukrainians
April 1919

Dnieper

River
July 1919

Crimea
April 1919

Black Sea

Turkey

Smolensk

Tver

Moscow

Vladimir

Vologda

Tula

Orel

Voronezh
Oct 1919

Kharkov

Donets R.

Don River

Rostov-on-Don

Aug 1918

TRANSCAUCASIA
Nov 1918

CAUCASUS Mts.

Tbilisi (Tiflis)

Erevan

Baku

Caspian Sea

Tambov

Nizhni Novgorod

Volga

Kazan
Aug 1918

Simbirsk

Penza

Samara

Saratov

Volga

Tsaritsyn

Volga
April 1919

April 1919

Ural River

Orenburg

April 1919

Ufa

Ekaterinburg
Aug 1918

URAL Mts.

Omsk

Trans-Siberian Railway

April 1919

Turkestan

Tashkent

N

Legend

August 1918
April 1919
October 1919

Scale
(Approximate Miles)
0   300

Map by Mollie Fletcher-Klocek, 2000

led, they also had the benefit of two important groups of fighting men: the Volunteer Army and the Don Cossacks. Denikin made dramatic advances northward, northeast, and northwest. By November, his troops reached Orel and were only about 235 miles from Moscow (they had started several hundred miles south), and appeared poised to attack the Red capital. They had, however, overextended their lines and were having great difficulty controlling conquered territory. They also were simultaneously engaged in fighting the Ukrainians, which diverted much needed troops. Moreover, they now faced a much larger Red Army, which was reinforced by troops transferred from the Siberian front (here, the Bolsheviks' control of the central heartland and its transport system proved its value). In contrast, Denikin had difficulty replacing his losses, especially those of the dedicated and skilled Volunteers, and no longer had the quality of soldiers who had won the early battles. A Red offensive drove Denikin back and by the beginning of 1920, thoroughly defeated his army, bottling up the remnants in the Crimean Peninsula. A third White offensive, by General N. N. Iudenich out of Estonia against Petro- grad in October, was also repulsed and that army quickly disintegrated.

By the beginning of 1920, the Red Army had, for all intents and purposes, won the civil war. They had defeated the two main anti-Bolshevik armies, as well as smaller threats elsewhere. The Allies, never a major factor (except, briefly, the Czechs), were in the process of withdrawing support from the anti-Bolshevik forces. The Bolsheviks prepared to finish off their various opponents, including independent nationalist governments such as in Ukraine and the Caucasus Mountains region. Before they could do so, however, Poland invaded in April 1920, in an attempt to annex parts of Ukraine, Belorussia, and Lithuania. After initial defeats, the Red Army rallied, transferred troops from other fronts, and drove the Poles back. At this point the Soviet leaders opted to invade Poland, hoping to spark a communist revolution there and perhaps in central Europe. This hope was probably entirely misguided, one of the products of ideology and the ongoing expectation of European revolution, rather than careful analysis of the situation. In any case, Polish workers did not rise to support a communist revolution, the Red Army was defeated as it neared Warsaw and hurled back. An armistice in October effectively ended the war, and they signed a peace treaty the next year.

The Soviet leaders could now finally turn to liquidating remaining armed opponents. In 1920 they crushed the remnants of Denikin's army, now commanded by Baron P. N. Wrangel, in the Crimea. Red troops drove outward from the Russian heartland in all directions, occupying all of Ukraine, mopping up the last pockets of serious resistance, and reasserting control over most of the outlying areas that had declared independence during the civil war years. Soon, most of the territory of Imperial Russia was under Soviet control, except for Poland, Finland, and the Baltic states of Latvia, Estonia, and Lithuania, which became independent, and a few small pieces of territory elsewhere. In 1921–22, the Red army crushed the last remaining armed forces opposing the Communist regime, the peasant armies often called "Greens," that had recently become an important force. That story, however, requires a review of war communism and Bolshevik policies toward the peasants.

WAR COMMUNISM: THE CLASS AND ECONOMIC CIVIL WAR

Lenin introduced the term "war communism" in 1921 to describe the Bolshevik economic and social policies of the civil war era. These policies grew out of a combination of Bolshevik ideology and economic-military pressures as the new rulers attempted to create a socialist society and a managed economy while fighting the civil war. The combination of communist ideology and pragmatic responses to problems produced the distinctive economic and social policies of the civil war, and in turn influenced both the war's outcome and the later Soviet Union.

The Bolsheviks came to power committed to creating a socialist society, meaning the replacement of private property and the market with social ownership and state direction and organization of the economy. The Bolsheviks therefore took steps immediately to establish control over the economy. Bolsheviks were, as Lenin noted, "centralizers by conviction," and they were obsessed with control in whatever context they operated, including the economy. One of the earliest acts of the new government was the creation on December 1, 1917, of the Supreme Council of the National Economy (VSNKh), whose task was to plan for and direct the entire economy. Coercion was implicit—sometimes explicit—in the system Lenin and the Bolsheviks had in mind.

Lenin initially approached the issue of nationalizing property cautiously. He expected to nationalize the banks and key industries (some of which were already state owned), but most initially would remain in private hands under strict state regulation. Worker radicalism and economic collapse, however, led to sporadic nationalization in late 1917 and early 1918, often by local officials in response to the workers' struggle to keep factories open and operating. At the same time the opening of the civil war further pushed the Bolsheviks in this direction as they undertook to mobilize economic resources for the war. They were not reluctant to do this, however, for it fit with their ideological goals. Therefore, in an effort to gain control of the situation, they decreed sweeping nationalization of industry, mining, and transportation on June 18, 1918. The state also undertook to control allocation of goods, introducing a nationwide system of consumer cooperatives for the receipt of essential food and other products, which were to be distributed according to a class-based rationing system. All of this assumed planned, or at least government control over production and distribution of goods. A major planning and managerial apparatus had to be developed to administer this.

As the civil war developed, a combination of ideology and economic need pushed the Bolsheviks toward ever more centralized control and direction of the economy, both in industry and in agriculture. The collapse of industry in early 1918 (the Russian exit from World War I and the end of the need for military production was a final devastating blow), followed by the beginning of civil war fighting, led the Bolsheviks to resort to strict central direction and draconian measures. On October 31, 1918, the Soviet government introduced universal compulsory labor for all males over age sixteen. The government also established higher pay for specialists and reintroduced piecework rates (pay per piece of work completed), harsh work rules and punishments for infractions, and other hated features of the old industrial order. The regime began to exhort the workers to "iron discipline" and "obedience" at the workplace. The Bolsheviks also broke up strikes, even using force to do so, and arrested worker spokesmen as saboteurs and counterrevolutionaries. Cheka-run labor camps backed this up. The issuance of labor books during the summer of 1919 gave the regime a way to keep a permanent record of employment and work behavior, similar to what the tsarist regime had used, and tightened its control over the workers. They brought the unions and other workers' organizations under Communist Party control and transformed them into agencies of the state.

The centralizing and authoritarian policies of the party conflicted with the workers' aspirations and activism. Issues of wages and working conditions continued to agitate them. The closing of factories in 1918–19 caused massive unemployment. The food crisis became desperate. Workers and others fled the cities—the industrial working class of Moscow fell from about 190,000 in 1917 to about 81,000 in January 1921, and Petrograd and other industrial centers suffered similar drops. The workers responded by demanding that the government take urgent measures to keep factories open, while opposing many specific policies of the regime. In short, they insisted that the government must act in the workers' interests as the latter perceived them. There were numerous clashes between workers and Bolsheviks, both violent and electoral. Workers' meetings criticized the Bolsheviks for blocking new elections to factory committees, soviets, and other organizations, for turning unions into government agencies, and for the economic disasters and other problems. Strikes broke out, and were in turn suppressed by force. These often led to large scale arrests of workers as the regime attempted to cut off incipient independent leadership. The decline in industry, and therefore in the need for workers, was another weapon the regime used to assert control—they could easily dispense with "trouble makers."

The clash of workers and the party/state created a dilemma for both. The party's self-identity was as "proletarian" and as representing the interests of the workers. This was essential to it as a Marxist party, and how it self-legitimized its "right to rule" and the policies of the state. Moreover, however despairing they were of worker behavior, the Bolsheviks recognized that workers were their key base of support and genuinely believed that their policies represented the workers' long-term best interests. At the same time, the workers, however angry with the Bolsheviks and Soviet state, had little alternative to supporting them. None wanted the old political-industrial regime back, and from mid-1918 onward they faced the threat of a White victory. The result was a curious situation in which both workers and Bolsheviks changed in important ways. Workers had only limited socialist political alternatives to the Bolsheviks (the SR and Menshevik parties were still legal and active, but tightly circumscribed by the regime). The Bolsheviks clearly lost support in the factories in 1918–19, although just how much is disputed. Some of that was due to disillusionment because of the harsh conditions of those years—life got worse, not better. Part was because worker-Bolsheviks left the factory floor in large numbers for the Red Army and for new jobs as factory, state, and party officials. Nonetheless, whatever the frictions in their relationship with the workers, ultimately the Bolsheviks successfully combined repression of dissent with positive appeals to the brighter future and warnings about the common threat from the Whites and capitalists. This was essential to their survival during these years. Overall, in periods of greatest political crisis and White threat, worker protests were muted, but when the political-military situation seemed more secure, workers vented their discontents.

The peasants and agriculture represented a special situation. In the six months after the October Revolution, the peasants finished carrying out a thorough revolution in the countryside. They expropriated and redistributed the land among themselves. Soon peasants held more than 90 percent of the land, the remainder being organized as cooperatives or state farms. Although the Bolsheviks in 1917 had encouraged the peasant revolution, it now brought special problems for the regime, especially one as focused on control and regulation as this one. The Bolshevik government wanted from the peasants the same three things its predecessors had: taxes, army conscripts, and food deliveries for the towns and army. These became more pressing during the civil war as the regime struggled to fill its army ranks and feed the army and the cities (where starvation threatened from 1918–22). Moreover, the peasant revolution worsened the grain supply situation because the former large estates had produced the most surplus grain for marketing, while peasant households tended toward a more self-sufficient economy, consuming a larger percentage of what they produced. The breakdown of industry worsened the situation because the shortage of consumer goods for purchases reduced incentives for peasants to produce and market surpluses.

To deal with the food issue, both the tsarist and the Provisional governments had developed plans for compelling peasant production and controlling distribution of grain and other foodstuffs at fixed prices, although they never successfully implemented them. The Bolsheviks undertook to do so with a law of May 1918 giving the People's Commissariat of Food Procurement dictatorial authority to centralize and fully control the acquisition and distribution of foodstuffs for the cities and the army. Bolshevik policy was based on a false, ideologically based assumption that there was a class of wealthy peasants and "rural bourgeoisie" who were hoarding vast amounts of grain. The problem, they thought, was how to force the peasants to turn over the foodstuffs, given that they could be expected to resist. One method, reflecting Bolshevik ideological assumptions, was the creation of Committees of the Poor Peasantry by a decree of June 11, 1918. Lenin had long held that sharp class distinctions existed among the peasants and that the poorest peasants were roughly the rural equivalent of the proletariat, and thus allies in the socialist revolution. This belief, coupled with the belief that there was a class of rich peasants (dubbed "kulaks") and that the villages were ripe for class warfare, set the stage for a policy of inducing civil war in the villages. The Committees of the Poor Peasantry would introduce class warfare into the villages and also be in charge of insuring the delivery of grain. These ideological assumptions were mistaken, for not only were they exaggerated to begin with, but the land redistribution of 1917–18 had a marked leveling effect in the village. It had reduced the numbers of both poorer and more wealthy peasants, so that about 85 percent of the peasants were now what was called "middle peasants," neither poor nor rich. The grain requisitioning and other Bolshevik control policies, moreover, reinforced peasant cohesiveness against "outsiders." Even the poorer peasants resisted them. The result was a rural civil war very different from what the Bolsheviks expected, as the villagers held together against outside predators, including Bolsheviks.

As a result, the government had to resort to more direct seizure of food-stuffs, using not only Red Army and Cheka units, but specially created "Food Detachments," ultimately numbering about 45,000. The latter's ruthless actions caused enormous resentment among the peasants. The state now estimated crop production, calculated its own needs, and then took the latter from the peasants. In return, it gave them what little industrial goods it had and, in theory, left an amount of grain assumed to be enough to live on and to sow the next year's crops. Believing that the peasants had more grain than they did and faced by hunger in the cities and army, the Bolsheviks squeezed ever harder. Sometimes food requisitioning armies, with their own quotas to fill, did not even leave peasants enough grain to live on or to sow for the next year's crop. In addition, the state levied new and heavier taxes on the peasants, plus new military conscriptions to fill the ranks of the Red Army. These Bolshevik exactions fed a spiraling rise of rural violence as the villagers resisted, both by reducing the amount of sown land and by arms, resulting in heavy losses on both sides. The Bolsheviks' ideologi-cally-based disdain for the peasants, the state's economic needs, and the re-gime's increasing propensity to use violence to solve problems, led them to resort to ever harsher measures. The peasants still resisted, with weapons and by evasion. The Bolsheviks in turn took this as proof of the need for "firmer" measures, which further alienated the peasants, and around and around in a vicious and increasingly bloody cycle.

Despite opposition to Bolshevik requisitioning, the peasants faced a po-litical dilemma. They did not enthusiastically support either side in the civil war, and mostly they wanted to be left alone by both sides. That, however, was impossible. Forced to choose, the peasants generally saw the Bolsheviks as the lesser of the evils, and also as the party that had passed the land distribution decree in 1917. So long as the Whites represented a threat, the peasantry gave a grudging support to the Bolsheviks, especially in areas where the White armies threatened in 1919. For the peasants, the purpose of revolution had been to drive out landlords and seize the land. Peasants feared that the White's demand for "return to legality" meant forcing them to relinquish all land taken thus far, as well as undoing other changes they had made in the countryside. The conservative ideology of the White lead-ers, and the presence of some noble landowners (although a minority) in their armies and leadership, led peasants to fear a landlord restoration if the Whites won. To this was added resentment at White requisitioning and con-scription that accompanied their occupation of areas, especially in south Russia. As a result, peasants both enrolled in the Red Army and formed their own "armies" to fight the Whites. Kolchak's offensive, for example, was hindered by the need to divert troops to fight peasant guerilla bands in his rear in Western Siberia (the main agricultural area under his control). At the other side of the country, Denikin had repeated trouble with peasant resistance, especially the peasant army of Nestor Makhno in southeast Ukraine. Well organized and supported by local peasants, Makhno's army fought under the black flag of anarchism against Reds, Whites, Germans, and various Ukrainian governments. He controlled a large area and set up an effective government. Makhno was a major thorn in the side of Denikin during the latter's 1919 offensive.

Once military defeat removed the White threat, the peasants no longer were willing to tolerate Bolshevik policies. The White defeat coincided with the beginning of near famine conditions, caused by the years of civil war and rapacious Bolshevik requisitioning of foodstuffs, and the combination set off widespread peasant revolts and the emergence of anti-Bolshevik peasant armies in 1920–21. By the summer of 1920, new peasant revolts blossomed across Russia, in addition to ongoing ones such as Makhno's peasant army in Ukraine. An especially large and most persistent peasant army emerged in Tambov province of central Russia, becoming known variously as the Tambov Revolt or the Antonov Revolt (after its main leader). Starting in a single village's resistance to requisitioning, it quickly spread into a brutal war of peasants killing local Communist officials while Red Army units burned villages and executed suspected peasant participants. Local SRs, still influential in the region, tried to offer leadership in the name of the original ideals of the revolution and of the slogan for "Soviet power." Indeed, in 1920 a new slogan, "Soviet power without communists," became widespread in Tambov and the country as a whole.

Under the leadership of Alexander Antonov and with the active support of the local peasantry, the Tambov peasant army became a formidable force that the government could not at first suppress (the war with Poland was still on). Moreover, peasant revolt spread to neighboring provinces, where revolts broke out under their own local leaders. These armies were drawn from the local peasantry (much of which had military experience by this time) and therein lay their strength. Not only did they firmly believe in their cause and were operating on home territory, but fighters could emerge out of and then merge back into the general population as conditions dictated, while the local population gave them food, supplies, shelter, information, and new recruits. Not until mid-1921 was the back of the Tambov peasant army broken. The main ingredient in its suppression was simple and brutal force, including mass executions, taking women and children hostage, burning villages, use of poison gas and armored cars, and ultimately overwhelming numbers of troops. The repressive force was helped by the devastations of famine and disease among the peasant population. The Red Army, which no longer had either White or Polish enemies to fight, also managed to destroy other peasant forces along the Volga, in Ukraine (including Makhno's army), and elsewhere by the fall of 1921. The concessions to the peasants embodied in the New Economic Policy of 1921, which over time helped pacify peasant hostility, were applied too late to have any role in the suppression of the peasant armies—that was done by force.

War communism was a peculiar attempt to replace markets and private ownership with decrees, state control, and nationalization of property, and thus to introduce "socialism" during the crisis conditions of civil war and economic collapse. The extent to which it did or did not "work" has been debated. The Bolsheviks did mobilize the resources necessary to win the civil war, and in this respect one might conclude that war communism "succeeded." But was the Bolshevik success because of or despite war communism? The economy was in a shambles by 1921, but was war communism the cause, or were the revolution and war the main causes of that? Such questions cannot be answered with certainty. What is clear is at the time of Bolshevik victory in 1921, the economy was wrecked and popular discontent—peasant revolt, workers' demonstrations, and the Kronstadt revolt—threatened the regime's survival just as much as White armies had earlier. Faced with this, Lenin called a halt to the mix of centralizing, authoritarian, and emergency economic measures now collectively called "War Communism." Under NEP, the government reduced the social and economic pressures on the population and gave them a breathing space. The ideological commitment to a total, "socialist" transformation of society did not cease, but was merely put in check for a while.

THE RED TERROR

Great brutality on all sides accompanied the Bolshevik Revolution and civil war. Henry Alsberg, an American correspondent, noted in late 1919 that there were no prisoners of war, because "after every battle—and this holds true of Bolsheviks and Denikin as well—all the captured officers are killed, and those of the soldiers whose papers show that they were volunteers meet a similar fate. The balance of the prisoners is given the choice of enlisting with its captors' army or being shot."[2] The opposing sides also used terror tactics against the civilian population, including the execution of known supporters of the opposition, killing people because of class or occupation, arbitrary execution of individuals or small groups as examples to intimidate others, and revenge killings, among other atrocities. The Red Terror (a term the Bolsheviks proudly used to describe their own actions) took particular aim at whole groups of people identified as "class enemies"—nobles, former government officials, army officers, merchants, and others of the educated and middle classes. Others who in some way fell afoul of the regime—peasants resisting grain or manpower requisitions, minority nationalist leaders, people labeled "saboteurs" or "speculators," even protesting industrial workers—also felt its force. Moreover, beyond those killed, others were locked up in prisons and concentration camps, where many of them died. The Whites also used terror, although less systematically and on a smaller scale. Their main victims were known or suspected Communist supporters, peasants and workers resisting White policies, and Jews in the Ukraine, where some White units engaged in anti-Semitic rampages. Peasant bands often inflicted horrible tortures and deaths on their enemies, whether Communists or Whites, when they turned against them, especially in 1920.

The Red Terror differed from the "White Terror" or killings by partisan bands most particularly in the Bolsheviks' efforts to develop a theoretical justification based on Marxism and the class struggle. The Bolsheviks argued that they were ushering in a new stage of human history, and that therefore "history itself" justified all of their actions, including repressions and killings, especially if framed in terms of "class conflict." Trotsky even wrote an elaborate and extensive justification of the use of terror in 1920, arguing that the Red Terror was a direct continuation of revolutionary struggle and thus justified. "The man who repudiates terrorism in principle . . . must reject all idea of the political supremacy of the working class and its revolutionary dictatorship . . . [and thus] repudiates the Socialist revolution."[3] While the civil war (and an attempt on Lenin's life in August 1918 by a suspected SR) intensified the use of terror and arbitrary violence against civilians, even before then Lenin and other Bolshevik leaders talked the language of violence against "enemies" and of the need for "terror" as an integral part of ruling. In early 1918, Lenin, defending the proposal that "enemy agents, profiteers, marauders, hooligans, counterrevolutionary agitators, and German spies are to be shot on the spot," told Issac Steinberg, the left SR minister of justice, during one of the latter's periodic protests against the lawlessness of the Cheka, "Do you think we can be victors without the most severe revolutionary terror?"[4] Later, during the civil war, Lenin and other Bolshevik leaders insisted on even greater bloodshed and repression. On August 9, 1918, Lenin ordered city officials in Penza "to carry out merciless mass terror against the kulaks, priests and whiteguards; suspects are to be shut up in a concentration camp outside the town." The same day, he sent another city the recommendation that they should "organize *immediately* mass terror, *shoot and deport the hundreds* of prostitutes, . . . officers, etc."[5] Terror and the leadership's language introduced into the party officialdom a legacy of striving to be "tough," a readiness to resort to force to settle problems, and a justification of killing masses of people, which had a lasting impact on the later Soviet political and social system.

CIVIL WAR, CULTURAL REVOLUTION, AND UTOPIAN DREAMS

After all that later happened in the Soviet Union, it is easy to forget the optimistic and reform features of the early Bolshevik regime, to forget how so many believed that they were ushering in a new and better era in human history. It is much easier to recall the repressive features of the Soviet regime, which in many ways came to define it. Yet, both were essential parts of the new regime from the very beginning. Many Bolsheviks—and others—saw the revolution as the beginning of a great cultural transformation, indeed as the road to utopia. The Bolshevik government moved quickly after taking power to legislate extensive cultural and social transformations. Building on the abolition of discrimination based on religion or nationality that the Provisional Government had begun, the Bolsheviks abolished all titles, ranks, and social distinctions. They stripped the Orthodox Church of control over marriage and divorce, which were made simple civil procedures, and of much of its role in education. They announced plans for universal education, health insurance, and other socially transforming actions, even though the economic conditions and civil war made implementation impossible at the time. The new Soviet leaders truly believed in the importance of a complete social and cultural revolution, and some even argued that it was more important than political or economic revolution, which they saw as only the means to this end. Therefore, in the early months, they issued a multitude of decrees designed to sweep away the old social order and begin the creation of a new socialist one, even if they did not have a clear picture or general agreement on just what that would be.

Bolshevik visions of a new society had a strong utopian streak (the Bolsheviks were utopians in many ways), with dreams of a completely remade society. Such a belief, in some degree, probably is inherent in revolutions and the belief that they are creating a new and better society sustains revolutionaries through the hard days. For the Bolsheviks, it was the idea of a socialist society in which private property and exploitation were abolished, but the details of the new society varied from person to person. Many Bolshevik leaders, such as A. V. Lunacharsky, People's Commissar for Enlightenment, welcomed revolutionary ideas for sweeping away "bourgeois" notions of art, education, marriage and family, religion, and other old social and cultural values, and their replacement by an as yet undefined "proletarian" form as part of a general social and cultural revolution. Alexandra Kollontai, a prominent Bolshevik and the People's Commissar for Social Welfare in the first Bolshevik government, theorized about a world in which women's roles were transformed by economic, sexual, and other equality, while traditional family structures were swept away, replaced by communal living and child-rearing practices. Many artists and intellectuals, advanced their own ideas about cultural revolution. The debate over exactly what the new culture would be was central to the intellectual effervescence of the civil war years and the 1920s, but everybody agreed that it would be radically different from the old. Creating a new "proletarian" or "Soviet" culture and a new type of person, "Soviet man," became a permanent goal of the Soviet regime throughout its existence, even after many of the utopian dreams had faded.

The pressures of the civil war had a contradictory effect on cultural revolution. On the one hand, it made implementing even the most modest visions extremely difficult. On the other, however, the rhetoric of the clash of historical epochs and class warfare encouraged the wildest dreams. Among those were ideas of a cultural-economic transformation through technology as extravagant as those accompanying the computer chip technology revolution of the late twentieth century. There were even attempts to implement some of these utopian visions, especially those that promised rapid economic transformation and involved state direction and control. In 1919–20, with the ruble worthless because of inflation and barter dominating economic transactions, many Bolsheviks were seduced by the utopian notion that the market and money would soon be replaced by a moneyless economy and state direction of production and distribution. This, they believed, could lead directly into a fully developed socialism. The perceived success of centralized control in winning the civil war encouraged some Bolsheviks to advocate even more vigorous measures of economic control in attaining their utopian goals. Trotsky advocated using the structure of the Red Army and methods of the civil war as models for a new economy. This included "labor armies," where workers would be conscripted for labor under military-type discipline and sent here and there as needed, as army regiments might. Despite popular opposition, these policies were introduced when some army regiments were transformed into labor armies in 1920 instead of being demobilized. Lenin became so enamored of mechanization and state planning that, in December 1920, he took the occasion of announcing planning for the electrification of the whole country to give one of his most technologically utopian pronouncements: "Communism is Soviet power plus the electrification of the whole country."

The peculiar combination of Bolshevik authoritarian control, disregard of individuals, fascination with technology, and utopian dreaming reached a bizarre culmination in Aleksei Gastev's Central Institute of Labor in Moscow in 1920, where they introduced ideas for the factory of the future. There they combined utopianism and authoritarianism with certain ideas about Western production efficiency (Henry Ford's production line and Frederick Taylor's time-motion efficiency studies and ideas of scientific management had already inspired a cult of "American efficiency" in revolutionary Russia). Hundreds of workers in identical uniforms performed identical mechanical production-line actions in unison, all calibrated according to Taylorism's time-motion efficiency studies. Man would either be replaced by machines or become machinelike, a near robot. It was the utopian dream run amuck. It was also a far cry from the freedom and dignity for which workers had revolted in 1917 and fought through the revolution and civil war.

Just as these ideas of cultural transformation were finding their most extreme and enthusiastic reception among party leaders, popular discontents forced the latter to face reality. Widespread peasant discontent caused massive revolts in late 1920 and early 1921, which accompanied a catastrophic drop in grain production. Industrial strikes and anti-Bolshevik resolutions shook the cities that winter, especially in "Red Petrograd," the cradle of the revolution. Finally, in March 1921, revolt broke out among the sailors of the Kronstadt naval base near Petrograd. Among the most radical political element of 1917 and one of the most reliable armed forces the Bolsheviks had in the civil war, the Kronstadters now criticized the government as no longer representing the will of the workers and peasants. They called for new elections to soviets, an end to many repressive policies, and a new revolution in the name of the ideals the workers, peasants, and soldiers had fought for since 1917. This forced the Bolshevik leaders to face economic and political realities. Although the Kronstadt sailors were falsely denounced as a new White plot and crushed by force, Lenin abruptly changed course with the New Economic Policy. War Communism and extravagant attempts at immediate cultural transformation were shelved in favor of allowing a partial "normality" to return to Russian social, cultural, and economic life, at least for the near term.

THE COMINTERN AND INTERNATIONAL CIVIL WAR

The Bolsheviks seized power not just to rule Russia, but to initiate a world revolution and to usher in a new world of remade mankind. Traditional Marxism saw history as moving through stages and envisioned a worldwide socialist revolution to replace the old bourgeois/capitalist era. Most Marxists saw this beginning in the most advanced industrial states and spreading quickly to areas such as Russia. Lenin, Trotsky, and others had argued, however, that the revolution might begin in Russia, the "weakest link in the capitalist chain," which would then spark revolution in the advanced industrial countries, who in turn would come to the aid of backward Russia. "We, the Russian working and exploited classes," proclaimed Lenin in January 1918, "have the honor of being the vanguard of the international socialist revolution." The Bolshevik Revolution, he said, had "opened a new epoch in world history."[6] Thus, the Bolshevik Revolution in Russia was, from the beginning, tied to the idea of an international revolution, which the Bolshevik leaders expected momentarily. They were so confident that Trotsky, as People's Commissar for Foreign Affairs, declared shortly after the October Revolution that he would simply "issue a few revolutionary proclamations to the people of the world and then shut up shop."[7] Although the Bolsheviks were soon forced to negotiate with the German and Austrian governments to get a peace treaty (a process they dragged out, hoping for the German revolution to take place), their faith in international revolution persisted and helped sustain them through the darkest days of the civil war.

Lenin and the Bolsheviks saw the events in Russia as the beginning of an international civil war of workers against capitalists. The prospects seemed especially bright following the end of World War I (November 11, 1918). The war had shattered the state structures of eastern and central Europe and left Europe exhausted, economically crippled, and in political turmoil. Civil wars in areas of the former Russian state that had declared independence, such as Finland, reinforced the notion of widespread civil wars on the path to universal proletarian revolution. The Bolshevik vision of international civil war found expression in the formation of the Communist International, or Comintern, whose founding manifesto (March 1919) declared that "The imperialist war [World War I], which used to oppose a nation to a nation, is being superseded, and has been partly superseded by, civil war, which opposes one class to another."[8]

The Comintern reflected the Bolshevik vision of international civil war. It had its roots in the divisions among European socialists after 1914 over their attitude to the war, but it was the Bolshevik Revolution and its dreams of world revolution that provided the catalyst. The radical left wing of European and American socialist parties reformed themselves as communist parties. This created a split between democratic socialist parties and the communist parties that lasted the rest of the century. The Comintern was founded in Moscow in March 1919 as the coordinating body of these communist parties. About the same time, Bolshevik belief in imminent world revolution received a boost when communists briefly held power in post-war Hungary and the German state of Bavaria, and drew strength from pro-communist demonstrations elsewhere. These events roughly paralleled the main White offensives in Russia, the period of the greatest military threat to the Soviet state, and thus reinforced the Bolsheviks' tendency to see the events inside and outside of Russia as parts of an intimately connected world civil war. Allied intervention in the Russian civil war confirmed the Bolshevik vision of themselves as engaged in a titanic, violent, worldwide struggle. Although hopes for immediate international revolution faded by 1921, as social and political stability returned to postwar Europe, the Comintern, based in Moscow and dominated by the Russian Communists, continued. It increasingly became an arm of Soviet foreign policy, the agency responsible for revolution abroad.

The idea of international revolution also provided part of the ideological basis for the unwavering Soviet hostility to the Western powers, which set the tone for international relations for most of the rest of the twentieth century. Allied intervention in the Russian civil war in 1918–19 did not create this outlook, which derived directly from Bolshevik ideology, but seemed to confirm the Soviet leaders' view of the world as divided into implacably hostile camps and that the forces of "international capitalism" were awaiting any opportunity to pounce. This became a permanent part of the Soviet view of the world and international relations, repeated over over again in propaganda to its own people and the world. It also helped shape the outlook of some post-Soviet Russians who believed that the collapse of the Soviet Union was not the result of its own internal problems, but rather in some way was engineered by the United States and "international capitalism." It continues to influence the foreign policy of the post-Soviet Russian state, many of whose leaders still think in terms of Russian opposition to "the West"—Europe and the United States—as the basic posture for Russian foreign policy. At the opening of the twenty-first century, some of the attitudes underlying the Bolshevik view of international relations have reemerged in the renewed Russian effort to position itself as the leader of the non-Western world against American and West European power and influence, attitudes that first surfaced and hardened during the civil war era.

By 1921, Lenin and the Soviet leaders stood successful against their domestic and foreign foes, although peasant revolts were still going on. However, they ruled over a country with a shattered economy, seething with discontent, and traumatized by years of war and civil war. Altogether, perhaps 25–30 million people died from war and war-related disease between 1914 and 1923. An even larger number were left permanently impaired from wounds, disease, and hunger. The expected international revolution had not happened. Moreover, many of the hopes for social and cultural transformation lay shattered as well. The world that so many had hoped for seemed far away. The leadership faced a wide range of questions about what to do now, about what kinds of policies were needed to deal with the many problems facing the country. They generally agreed that the New Economic Policy was a temporary measure, and that the ultimate goal was a socialist society, but concurred on little else, including how long NEP would last or how to go about building that society. The political leaders of the Soviet Union, soon without Lenin's leadership (he fell ill in 1922 and died in January 1924), fought out the answers to those questions through the power struggles of the 1920s that led to Stalin's rise to supreme power.

NOTES

1. By the harsh terms of the Treaty of Brest-Litovsk, signed on March 3, 1918, Russia officially ended the war, but also lost massive amounts of territory, people, industry, and grain producing regions. The onerous terms perhaps vindicated those political leaders of 1917, of varying political persuasions, who had argued against a separate peace with Germany precisely because of the staggering cost it would have for Russia. The cost to any political regime which did not make peace, however, was loss of power, and that was the one price Lenin was unwilling to pay.

2. Henry Alsberg in *The Nation*, given in Rex A. Wade, *Documents of Soviet History*, vol. I, *The Triumph of Bolshevism, 1917–1919* (Gulf Breeze, FL: Academic International Press, 1991), 404.

3. Rex A. Wade, *Documents of Soviet History*, vol. II, *Triumph and Retreat, 1920–1922* (Gulf Breeze, FL: Academic International Press, 1993), 83.

4. Cited in W. Bruce Lincoln, *Red Victory. A History of the Russian Civil War* (New York: Simon and Schuster, 1989), 135.

5. Evan Mawdsley, *The Russian Civil War* (Boston: Unwin Hyman, 1987), 81–82.

6. V. I. Lenin, *Collected Works* vol. 26 (Moscow: Progress Publishers, 1964), 472, 479.

7. Leon Trotsky, *My Life* (New York: Scribner, 1930), 391.

8. Quoted in Rex A. Wade, *Documents of Soviet History*, vol. I, *The Triumph of Bolshevism, 1917–1919* (Gulf Breeze, FL: Academic International Press, 1991), 322.

Nevsky Prospect, the main street of St. Petersburg/Petrograd, before the revolution. Nevsky Prospect was the traditional focus of popular demonstrations, including those during the February Revolution and 1917. (Library of Congress)

Demonstration for women's rights, Nevsky Prospect, April 1917. The women demonstrators in the middle of the street, carrying the banners, are mostly obscured by the onlookers. The closest banner says, "Russian League for Equal Rights for Women" (a feminist organization), and the back one reads, "Voting Rights for Women." (Courtesy of Jonathan Sanders)

May Day celebration, Petrograd, 1917 (April 18), Winter Palace Square. The banners of the soldiers' group read, left to right, "'Long Live a Democratic Republic," "Land and Liberty" (the long-time peasant and SR Party slogan), and "We Repudiate the Old World," with another banner within it proclaiming "Freedom." (Library of Congress)

Worker Red Guards and an armored car, 1917. (Al'bom Revoliutsionnoi Rossii, n.p., 1919)

Nicholas II and his family, shortly before the revolution. (Library of Congress)

Alexander Kerensky, hero of the early months of the revolution, Minister-President from July–October. (Library of Congress)

Prince G. E. Lvov, Minister-President after the February Revolution, 1917. (Library of Congress)

Vladimir Lenin, the Bolshevik leader. (Library of Congress)

Czech troops in a fortified train along the Trans-Siberian Railroad. Armored and fortified trains played an important role in the civil war. (National Archives)

5

Ethnicity and Nationality in the Revolution and Civil War

The revolution opened up a new world of opportunities for the non-Russian peoples of the empire, who made up approximately half of the total population. In addition to the same chances for fulfilling social, economic, and political aspirations that the revolution gave the Russian population, it gave nationalist spokesmen an opening to organize, propagandize, and attempt to mobilize the population along lines of national identity. It also allowed nationalists an opportunity to assert their claims to political and cultural authority. As a result, a wide variety of nationality movements burst forth, ranging from those with modest claims for cultural autonomy and respect for religious and ethnic differences to others demanding national-territorial autonomy within a federal republic. The call for national-territorial autonomy was especially prevalent among the larger nationalities, while smaller or scattered groups looked to cultural autonomy.

In the winter of 1917–18, after the Bolshevik Revolution and the disintegration of central governmental authority, several nationalities moved toward complete independence. The civil war of 1918–21 involved major fighting by the nationalities against both Reds and Whites (as well as among themselves) that helped shape the outcome of the civil war. The Whites' refusal to accept any kind of nationality-based autonomy, much less independence, made it impossible for them to cooperate with nationalist governments and armies against the Bolsheviks and thus contributed importantly to the latter's victory. Moreover, the nationalist eruption of 1917–21 directly influenced the political shape of the Soviet Union, forcing the communist leaders to create it as a federal republic. Although long assumed to be largely an arrangement to soothe ethnic sentiments and win support when the regime was weak, with little long-term political significance for the state as a highly centralized communist regime, it turned out to have major practical long-term consequences. By reinforcing "national" identities and creating the political boundaries, administrations, and identities of "republics," it contributed significantly to the revival of nationalist assertiveness that resulted in the dissolution of the Soviet Union in 1991.

THE "NATIONALITY QUESTION"

The "nationality question" was complex, encompassing a large and diverse population: more than one hundred ethnic and nationality groups of widely differing size, culture, language, beliefs, and economic development, including about twenty major nationalities. These people had been incorporated into the Russian empire as it expanded and mostly lived in their ancestral homelands. ("Ethnic" in Russia did not have the now common Western, especially American, connotation of recent immigrants to a country who retain some values of or attachments to their former homeland.) The sense of ethnicity and nationality identity varied widely. Some groups or individuals had a strong sense of national identity, while others thought of themselves by tribal or local region. Some had a sense of being "Ukrainian," "Estonian," or other, but that was primarily cultural or linguistic and did not translate into any political identity that required some sort of autonomous or independent state. Some of the educated elites were thoroughly "Russianized" and had little nationality sentiment, although the same educated class also produced the leading advocates of nationalism. Tsarist Russia, however, had vigorously repressed nationalist sentiments wherever they appeared. As a result, nationality-based movements had to begin from the ground up in 1917, and initially had difficulty mobilizing the peoples in whose name they claimed to speak. In time, however, nationalism became an important force in the revolution and civil war, leaving a powerful legacy for the later history of the Soviet Union, including its breakup in 1991.

Assessing the importance of ethnicity and national identity in motivating people during the revolution and civil war is difficult. People had multiple identities and aspirations: a Ukrainian peasant could identify with the grievances of all peasants against landlords, including Ukrainians, but could also support Ukrainian cultural or political movements against other nationalities (such as Polish landlords, Russian officials, or Jewish merchants). If drafted into the army, he tended to identify with all other soldiers against the war and in hostility toward officers, but might also support the formation of specifically Ukrainian regiments with Ukrainian officers. Similarly, a Tatar factory worker in Kazan could respond to the issues of 1917 as a worker, as an ethnic Tatar, or as a Muslim, not to mention other possible identities based on gender, political beliefs, former life as a peasant, and other factors. When the Ukrainian peasant or Tatar worker was confronted with a need to choose among parties and programs, which identity prevailed? And, did it change according to time and circumstances?

The interaction of nationality or ethnicity with social class was especially complex. Where ethnicity and social-economic identity coincided, this produced successful ethnic-based parties that also were advocates of major social change and socialist in doctrine. Some, such as Latvians and Georgians, combined Marxist doctrines with a nationalist orientation in a situation where a minority population from another nationality dominated local economic and political power. In places such as Ukraine, nationalist leaders combined ethnic identity with the peasant orientation of the SR party and the peasantry's concern with land distribution. In such cases, it is difficult to distinguish to what extent their appeal rested on nationality or social-economic grounds. It appears that in most cases in 1917, social concerns eclipsed national content: nationalist parties without strong social reform platforms usually did poorly, while non-nationalist, "all-Russia," socialist parties often did well even in minority areas. Together, socialism and nationality were a potent political mixture. If skillfully developed by local elites, the combination offered both local power and a chance to advance national autonomy, whether cultural or territorial.

The nationality question also intersected with demands for civil rights and constitutional democracy. When brought together, they led to a demand for self-determination along ethnic lines. This ran counter to the basic political assumption of the Russian Empire, in which, although there were definite notions that some groups—Russians, in particular—were superior to others, the binding assumption was of a multiethnic empire held together by common loyalty to the ruler, backed by military force and a network of laws and administrative bureaucracy. Thus, the overthrow of the monarch in 1917 required a reconceptualization of the political relationships among the peoples of the state. Ethnically Russian or Russianized political leaders tended to assume that nothing much had changed, simply replacing the ruler with "the state" as the focus of loyalty. In contrast, spokesmen for the larger ethnic groups, especially along the western frontier, responded with assertions of their right to national self-determination.

For almost all nationality spokesmen and movements in 1917, at least until the October Revolution or even until the Constituent Assembly in January 1918, the objective was some kind of autonomy within a federal state. Most looked to some kind of territorial autonomy, embodied in slogans

European Russia, Major Nationalities

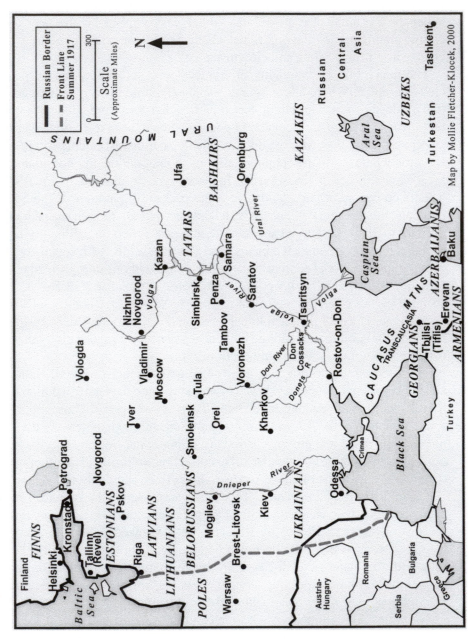

Map by Mollie Fletcher-Klocek, 2000

such as "A Free Estonia [or Ukraine or other] in a Free Russia." This meant a demand for the reorganization of the state as a federal republic in which administrative boundaries would be drawn along nationality lines, and that these regions would have significant autonomy. It usually included calls for use of the local language in schools, courts, and other institutions, the staffing of key government posts by people of the local nationality, grouping of soldiers into nationality-based military units, development of the local culture, and other related demands. It assumed that this was possible now that a democratic—free—Russia had replaced the tsarist regime. Calls for a "free Ukraine," or demands that the local nationality's political assembly possess "all authority" in the region, were not calls for full sovereignty or independence, but rather for extensive local autonomy and self-governance along ethnic lines within a radically decentralized, democratic, federal Russian state. The push for such ethnic autonomy within a federal state also reflected the prevalent idea of the importance for small nationalities to exist, for safety and prosperity, within larger political states; the multinational state was then a more widely accepted idea, especially in eastern Europe, than it is in our time. It is also important to recognize that the Russian language has two words for "Russian." *Russkii* referred to the nationality, language, and culture. *Rossiiskii* referred to the state. Thus, it was easy to distinguish between Russians as a people or nationality and Russian as reference to a state, a distinciton not linguistically clear in English and most other languages, but which makes more comprehensible discussion of an ethnic-based state within a "Russian" state.

The Provisional Government and the Soviet leaders in Petrograd and Moscow, many of whom were Russianized members of minority nationalities, were not sympathetic to even these limited nationality movements and demands for autonomy. Both the socialist and liberal political parties of Russia had opposed tsarist discriminatory policies and supported the civil and cultural rights of the minority peoples. At the same time, however, most political leaders at the center—Russians especially, but also many of other ethnic origins—insisted upon maintaining the political unity of the state. The Kadets were especially emphatic about preserving the authority of the state and opposed federalism. The SRs and Mensheviks were more ambivalent. Both supported the right of self-determination in theory but were uncomfortable with it in practice. The resolution on the nationality question passed by the Menshevik-SR dominated First All-Russia Congress of Soviets in June, while accepting the abstract right of self-determination of peoples, opposed any efforts at territorial autonomy or separation before the Constituent Assembly. Moreover, Petrograd authorities failed to recognize the seriousness of the new nationalist assertiveness, believing that through

civil rights, toleration, democracy, and elected local and national governments, the "nationality question" would fade away in the new free Russia.
Only in late September did the Provisional Government, already badly
weakened, make concessions to the growing demands for nationality autonomy, recognizing the right of self-determination. It also promised to issue laws giving minorities "the right to use their native languages in
schools" and elsewhere, months after this had become a staple of demands
from minority spokesmen.

In contrast to the Provisional Government and to the Kadets, Mensheviks, and most SRs (all of which parties were in the government and had responsibility for the preservation of the state), the Bolshevik party in 1917
created an accommodating image on the nationalities question. Lenin had
long argued that while nationalism was ultimately detrimental to the interests of the working class, whether it was progressive or regressive depended
on specific circumstances. For some peoples, he argued, national independence or autonomy was a prelude to socialist internationalism: let people
who had never enjoyed independence have it and thus learn the superior
benefits of socialist universalism. The right of independence did not mean,
however, that it was wise or even permitted in all circumstances. In 1917,
Lenin adapted these ideas to the reality of the situation in Russia, where nationalist sentiments were growing. He defended the right of national self determination—whether independence or autonomy—and repeatedly
attacked the Provisional Government on behalf of Finnish and other nationalist movements. The Bolshevik party conference in April, at Lenin's strong
insistence and over the opposition of some party leaders, affirmed the right
to secede. At the same time, however, the party resolution stated that demands for secession must always be considered from a class perspective on
a case-by-case basis. In the long run, this was used to justify the forced
reincorporation of some nationalities into the Soviet Union. In the short run,
Lenin's nationality program facilitated periodic cooperation with some na-
tionalist-oriented parties and helped win popular support in some regions.
His program rested on both practical acceptance of the force of nationality
and federalism in 1917 and a confidence that ultimately the success of
Bolshevik socialism would render nationalism meaningless. First, however, the Bolsheviks had to win and retain power, and that meant temporary
compromises even by those Bolsheviks less tolerant than Lenin on this
question. Nonetheless, local Bolsheviks often opposed autonomy for their
regions in defiance of central party policy. There were many contradictions
in Bolshevik policies and behavior toward the national minorities, even before they came to power.

In general, Russian and central political leaders on the one hand, and minority nationality spokesmen on the other, saw the revolution, and especially what freedoms it entailed, differently. Most Russian political leaders stressed that democracy and freedom could be guaranteed only by preserving intact the Russian state, perhaps even a centralized one. Minority nationalists, on the other hand, saw the democratic promise of the revolution being fulfilled only through some major restructuring of the state toward autonomy and federalism, and even meaning independence if that is what a people wanted. Without that, they argued, freedom and democracy had no meaning. Many came to think that while the new government might be different from the Imperial government on most issues, it differed little from the old one in its attitudes toward minorities and still represented Russian, "Muscovite," domination, and was hostile to "our" aspirations. The result was that growing nationalist movements among the larger nationalities along the western and southern borders threatened the unity of the Russian state. It is impossible in a short space to examine all of these, but we can sketch the impact of the revolution and the drift toward separatism in a few important and representative cases.

UKRAINE

Developments in Ukraine were especially important. Its large territorial size and population (just under a fifth of the total population of Russia in 1917), economic importance, and strategic geographic location made it a key area. A nationalist movement emerged among the small class of Ukrainian intellectuals in the nineteenth century, but met vigorous repression from the tsarist authorities. The February Revolution gave Ukrainian nationalists the opportunity to agitate on behalf of their views, and many organizations quickly emerged. The most important of these was the Ukrainian Central Rada (Council), formed on March 4, 1917, by Ukrainian intellectuals in Kiev. Led by socialist-oriented parties, the Rada represented a fusion of nationalism and moderate socialism and became the dominant institution of Ukrainian national politics in 1917, and eventually the government of Ukraine. Its initial program was summarized by the banner that festooned its meeting hall: "Long live autonomous Ukraine in a Federated Russia." It called for territorial-national autonomy for Ukraine within a new federal state, recognition of the Central Rada as the governmental authority in Ukraine, staffing of key governmental posts by ethnic Ukrainians, organization of Ukrainian military units, convening of an all-Ukraine constituent assembly, and use of Ukrainian language in schools, courts, and other public institutions. These issues were common to most nationalist movements in 1917.

The Ukrainian Central Rada soon came into conflict with the Provisional Government, which refused to recognize its claims to speak for all Ukrainians. The Central Rada responded by issuing its first "Universal" on June 19, 1917, proclaiming "Without separating from all of Russia, without breaking with the Russian state, let the Ukrainian people have the right to manage its own life on its own soil."[1] The Rada followed this by establishing a General Secretariat to function as its executive body, a government for Ukraine in effect. This brought cries of outrage from the Petrograd press, some seeing it as part of a German plot to dismember Russia. Relations between the Rada and Provisional Government continued to deteriorate throughout 1917, as the Rada pushed ever more vigorously for recognition of its authority while the Provisional Government resisted or made grudging concessions. During these disputes, the Rada remained committed to the idea of autonomy within a federal Russian state.

Even as the Central Rada asserted its authority vis-à-vis the Provisional Government, it faced serious problems in mobilizing popular support in Ukraine. Such problems dogged it and other Ukrainian national movements through the civil war as well. Central was the problem that the ethnically Ukrainian population was primarily peasant, and therefore dispersed across the countryside and difficult to mobilize. More important, that peasant population had only a weakly defined—if any—sense of Ukrainian identity. If asked to identify themselves, most peasants did so in religious terms (Orthodox Christian) or by regional terms (Hutsuli, etc.), and had little sense that their future rested with being "Ukrainian" or with any Ukrainian state. The Ukrainian peasants were interested in the land and other peasant issues and their behavior reflected that. As a result, they voted overwhelmingly for Ukrainian *socialist* parties, as in the Constituent Assembly elections in November 1917. In all probability, they did so on the reasonable assumption that those who spoke their local language were more likely to defend their interests. Class and ethnic identity came together for most Ukrainians in 1917. Ukrainians were overwhelmingly peasant, while landlords, government officials, and merchants were predominantly Russians, Poles, and Jews; nationality identity coincided with social-economic interests and cultural differences. Since the Rada and most successful Ukrainian parties also were socialist and supported land distribution, peasants found it easy to support them on both ethnic and social-economic grounds. As events were to prove during the civil war years, however, this conjuncture of interests did not necessarily translate into *active* peasant support for Ukrainian national governments.

The problems of Ukrainian nationalists (and some others) were magnified by another demographic reality—the cities were dominated by non-Ukrainians, who were either hostile or indifferent to Ukrainian national aspirations. Russians, Jews, Poles, Germans, Tatars, Greeks, and others, representing 20–25 percent of the population in Ukraine, dominated the cities and government, the professions, and commerce, while Ukrainians were primarily rural and peasant. In Kiev, the presumed capital of Ukraine and where most of the Ukrainian congresses and organizations met, Ukrainians made up only 16.4 percent of the civilian population in 1917, and they were a minority in nine of the ten largest cities of Ukraine. Concentrated in the cities and more easily mobilized, the non-Ukrainians were influential beyond their total numbers. The lack of Ukrainian influence in the cities translated into lack of power in the most important political assemblies, the urban soviets. These city soviets were concerned primarily with social and economic issues and the war, and tended to be either opposed or indifferent to Ukrainian nationalist concerns. The Russian population especially opposed the ambitions of the Ukrainian Rada and rejected calls for territorial autonomy and federalism, and many even rejected the notion that the closely related Ukrainians were a distinct nationality (frequently using the term "Little Russians" to describe Ukrainians). Most Jews, Poles, Tatars, and other minorities also were hostile or indifferent to Ukrainian nationalist appeals, and tended to stress the importance of individual civil rights and toleration for group culture, religion, and language. Most believed these could better be achieved within a multiethnic Russian state than within an autonomous, much less independent, Ukrainian state.

Despite these liabilities, and with the general if rather passive support of the peasantry, the Central Rada continued to attempt to mobilize popular support and to assert its claim to governance. This prepared the path for a declaration of independence after the October Revolution and for the civil war in Ukraine to include important nationalist features.

THE BALTIC, CAUCASUS, AND ELSEWHERE

Nationality movements in the Russian Empire shared many common features, and so the Ukrainian case study suggests many of the main features of them generally. Still, each major nationality had its own special situation and each movement its own characteristics. The neighboring Latvian and Estonians were both peoples incorporated into the Russian state during the eighteenth century and divided among multiple administrative districts. Both were traditionally peasant peoples, but with recently developed urban working and middle class populations. The minority "Baltic German" population had long dominated the area politically and economically, and thus emerging national consciousness was directed more against them than Russians. In both areas, strong national movements developed rapidly in 1917 and demanded the creation of separate administrative entities based on ethnic lines. They prospered by combining extensive socialism with ethnic identity and calling for autonomy within a federal Russian state, use of native language in schools and administrations, ethnic military formations, and other demands common to most nationality autonomy movements. In Latvia, the Bolshevik-dominated Latvian Social Democratic Party combined national identity and demands for radical social-economic reform to become the principal party by summer 1917. In Estonia, the nationalists were a combination of liberals and moderate socialists, and were challenged by city soviets representing mostly Russian and other non-Estonians and inclined toward the Bolsheviks and Left SRs. In both Latvia and Estonia, workers and peasants appear to have been concerned primarily with economic issues and to have supported parties with strong social platforms. How important nationality issues were is hard to gauge as all successful parties, including Bolsheviks, used the Estonian or Latvian language and stressed national language use and local autonomy in their platforms.

Across the Russian state in the Caucasus Mountains region, the demand for national political autonomy was weaker and a clear nationalist movement developed somewhat more slowly, although ethnic-nationality identity was quite strong. The situation differed among the three major populations. Armenians, an ancient and distinct Christian people, were spread across the Russian, Turkish, and Persian borders, and had been profoundly affected by the massive massacres of Armenians in Turkey before and during World War I. Their large merchant class, dispersed among the cities of the area, also gave Armenian identity a peculiar twist. The result was the emergence of a dominant political movement that stressed cultural-national identity and ethnic survival above all else, with only mild socialist tendencies. Most important, their survival depended on Russian protection from the Turks, and so autonomy sentiments were muted throughout 1917, emerging only with the collapse of Russian state authority at the end of 1917. In Georgia, a national movement somewhat similar to that in Latvia unfolded. A Marxist party, in this case Mensheviks, already had succeeded in blending national identity with class (Georgians were mostly rural, while the capital city of Tiflis [Tbilisi] was dominated by an Armenian merchant class and Russian political administrators). Despite the heritage of their own Orthodox Christian church and language, and a historic Georgian state before being annexed by Russia at the beginning of the nineteenth century, nationality-based autonomy had only weak appeal in Georgia. The dominant Menshevik party rejected nationalist separation, and that plus the security provided by Russia worked against separatist sentiment. The latter emerged only after the Bolshevik seizure of power and collapse of central authority forced the issue in the winter of 1917–18. The third major population group, Muslim by religion, Turkish ethnically, and culturally influenced by Persia, had an even weaker sense of identity and was just beginning to be collectively called Azerbaijani. Although they too were forced to form an independent state after the breakup of Russia in early 1918, this flowed more from events than as a result of a vigorous nationalist movement.

The large Muslim and mostly Turkic-speaking population of Russia was united by a common religion, but divided in many ways: by spoken language, history, geography, social- cultural characteristics, social-economic class, nomadism, ethnicity, and a sense of being different peoples. In many areas, especially Central Asia, identities were not well fixed in modern nationality terms. Although Central Asia produced movements for territorial autonomy along ethnic lines, as well as an unsuccessful pan-Muslim movement, the most important conflicts of 1917 were between Muslim modernizing reformers and culturally conservative, clerical-led forces. There were, however, major conflicts between "natives" and Russian settlers (especially in Central Asia), between Russians and Tatars along the Volga River, and between Armenians and Azerbaijani in the Caucasus, as well as among other groups. Nonetheless, nationality-oriented movements gained strength through the course of the revolution and civil war, with great importance not only for the civil war, but for the contemporary history of these areas and the modern states now existing there, and their relationships with Russia.

The situation and behavior of one of the largest minorities, the Jews, was unique. Russia's Jews greeted the overthrow of tsarism enthusiastically. Jews had been especially subjected to official discrimination as well as anti-Semitic riots—pogroms—in late Imperial Russia. More than any group, they benefited directly and immediately from the abolition of laws discriminating against people on religious or nationality grounds. The end of the restrictions led to a remarkable outpouring of activity: publication of newspapers and books in Hebrew and Yiddish, Jewish musical societies, Yiddish and Hebrew theatrical performances, expansion of religious schools, establishment of self-governing councils, and other expressions of Jewish identity and culture. Individuals obtained the freedom to pursue previously restricted professional and educational opportunities and to hold important public positions. At the same time, the revolution forced Jews to debate their identity as a people, perhaps as a nationality, and how they as an identifiable group should respond to the revolution. This was complicated by the fact that Jews were scattered geographically along the western edge of the state rather than occupying a traditional homeland in which they were the majority, as other groups did. Moreover, more than a third of Russia's Jews were in territories under German occupation. Given their dispersed settlement, most Jewish leaders argued for some kind of national-cultural autonomy rather than national-territorial autonomy, as most large minorities did. National-cultural autonomy assumed that the Jews were a nationality who should have some kind of regional and nationwide assemblies within a federal Russian state to speak for all Jews no matter where they lived, as well as communal self-governance for their communities within the cities and towns where they resided. A special and internally divisive Jewish issue was the Zionist call for emigration from Russia to set up a Jewish homeland in Palestine.

THE NATIONALITIES IN THE CIVIL WAR

The October Revolution, the Bolsheviks' dispersal of the Constituent Assembly, and the beginning of civil war affected the nationalities enormously. First of all, nationality spokesmen had to decide whether to recognize the new Bolshevik regime. Then, once the dispersal of the Constituent Assembly ended the possibility of that institution determining the question of federalism as the basis for the new Russian state, they had to decide whether to assert greater or even full independence. Then the beginning of civil war forced them to defend themselves against one side or another and even against each other, drawing them into the general whirlwind of war and chaos that characterized the years 1918–21. A brief survey of a few areas illustrates the main issues.

In Ukraine after the October Revolution, the Rada issued its Third Universal on November 7, 1917, proclaiming itself the government for Ukraine, although still within a Russian confederation. After the dispersal of the Constituent Assembly in January 1918, it proclaimed Ukrainian independence in the Fourth Universal. In the meantime, the Bolsheviks in Ukraine had gathered at Kharkov to proclaim a Ukrainian Soviet Republic. Tension between the central Soviet government and the Rada led to a Bolshevik armed invasion, which defeated the Rada's new army and captured Kiev on February 9, 1918. By this time, however, the Rada had signed a peace treaty with Germany and Austria-Hungary, and soon afterward German troops entered Ukraine and drove out the Bolsheviks. Then the Germans dispersed the Rada (which was socialist) and set up a conservative government headed by General Pavlo Skoropadsky. His government and German requisitioning soon alienated the peasants as well as many others, and opposing Ukrainian movements quickly appeared. Following the collapse of Germany in November 1918, Skoropadsky was overthrown and the Directory, a coalition of parties of generally socialist and nationalist orientation, was created. The Soviet government took advantage of the German withdrawal to invade. It defeated the Directory's troops and entered Kiev for the second time in February 1919. During 1919, multiple armies—Red, White, peasant, local partisan bands, those of various Ukrainian "governments"— struggled for control of Ukraine in whole or part. During its advance north, General Anton Denikin's White army considered Ukrainian nationalist governments and forces to be just as great an enemy as the Bolsheviks and diverted important forces to fight them. Kiev changed hands several times in 1918–19, while Ukrainian forces fought both the Bolsheviks and Whites. The Polish invasion in 1920 added a new dimension, with some Ukrainian forces again taking Kiev from the Bolsheviks with Polish help, only to be driven out again in June 1920. This time, the Bolsheviks held Ukraine for good, creating anew the Ukrainian Soviet Republic.

In the Baltic region, a similarly confused situation prevailed, but with a very different outcome. By October 1917, power in Estonia was divided between the Maapäev, representing Estonian nationalist movements of mostly liberal and moderate socialist outlook, and the urban soviets dominated by the Bolsheviks and radical left. The situation was still clouded when German troops occupied the area in February 1918. In Latvia, the Bolsheviks dominated the situation at the time of the October Revolution and supported Lenin's Soviet government, but the Germans also overran all of Latvia in early 1918. After the end of World War I in November 1918, a multisided struggle began among Reds (Latvian, Estonian, and Russian), Latvian and Estonian nationalists, anti-Bolshevik Russians, Germans, Poles, and Allied (especially British) forces. At the end, in early 1920, with German and Allied backing, the nationalists prevailed and the Soviet Union recognized the independence of Estonia and Latvia (as well as Lithuania). In Finland, strong nationalist sentiments had combined in 1917 with deep social divisions to create a volatile situation, but one in which all sides asserted Finnish political authority. The elected parliament, with a nonsocialist government, sought and received Soviet recognition of Finnish independence in late December 1917. Social-political tensions in Finland, however, led to an attempted seizure of power by leftists in January 1918, with Soviet backing. This provoked a bitter Finnish Red-versus-White civil war, in this case won by the Whites (anti-leftists) led by General Gustav Mannerheim, which confirmed Finnish independence.

In the Caucasus Mountains region, the situation was even more complex, due to the multiplicity of ethnic groups. During 1917, political leaders of the area, mostly moderate socialists of various nationality-based parties, struggled to avoid ethnic conflict even as they consolidated their own ethnic power bases. They responded to the October Revolution and dispersal of the Constituent Assembly by creating multinational political bodies to hold power temporarily, such as the Transcaucasian Commissariat, but failed to establish a real authority in the region against the centrifugal pull of national/religious identity and Bolshevik and Turkish pressure. In May 1918, the Georgians gave up on broader political solutions and declared an independent Georgia, followed quickly by the Azerbaijani and Armenians. During the following years a chaotic situation unfolded: territorial wars among the three new republics; wars with White and Red Russian forces; conflict with their own smaller minorities and nearby ethnic groups; intervention from Turkey, Germany, and then Britain; inexperienced leaders and the problems of state building, and economic collapse. Once the main Russian civil war and outside intervention ended, the three struggling republics faced the victorious Soviet Russia. Because the Bolsheviks were very weak in the area, the Soviet government had to resort to military invasions by the Red Army with only a flimsy pretext of answering the call of local communists. Azerbaijan was taken in April 1920, Armenia in December, and Georgia in February 1921.

In Central Asia, the local soviets, most importantly in Tashkent, were radical and immediately supported the October Revolution. They were strictly a Russian affair, however, with the local Muslim majority excluded. Therefore, Muslims rallied around their own organizations and demanded autonomy. During 1918–20 complex ethnic, political, and military struggles among Russians/Bolsheviks/anti-Bolsheviks and Central Asians/Muslims created chaotic political and social conditions, complicated by the fact that the circumstances and attitudes differed significantly by ethnic group within the larger Muslim area. Only gradually during the period of 1919–24 was Soviet power firmly established over the whole area, mostly by force but also by working with some local groups. Further north, among the Tatar and Bashkir Muslims of the central Volga River and the Ural Mountains region, the situation was rather different, with Russian and Muslim populations intermingled more than in Central Asia. Moreover, this area was central to the Russian civil war of 1918 and 1919. The Soviet government therefore made an earlier and greater effort to win Muslim support there. It appealed to national sentiment by decreeing a "Tatar-Bashkir Republic" within the Russian Soviet Republic in March 1918. They were helped by White attitudes, especially those of General

Kolchak's government, which opposed autonomy movements and alienated the Tatars and Bashkirs. The Bolshevik government skillfully steered a cautious path in the Tatar and Bashkir areas, trying to keep their support (or at least nonopposition) while preventing development of a strong Muslim political movement outside of Bolshevik control. Once the Whites were defeated, separate Communist-led autonomous Tatar and Bashkir republics were created within the Russian Republic.

By the end of the civil war, the Soviet government had brought most of the minority nationality areas under its military and political control (except in the Baltic regions where independent states emerged and in a few other places). The process, however, had involved creating theoretically independent soviet republics in places such as Ukraine, Belorussia, Georgia, Armenia, and Azerbaijan, plus "autonomous republics" for smaller nationalities within the Russian Republic, such as the Tatars. Each of these was ruled by the single Communist Party, which was not only headquartered in Moscow, but highly centralized. This politically anomalous situation needed to be resolved, and prompted vigorous debate in Bolshevik leadership circles about the role of nationality in the new political structure. Lenin, who generally was more sensitive to nationality identity issues than his colleagues, argued for some sort of federal system that allowed for the nationalist sentiments of the time. Much of the party leadership, including Joseph Stalin, who was People's Commissar for Nationalities, opposed concessions to nationalism and argued for a unitary state in which internal administrative subdivisions ignored nationality. In what proved to be his last major political victory before illness felled him, Lenin won out. The result was the approval in 1922 of the formation of the Union of Soviet Socialist Republics as a federal state, finalized in the constitution of 1924. The Communist leaders believed that within this state, the nationalist impulses of Ukrainians and others from the revolutionary and civil war years could be accommodated until such time—confidently expected—as national identity ceased to be important. Instead, it laid the ground for nationalism to reassert itself, more successfully, in 1990–91, and contributed to the breakup of the Soviet Union. The new republics that in 1924 (and after) constituted the Soviet Union's federal structure, and then emerged as independent states in 1991, were very similar to where strong nationalist movements had materialized in 1917. Unresolved problems with nationalist/religious assertiveness of some of the "autonomous republics," such as Chechnia, continue to plague the Russian state into the twenty-first century, as do relations with Ukraine and the other republics that declared independence in 1991.

European Russia, 1924 Boundaries

RUSSIA 1924

URAL MOUNTAINS

Russian Central Asia

Turkestan

Map by Mollie Fletcher-Klocek, 2000

Scale (Approximate Miles)
300
0

N

Omsk
Ekaterinburg
Ufa
Orenburg
Ural River
Kazan
Samara
Simbirsk
Penza
Saratov
Volga River
Tsaritsyn
Volga
Caspian Sea
Aral Sea
Tashkent
Baku
Erevan
Tbilisi (Tiflis)
TRANSCAUCASIA
CAUCASUS MTNS
Turkey
Black Sea
Rostov-on-Don
Don Cossacks
Don River
Donets
Crimea
Odessa
Ukraine
Kiev
Kharkov
Dnieper River
Voronezh
Tambov
Tula
Orel
Smolensk
Minsk
Belorussia
Brest-Litovsk
Warsaw
Poland
Lithuania
Riga
Latvia
Estonia
Tallinn (Revel)
Pskov
Kronstadt
Helsinki
Finland
Baltic Sea
Petrograd
Novgorod
Tver
Vladimir
Moscow
Vologda
Nizhni Novgorod
Volga
Russian Border 1924
Romania
Bulgaria
Greece
Yugoslavia
Hungary
Czecho-slovakia

NOTE

1. Taras Hunczak, ed., *The Ukraine, 1917–1921: A Study in Revolution* (Cambridge: Harvard University Press for the Harvard Ukrainian Research Institute, 1977), 382–95, gives the four Universals issued by the Rada in 1917–January 1918, defining its status vis-à-vis the Russian state.

6

Legacies

The Bolshevik Revolution has left a large and varied legacy, as well as a great deal of debate, which continues to affect the world today. First, there was impact on Russia itself and on the new state that came out of the revolution, the Soviet Union (or, formally, the Union of Soviet Socialist Republics—USSR), and eventually on post-Soviet Russia. The Bolshevik Revolution, to an unparalleled degree, swept away the old elite—political, social, economic, and cultural—and its values and institutions. Not only did it destroy the old political system and ruling class, but it also drove out the landowning class, which was not merely dispossessed, but in large part destroyed physically, either dead or fled abroad. The old middle class, especially the commercial element, was almost as completely eliminated, and its survivors found their condition radically altered. Property was confiscated and nationalized on an unprecedented scale, and the new system of state ownership and direction of the economy was equally novel. Politically, the Bolshevik Revolution ended the trend toward a more open, pluralistic, and democratic society that had been evolving in Russia and seemed to have reached fulfillment in 1917. Instead, the Bolsheviks, while retaining the outward forms of democratic and constitutional procedures, hollowed them out and created one of the most fully developed dictatorships of human history and the prototype of the modern authoritarian society. The earlier great revolutions of the modern Western world—the British, American, and French—incorporated more of the old elite and prerevolutionary values and institutions into the postrevolutionary order than did the Russian. In Russia, the Bolsheviks, more consciously and more successfully, built something very different from the old order. To be sure, much remained—Russia would have continued to be a "Great Power" in any case, for example—and the respective elements of continuity and change between tsarist and communist Russia have been the subject of debate ever since, but by any measurement, the changes were astonishingly sweeping.

A sense of the degree to which the Bolshevik victory in the revolution and civil war sent Russia along a path of development very different from what it would have traveled had victory gone to either the liberal and moderate socialist democrats who held power in the first part of the revolution, or to the conservative White generals who contested the civil war, can be seen by a brief look at alternatives, by a kind of "what if" look at Russia. Certainly, the Red Terror and the ideological justifications developed for it helped prepare the ground for the "Great Terror" of the 1930s and the continued use of repression against "class enemies" throughout Soviet history. Nothing similar existed in the thinking of their rivals, despite the actual brutality of some White Army commanders during the civil war, and it is impossible to imagine a government created by the Bolsheviks' rivals carrying out the massive terror and forced labor camps of Soviet history. Nor would any other regime have felt it necessary to destroy the old elites so thoroughly, although they might have partially dispossessed them, especially landowners. On another theme, the other parties would not have tried to transform "man" himself (and herself), to produce the "new Soviet man" of later Soviet propaganda, as the Bolsheviks did. Not even the most restrictive tsars controlled intellectual life to the extent that the Bolsheviks did, nor can one conceive of any of the political alternatives to the Bolsheviks establishing a similar kind of control over thought, beliefs, and expression. Any Russian government of the twentieth century would have pushed industrialization and would have had to use some of the same approaches (as had the industrialization of the 1890s), but it is hard to imagine any other regime as committed to centralized economic control or resorting to Stalin's tactics for industrialization. These and other "what if" scenarios can be debated indefinitely, and make for fascinating speculation, but what is not in doubt is that Soviet Russia was a very different place, with fundamentally different political, economic, social, and cultural features, than the Russia that any other outcome of the revolution and civil war would have produced.

Another example of the legacy, again on a comparative basis, is in the anti-Western attitude that was so much a part of the Soviet outlook and policies. Although an element of anti-Western sentiment ran through prerevolutionary Russian thought, there also was an even stronger current of seeing Western achievements as models for Russia, and a powerful Westernizing tradition had long existed. The people who first came to power in

1917, the liberals and moderate socialists, admired Western Europe and most of them hoped to reshape Russia along Western-inspired lines of democracy, parliamentary government, rule of law, and individual rights. Even socialists, who rejected Western capitalism, saw themselves as following the general path of European democratic socialism and broader Western values. Similarly, the White generals saw themselves as part of the larger Europe and within the slowly modernizing and Westernizing tradition of prerevolutionary Russia. The Bolsheviks, on the other hand, although subscribing to the Western philosophy of Marxism and admiring some features of the West, especially its technical achievements, were fundamentally hostile to the West's basic political, social, and economic institutions and values. They saw themselves as leaders of a world revolution in the name of an alternative set of political-economic principles. This produced not only many characteristics of the Soviet Union, but a foreign policy and international relations—including the Cold War—different from what any alternative outcome of the revolution would have produced. This anti-Western sentiment reached its highest point during the Stalin era, but was a feature before and after as well. Indeed, the whole Cold War could not have happened, or would have been a very different Russia-Western confrontation, without the Bolshevik Revolution and the foreign policy and revolutionary objectives of Soviet Russia, and the reactions they inspired abroad.

The revolution also provided the foundation myth of the Soviet Union and its sense of special mission. Soviet leaders saw the October Revolution as the event that legitimized their regime (and therefore attempted to control historical writing about it). Communist leaders, all the way to Mikhail Gorbachev at the end, saw the Russian Revolution as opening a new era in human history. This, they believed, gave the Soviet Union a special mission in the world. The idea of a special mission arising out of the revolutionary heritage, self-proclaimed but also granted by many others, became a key ingredient in the Soviet view of the world, their place in it, and the conflict with the Western powers in the 1920s and 1930s. The Soviet victory in World War II and their new postwar position as one of the two superpowers reinforced this sense of special mission, and it helped fuel the Cold War. Moreover, the revolutionary mission, a constant feature of Soviet internal propaganda, became an important part of the identity not only of the Soviet Union as a state, but of many of its people, and gave them a sense of purpose. The collapse of the Soviet Union in 1991, and with it a retrospective discrediting of the Bolshevik Revolution that had created the Soviet system, damaged also the revolutionary mythology and sense of a special historical mission. This has left many Russians disoriented as they seek a new national identity to replace the old Bolshevik-inspired one. The promises of the Communist

Party were so extravagant and the propaganda so pervasive that they stifled alternative visions of society, visions that might have helped sustain Russians through the hard present times. They also contributed to the cynical selfishness and corruption of the post-Soviet era. This legacy, this belief in a great mission, also has left not a few Russians discontented and yearning for the old days when they confidently believed in a great historical role for Russia in the world (and had the military power to back it).

The Bolshevik Revolution's worldwide impact was enormous, although not necessarily in the way its founders intended, and transformed the globe in important ways. Many people throughout the world accepted the Bolshevik/Communist leaders' vision of their revolution as the beginning of a worldwide upheaval and a total transformation of political, economic, and social systems. Communist movements, inspired by the Bolshevik Revolution, split off from existing socialist movements or were founded from scratch around the globe. In early 1919, they formed the Communist International (Comintern, Third International), under Soviet leadership, beginning a worldwide communist movement that became one of the most powerful movements of the twentieth century. Knowing what kind of dictatorships the Soviet Union and its communist offspring became, it is easy to forget how, in the first flush of optimism, and in reaction to the slaughter of World War I, many saw communism as a path to solving the problems of war, poverty, and inequality found in the capitalist and liberal democratic world. They believed that it would usher in a new era of freedom, prosperity, and justice. For most, that dream proved short-lived, perhaps two or three decades, but some continued to believe in it to the end of the century.

Outside Europe and North America, communism linked up with the anti-Western and anticolonial movements in what later came to be called the "Third World." The Bolshevik Revolution and the Soviet Union became models for many Third World intellectuals and political leaders, especially after 1945, when a newly powerful Soviet Union presented itself to the world as an alternative model for economic and social development and as an alternative type of political system. Indeed, imagining the Third World revolutions of the second half of the twentieth century without the Bolshevik/communist inspiration is difficult. They certainly would have been different revolutions. Although countries such as China, Vietnam, and Cuba had to adapt communism to local conditions, and in the process altered it, they made their revolutions in the name of the communist revolutionary tradition begun by the Bolsheviks and saw themselves as continuing it. Other revolutionaries in Asia, Africa, and Latin America drew more selectively on the Bolshevik revolutionary tradition and communism, but were nonetheless influenced by them to varying degrees.

Nor should we overlook the impact of the Bolshevik Revolution on non-communist political movements, as the Bolsheviks inspired revulsion as well as admiration. Bolshevism/communism powerfully affected, and in significant ways reshaped, conservatism as a political movement. Anti-communism became a central tenet of conservative thought and programs. At times it perhaps became the dominant element, such as in the "Red Scare" of 1920, and in the activities of Joseph McCarthy in the early 1950s. One of the often-made political analyses of the 1990s was to ask what the collapse of the Soviet Union meant for conservatism, what might replace anticommunism and anti-Soviet postures as centerpieces of conservative political parties in the United States and Europe. Other political movements, liberalism and democratic socialism in particular, also had to redefine themselves vis-à-vis the Bolshevik Revolution, communism, and the Soviet Union. Conflict over communism tore European and American trade union movements apart, and the Westesrn intellectual communities as well. The rise of fascism and Nazism is not understandable without comprehension of the role of anticommunism in their programs and among their supporters. Hitler, Mussolini, and other fascists shaped much of their appeal around the fear of the spread of Bolshevism; some observers have even suggested that without communism, those movements would never have gained the following that they did. After World War II, anticommunism was also an important part of many of the military dictatorships of Latin America and the Third World, and a key reason for American alliance with many of them during the Cold War era.

The Bolshevik Revolution's impact on socialism as a political movement also deserves special attention. There have been two stages to the debate on this issue. The first began immediately after 1917. Socialism was an important political movement before the revolution, especially in Europe, and remained one afterwards. The Bolshevik Revolution, however, split socialism into sharply defined (and antagonistic), democratic and reformist versus revolutionary, communist, and authoritarian wings. Revolutionary socialism was revitalized and quickly became closely identified with communism and the Soviet Union. The collapse of the Soviet Union opened a new debate, which promises to be long-lived, about what that collapse means for the future of socialism generally. Some have argued that it means the (final?) discrediting of socialism as an ideology or political movement, while others (often with anxiety) have contended that it freed socialism from the albatross of Soviet communism, allowing democratic and nonrevolutionary forms of socialism a new opportunity to flourish. This controversy has been more important in Europe and the Third World than in the United States, where socialism has been less influential. Ultimately, the entire debate leads back to the Russian Revolution and civil war, to decisions made then and the consequences that followed.

The Bolshevik Revolution has had a far-reaching, if somewhat paradoxical, impact on the intellectual, and cultural currents of the twentieth century. Most directly, of course, it shaped the social, intellectual, and cultural features of the Soviet Union. Its influence was hardly limited to that country, however. The revolution, through the Bolsheviks' extravagant claims about building the future, stimulated both utopian and anti-utopian thought. Initially, it stimulated the arts in Russia, but quickly led to creative sterility inside the Soviet Union as the official doctrine of Socialist Realism was imposed. Art in the West also was significantly, if temporarily, influenced, as witnessed, for example, by paintings, photography, and films of the 1920s and 1930s. Yet, in the long run, Bolshevism's impact was limited. The main direction of art in the twentieth century was abstraction, which was anathema to the Communists, and even "realistic" art swiftly moved away from both the style and messages of Bolshevik-inspired Socialist Realism. Similarly, despite some minor influence on literary trends of the mid-century, the Bolshevik Revolution failed to stimulate a great literary tradition. It had a greater influence in the intellectual world, especially on political thought, but fell far short of the impact of the French Revolution (and to a lesser extent the American and British revolutions). To take one ironic example, while one cannot imagine Marx without the French Revolution, nothing similar can be said of the Bolshevik Revolution's impact on the world of thought. It was, perhaps, more successful in spawning a revolutionary romanticism, especially in Europe and Latin America, that in turn affected politics, thought, and culture. The Bolshevik Revolution also had a significant, if diverse, influence on popular culture in the West. Popular literature and Hollywood films of the 1920s and 1930s reflected a fascination with this mysterious new society, and then, with the coming of the Cold War in the late 1940s, communism and the Soviet Union provided the inspiration for a vast outpouring of novels and movies (of which John Le Carre's spy novels and Tom Clancy's *Red October*, novel and movie, can stand as examples). Its influence on diverse currents of thought and behavior continues, in often unpredictable ways. As late as 1999, Hollywood, seemingly far removed from such issues, found itself embroiled in bitter controversy over the earlier pro- and anticommunist activities of prominent film directors, writers, and actors, while in early 2000, a stage play about growing up a "Red Diaper Baby" in an American Communist family was playing in Washington.

A final legacy, one only recently recognized, was the effect of the revolution and civil war on the nationalities that made up the former Russian Empire and how that would affect the state structure of the region in the twenty-first century. The revolution of 1917 unleashed a powerful nationalist wave that had two immediate results. First, some peoples along the western edge of the old state took advantage of its collapse to call for self-determination and then to create independent states, while others attempted to do so, but failed. Second, the power of nationalism in the revolution and civil war forced the Soviet leaders to structure the new state, the Union of Soviet Socialist Republics, as formally a federal state made up of constituent republics (along with smaller "autonomous" republics and regions). National identity was now recognized by internal borders and in the names of constituent "republics." This was a major change from the unitary structure of tsarist Russia. Although in the following decades the Communist Party declared nationalism to be a declining force, and Western scholars dismissed its importance in the Soviet Union, in fact the nationalist surge of the revolution and civil war survived in altered form. The division of the Soviet Union into ethnic-based republics with distinct boundaries and administrations, and serving as repositories of national identity, set the stage for nationalism once again to assert itself if the central state power weakened. This it did again in 1989–91, just as it first did in 1917–21. Identities and boundaries that were developed because of the Russian Revolution proved to have laid the groundwork for the new independent states that emerged out of the wreckage of the Soviet Union—Ukraine, Belarus, and the new states in the Baltic, the Caucasus, and Central Asian regions. They also prepared the ground for the assertiveness of "autonomous republics," such as Chechnia and Tatarstan, within the post-1991 Russian state, with the attending ethnic conflicts (of which two or three dozen were ongoing at the opening of the new millennium in 2000). The long-term working out of the nationalist legacy remains uncertain, but is one of the major issues of the early twenty-first century.

Whatever its varied legacies, what the Bolshevik Revolution did not do was fulfill the revolutionary dreams of 1917 for freedom, democracy, economic well-being, civil rights, and justice. It did, it should be recognized, address some of the popular concerns. In particular it speeded the spread of literacy, created a well-educated population, and built a system of medical care, old-age pensions, guaranteed employment, and other social welfare programs that were very popular with the population (and exceeded what any alternative regime probably would have done). Despite these achievements, however, for the most part it failed to fulfill the aspirations of the revolution of 1917. Moreover, it failed to take its expected place in the revolutionary tradition. Many (including the early Bolsheviks) saw it as extending the line of progress of the British, American, and French Revolutions toward greater freedom, democracy, equality, justice, dignity, and well-being. In this it failed, proving to be an aberration from, rather than an extension of, those revolutions. Nonetheless, the legacies of the Bolshevik Revolution, for good or ill, are many and varied, are with us still, and will remain with us for a long time yet to come. Fascination with the Russian Revolution, its dreams, failures, and threats, remains an important part of its legacy to our world.

Biographies: The Personalities of the Revolution and Civil War

Denikin, Anton Ivanovich (1872–1947)

Denikin was a prominent Russian general and one of the two most important leaders of the White armies in the civil war. Born December 4, 1872, in Russian Poland to a Russian father and Polish mother, he entered the army and attended the prestigious General Staff Academy. Contrary to the image of the White generals as aristocrats (as some were), Denikin was among those of humble origins—his father had been born a serf. He distinguished himself as capable and courageous in the Russo-Japanese War and World War I, reaching the rank of lieutenant general. After the failed offensive of June 1917, Denikin was one of the most outspoken critics of the changes made in the army since the February Revolution. He spoke out for restrictions on the soldiers' committees, restoration of officer authority, and restoration of the death penalty as necessary steps to preserve the army.

After the October Revolution, Denikin made his way to south Russia where he helped organize the Volunteer Army. On the death of General Lavr Kornilov, he become its commander in April 1918, and in October also took responsibility for the government and civil administration of the areas under its control. By early 1919, he brought most anti-Bolshevik armies in south Russia under his control as commander-in-chief of the "Armed Forces of South Russia" (AFSR). In May 1919, Denikin launched his major offensive, driving north toward Moscow and Kiev with an army of 300,000. He conquered most of Ukraine and south Russia, reaching Orel, about 235 miles from Moscow, and was the greatest military threat the Reds faced. By fall, however, he had overextended his small army, and Red counterattacks in October drove Denikin's armies back. Pushed back into the Crimean Peninsula, Denikin handed over command of the remains of the army to General Baron P. N. Wrangel in April 1920.

As a political leader, Denikin saw himself as "above politics," in the tradition of Russian officers. Although personally a republican and one of the most politically liberal generals, he realized that his army was divided between republicans and monarchists and that to espouse either position would cost a large part of his army. Consequently, he insisted that the political future of Russia could be decided only after the defeat of the Bolsheviks and convening of a Constituent Assembly. He did, however, insist on maintaining the territorial unity of the Russian state, one Russia indivisible. This cost him potential allies among the nationalities, most importantly the Ukrainians, against whom he was engaged in fighting almost as much as the Bolsheviks. Denikin was more inclined to some moderate social reforms to meet the aspirations of workers and peasants than were most of his fellow generals, but his efforts to generate support through reform failed. In part, this was because his reforms were half-hearted and he had, ultimately, less to offer the populace than did the more sweeping reforms of the Bolsheviks. Moreover, any chance his reforms had were destroyed by the actions of some of his monarchist-oriented generals, who allowed looting and brutality toward the populations of areas they brought under their military control and who also allowed returning landlords to reassert themselves. As a result, Denikin was unsuccessful in rallying the popular support needed to win the war.

Denikin emigrated to Western Europe, living mostly in France, and then to the United States in 1945. In emigration, he wrote his memoirs and a five-volume account of the Russian Revolution and civil war, part of which was abridged as *The White Army*. He died in Ann Arbor, Michigan, on July 8, 1947.

Kamenev, Lev Borisovich (1883–1936)

Kamenev was one of the "Old Bolsheviks" and one of Lenin's closest associates. Born in Moscow on July 18, 1883, to a professional family, he became involved in radical politics while a student at Moscow University. He later took the revolutionary pseudonym "Kamenev" (real name, Rosenfel'd). He went abroad in 1902, where he joined the *Iskra* group, which was attempting to create a unified Social Democratic party. He supported Lenin in the party split and began his career as a Bolshevik party organizer and leader. After returning to Russia, he was arrested in 1907 and soon again went abroad. He then became a prominent member of the party leadership and, along with Grigorii Zinoviev, with whom his history is closely linked, one of Lenin's closest and most reliable collaborators. The three men and their families often lived close together (Kamenev had married Olga Bronshtein, Leon Trotsky's sister). Kamenev returned to Russia again in January 1914 to be Lenin's man overseeing Bolshevik operations in Petrograd. In November, he was arrested and sent to Siberia, where he remained until the February Revolution.

Kamenev returned to Petrograd on March 12, 1917, along with Stalin, and the two asserted their leadership over the party. Their policy of partial cooperation with the Provisional Government and the Mensheviks in the Petrograd Soviet was much more moderate than either that of the Petrograd Bolshevik leaders they displaced or what Lenin was developing on his way back from Swiss exile. Kamenev initially opposed Lenin's April Theses. Nonetheless, he was elected to the newly constituted Central Committee (nine members, the top policy body of the party). There he became the leading spokesman of the more moderate wing of the Bolshevik Party (if one can so characterize any Bolsheviks). He continued to be more open to cooperation with the other socialist parties and opposed Lenin's attempt to boycott the Moscow State Conference in August and the Bolshevik walkout from the Preparliament in September. Most of all, with Zinoviev, he led the opposition to Lenin's call for an armed insurrection, even issuing an appeal to the party for restraint and warning of the danger to the revolution from a premature uprising. With the Bolsheviks and other radical elements daily growing in popular support, Kamenev argued, it was preferable to wait for the Second Congress of Soviets or the Constituent Assembly and a peaceful transfer of power. His passionate arguments and party standing probably were one reason Lenin failed to get the party clearly committed to, much less organized for, a seizure of power before the October Revolution. Although he resigned from the party's Central Committee on October 20, Kamenev returned to Bolshevik headquarters to help direct its operations after Kerensky's move against the Bolsheviks on October 24. When the Congress of Soviets opened October 25 with a Bolshevik-led majority, he took the chairmanship. He also became chairman of the Central Executive Committee, established by the Congress on October 26, and thus in effect the titular head of state.

Kamenev continued to oppose Lenin (and now Trotsky) on the question of organizing power. During the Vikzhel negotiations, he led the Bolshevik faction that seriously strove to create a new, multiparty government. After that failed, in part because of Lenin's and Trotsky's intransigence, Kamenev again resigned from the Central Committee of the party, as well as from the

Central Executive Committee. Although temporarily removed from his main positions of political power, Kamenev continued to play an important role. He had a key role in peace negotiations with Germany and then, in February 1918, went to Britain and France to drum up support for the Soviet government and for international socialist revolution. During the civil war, he carried out a variety of diplomatic and domestic political tasks, as a kind of troubleshooter. He also resumed his old position at the top of the party hierarchy and as one of Lenin's closest associates. In 1919, he became a member of the five-man Politburo, the new top party organization, even chairing it in Lenin's absence. He became chairman of the Moscow Soviet, by then the most important city soviet in Russia, and held a number of other party and government positions.

When Lenin suffered a stroke in 1922 (an illness from which he never recovered), Kamenev joined Zinoviev and Stalin in the "triumvirate" that took effective leadership of the party. At first, the triumvirate focused on removing Trotsky, the man seen as their main rival, engaging in a major war of words as well as political maneuvering. Hardly had they succeeded than Zinoviev and Kamenev became concerned over the growing power of Stalin (which they had helped or acquiesced in). After an unsuccessful attack on Stalin at the Fourteenth Party Congress in 1925, Kamenev lost some of his offices. Continued conflict led to further loss of offices and power in 1926, and in 1927 he was expelled from the party and exiled to a small provincial city. His career in the following years followed a path of ups and ever sharper downs. In 1935, at the start of the "Great Terror," he was imprisoned, and in 1936 brought before the most infamous of Stalin's "show trials." Charged with being an accomplice of a "Trotskyite-Zinovievite Terrorist Center," he confessed to this absurdity, possibly in an effort to save his family, and was secretly executed in August 1936.

Kerensky, Alexander Fedorovich (1881–1970)

Kerensky was, as many different observers noted in 1917, the right man at the right place at the right time. A young man of thirty-five in February 1917, he quickly became the popular hero of the February Revolution and the Provisional Government, the subject of public adulation. In the words of one conservative, "He grew in this revolutionary bog, in which he was used to running and jumping, while we had not yet learned to walk." When the Petrograd Soviet was formed on February 27, he was elected vice-chairman. He entered the Provisional Government when it was formed on March 2, becoming the only person in both the Soviet and the government, which reinforced his key political position. Although he never played a major role in the Soviet, he increasingly became the key figure of the government, serving in succession as Minister of Justice (March–April), Minister of War (May–August), Minister-President (July–October), and adding the title of Commander in Chief of the army in September.

Kerensky was born on April 22, 1881, at Simbirsk (later renamed Ulianovsk in honor of Lenin, who also grew up there). Kerensky's father was a schoolteacher and administrator, among whose pupils, by a quirk of history, was Vladimir Ulianov, the future Lenin. Kerensky studied history and law at St. Petersburg University and became an attorney, joining a legal aid society that provided free legal assistance to the poor. During university days, he became associated with radical political circles, especially the Socialist Revolutionary Party. This led to his arrest in December 1905 and temporary banishment from the capital. In 1906, he became a defense lawyer in political cases and began to make a name for himself. In 1912, he was appointed to a special commission established by the Duma to investigate the Lena Gold Field massacre, where about two hundred striking miners had been shot. By this time he was a well-known public figure, associated with defending popular causes and ordinary people against government or employer repression. In 1912, Kerensky, whose political affiliation was loose, was asked to stand for election to the Fourth Duma on the Trudovik ticket. The Trudoviks (variously translated as Toilers,' Labor, or Workers' Party) represented the moderate wing of the SR party and of the nonparty populist movement. In the Duma, his energy and untiring criticism of government abuses made him a leading spokesman of the radical wing.

When strikes began in February 1917, Kerensky urged his fellow Duma leaders to make connections with the demonstrators in the name of revolution. After the revolt of the soldiers on February 27 transformed the upheaval, Kerensky plunged into the revolutionary thicket. During the last days of February and early March, he seemed to be everywhere—giving a speech here, haranguing soldiers there, scurrying in and out of meetings, issuing orders, dramatically arresting members of the old regime, and equally dramatically rescuing others from mob violence. He was the popular hero of the February Revolution. Indeed, more than any other political figure of 1917, he identified completely with it and in turn came to be identified with it, both in 1917 and after (ever since, the Provisional Government has sometimes been called the "Kerensky government"). He was variously dubbed the "people's tribune," the "people's minister," the "knight of the revolution," "the symbol of democracy," and "the first love of the revolution," to name several. His face adorned postcards, and a medallion circulated bearing his likeness. During the negotiations between the Duma committee and the Petrograd Soviet for formation of the Provisional Government,

Kerensky was one of the socialist Duma members invited to join the government. In keeping with a Soviet decision, the others declined, but Kerensky, in a sudden and dramatic appearance on the floor of the Soviet, appealed to the membership to approve his entry as their representative. "Do you trust me," he cried out, and received a thunderous roar of assent.

Within the new government, Kerensky quickly asserted himself in pushing a wide range of reforms and policies, and his immense popularity gave him enormous authority. The government soon divided between the more conservative government members around Paul Miliukov and Alexander Guchkov, who attempted to assert government authority and to diminish the Soviet's role, and a group around Prince Lvov that quickly determined the need to work closely with the Soviet because of its enormous popular support. Kerensky associated with the latter group. When the April Crisis led to Miliukov's resignation and the reorganization into the "first coalition," Kerensky became Minister of War and his influence and popular prestige grew. During this period, he became the embodiment of coalition government. He also became the government's focal point for preparations for the June Offensive, taking long tours of the front to stimulate fighting enthusiasm among soldiers.

Despite the unpopularity of and disastrous outcome of the offensive, Kerensky's personal reputation survived, in part because political blame focused on the Bolsheviks after the July Days. Kerensky became Minister-President of the new, "second coalition" government. Moreover, as other leading political figures left the government, Kerensky became increasingly dominant within it. Even as Kerensky achieved complete leadership of the government, however, both its and his own popularity eroded. The Provisional Government was failing to solve problems and to fulfill popular aspirations, and Kerensky's identity as the government leader led to a rapid drop in his popularity. The Kornilov Affair in late August completed the destruction of Kerensky's reputation. The crowds that earlier had cheered him as the hero of the revolution, now cursed him.

Kerensky remained head of the government after the Kornilov Affair, but his popularity was gone and his personal authority swiftly declined. He was now seen only as a stop-gap head of state until others could decide on a new government (a view he did not share). Some partisans of coalition still clung to him as its embodiment, but both popular opinion and most political leaders were moving away, looking for the next stage of revolutionary development. His decision to move against the Bolsheviks before the Second Congress of Soviets met sparked the October Revolution, which swept him from power.

After the October Revolution, Kerensky spent several weeks underground, trying unsuccessfully to organize an anti-Bolshevik movement. By that time he lacked political credibility with all groups and was very unpopular. In May 1918, disguised as a Serbian officer, he made his way out of the country. He played no significant role in the civil war. Kerensky lived the rest of his life in exile. During the 1920s and 1930s, he was active in emigré politics in France and Germany. In 1940 he fled the Nazis, coming to the United States, where he lectured and wrote. In the 1950s and early 1960s, he collaborated with Robert Paul Browder to edit and publish a large, three-volume set of documents, *The Russian Provisional Government, 1917*, and wrote his last memoir account (he had already written several), *Russia and History's Turning Point* (1965). He died on June 11, 1970, an event which even Soviet newspapers noted, although with a brief, one-line statement.

Kerensky was both the heroic and the tragic figure of the Russian Revolution of 1917. Thin, pale, with flashing eyes, theatrical gestures, and vivid verbal imagery, he was a dramatic and mesmerizing speaker with an incredible ability to move his listeners. One observer wrote that "Not only does he burn, he kindles everything around him with the holy fire of rapture." Announcement of his appearance at the "concert-meetings" that were so popular in 1917 drew huge crowds to hear him. The popular idol of the first weeks, he became the personification of the Provisional Government. Although he described himself as a socialist (which before 1917 was a sort of badge identifying opposition to tsarism), he was the mildest of socialists and really stood at the point where moderate socialism blended into the left wing of liberalism. Thus, he was the perfect embodiment of the coalition politics of 1917. As the year wore on, however, Kerensky's oratory could not compensate for the government's failures. The same speeches that in the spring made him a hero now earned scorn and a reputation as an empty babbler. The new paper currencies issued by the Provisional Government under his leadership were popularly called "Kerenki," and because inflation quickly made them worthless, his name thus took on something of that meaning as well. It was a tragic end for the hero of February.

Kolchak, Alexander Vasilievich (1874 or 1873–1920)

An admiral of the Russian navy, Kolchak became the principal White leader in Siberia and the east during the civil war. Born November 4, 1874 (sometimes he gave his birth as 1873), Kolchak followed his father into a naval career, serving with distinction in the Russo-Japanese War and other capacities, including as a polar explorer. During World War I, he first directed anti-German mine warfare in the Baltic and then, in 1916, became commander of the Black Sea Fleet. After the revolutionary mutinies against officers reached the Black Sea Fleet in June 1917, Kolchak threw his sword into the sea rather than surrender it, and then resigned his post. In July, the Provisional Government sent him on a naval mission to the United States, which led to nothing. He was at sea in the Pacific Ocean at the time of the October Revolution. He spent the first half of 1918 in various places, including an effort to enlist in the British navy for service against Germany.

In October 1918, the main anti-Bolshevik government in Siberia, the Directory (Provisional All-Russia Government) at Omsk, appointed Kolchak its minister of war. Many of its supporters believed that a strong military leader was necessary, and some looked for a dictator. During the night of November 17–18, conservatives overthrew the civilian leaders of the Directory—which included liberals and moderate socialists—and declared Kolchak to be "Supreme Ruler" of Russia, in effect dictator. This changed the nature of the Russian civil war in the east from one of Bolsheviks versus moderate socialists and liberal democrats to one between Bolsheviks and conservative military dictators, into Reds versus Whites. As military dominated movements had already emerged in south Russia and in the Baltic region, the whole civil war now took on this complexion.

Kolchak focused his efforts on building an army, largely ignoring political and social issues. He failed across the board. The army proved to be poorly organized and led, and was especially brutal in treatment of the civilian population. At the same time, the government was corrupt and inefficient. These features alienated most of the population, especially the peasants of Western Siberia and the workers of the Urals, who throughout the critical phases in 1919 harassed Kolchak's army with guerilla warfare. The obvious role of the British in arming and training his army, even to using British uniforms, alienated many others. Despite these problems, and with Allied prodding, the other White generals in 1919 recognized Kolchak's nominal supreme leadership (Denikin was especially lukewarm). This proved to have little practical effect, even in coordination of military strategy.

In March 1919, Kolchak launched an offensive westward, moving across the Urals and toward the Volga River. The Red Army counterattacked in May, and soon Kolchak's army was in rapid retreat and began to disintegrate. In November, Kolchak lost Omsk, his "capital," and the British had already withdrawn their support by that time. As Kolchak retreated eastward, his army disintegrated and for practical purposes he was the prisoner of the Czechs, who had been a key component of the anti-Bolshevik forces in the east, but who had always disliked Kolchak's dictatorship. The Czechs still hoped to complete their journey across the Trans-Siberian railroad to

Vladivostok and then to France and home, but faced nearly impossible obstacles ahead. When the authorities in Irkutsk (a combination of Bolsheviks, Mensheviks, and SRs) demanded that Kolchak and the imperial gold reserve that he was carrying be turned over to them, the Czechs in effect bartered him for safe passage on to Vladivostok and home. He was executed on February 7, 1920.

Ineffective as the military commander of large armies and poor at selecting good subordinate commanders, Kolchak proved a military failure (even allowing for the difficult task he faced). He also proved an inept political leader. He failed to create a stable administration in territory that he controlled and his policies alienated the population. His staunch defense of the principle of the territorial integrity of the Russian state meant that he could not reach any agreement and thus alliance with anti-Bolshevik forces in the west, especially Poles and Ukrainians, who would have been invaluable allies against the Bolsheviks.

Kornilov, General Lavr Georgievich (1870–1918)

Born August 18, 1870, in Ust-Kamenogorsk, Siberia, to a Cossack junior officer and a (probably) Buriat-Mongol mother, Kornilov became the central figure in the main "counterrevolutionary" episode of 1917, the "Kornilov Affair" in August. With prominent high cheekbones, dark slanted eyes, black hair and moustache, and by 1917 accompanied by an exotic bodyguard of Caucasus mountaineers, Kornilov made a dramatic appearance on the stage of the Russian Revolution. He already had acquired a reputation for bravery during the Russo-Japanese War of 1904–1905, served in both exploratory expeditions and espionage activities in Central Asia and Persia (aided by his "oriental" looks and a gift for languages of the area), and built a reputation as a dashing young Russian general. He was captured on the Austrian Front during World War I and then escaped, making his way, disguised as a peasant, to Russian lines, and became something of a national hero. After the February Revolution, he was appointed commander of the Petrograd garrison. During the April Crisis, he ordered troops out to control the demonstrations, only to have his order countermanded by the Petrograd Soviet. Angered, he requested transfer back to the front. He commanded the Eighth Army during the June offensive. During the German counterattack and Russian retreat, he personally ordered (illegally) the shooting of looters.

After the offensive's failure, Kornilov emerged as a vigorous advocate of using harsh measures to restore discipline in the army, including restoration of the death penalty and ending soldiers' meetings at the front. This drew the attention of a wide range of people interested in "restoration of order," mostly conservatives and liberals, but also some socialists, who found him more acceptable than most generals (he had a reputation for being more "democratic" because of his humble background and good relations with his troops). The Kadet Party pressured Alexander Kerensky, now head of government, to appoint Kornilov supreme commander in chief of the army, which Kerensky did on July 18. The problems that lay ahead were signaled by Kornilov's remarkable acceptance conditions, especially that he would be "responsible only to my own conscience and to the whole people," and his insistence on a free hand to restore military discipline. Kerensky did not really trust Kornilov, but hoped to use him both to appease the right and counterbalance the left. Kornilov in turn disdained the Petrograd politicians, believed treason was rampant, and generally had only a poor understanding of politics and political parties. Intermediaries, especially Boris Savinkov, a former SR terrorist who was now the assistant minister of war, tried to convince Kerensky and Kornilov that the salvation of the country rested on their cooperation.

During August, tensions surrounding Kornilov grew. He pressured the Provisional Government to impose the death penalty in the rear as well as at the front, to deal harshly with strikers in defense industries, and take other measures to "restore order." Resistance to these—they would have been extremely unpopular and probably impossible to implement—strengthened his distrust of the Petrograd political leadership. Conservative newspapers hailed him as the prospective savior of Russia, while left papers and orators warned that he was a prospective counterrevolutionary military dictator. Many saw him, favorably or unfavorably, as the potential Napoleon of the Russian Revolution. Indeed, those looking to break the power of the soviets and change the political structure began to organize around him. The degree of his knowledge and approval of these efforts remains unclear.

Starting as early as August 7, 1917, Kornilov began to move troops he considered especially dependable toward Petrograd under the command of General A. I. Krymov. The official purpose—and perhaps a genuinely believed one—was to defend against a supposed Bolshevik conspiracy and against a possible German thrust toward the city. In any case, it appears that Kornilov was becoming increasingly convinced of the need for a move against the left, with or without Kerensky's cooperation. An exchange of messages through intermediaries and via a sort of teletype machine explored restructuring the government and discussed the respective role of the two men. They also revealed their suspicions of each other, and convinced Kerensky that the general planned a coup. On August 27, Kerensky suddenly dismissed Kornilov. Thunderstruck, Kornilov denounced Kerensky and launched Krymov's force toward Petrograd. This quickly collapsed as delegates from the Soviet convinced Krymov's soldiers that they were being used for counterrevolution. By August 30, the "Kornilov revolt" had collapsed. Krymov shot himself and Kornilov and some other generals were arrested, but held in safety near the front by Kornilov's own special guard detachment composed of non-Russian mountaineers from the south.

The Kornilov Affair had enormous repercussions. The Bolsheviks and radical left had warned against a military coup and now seemed vindicated. Their political stock soared, and they soon took over the Petrograd and other soviets, preparing the way for the October Revolution. Kerensky, the moderate socialists, and the liberals, in contrast, were discredited because of their earlier support of Kornilov.

After the October Revolution, Kornilov and other imprisoned generals fled south to the Don Cossack region, where they organized the "Volunteer Army" to fight the Bolsheviks. During fighting on April 13, 1918, before the civil war fully developed, Kornilov was killed by artillery fire. His name, however, had already become, and remained, embodied in the terms "Kornilovite" and "Kornilovshchina," synonyms for counterrevolution in Russian, especially Bolshevik, usage.

Lenin, Vladimir (1870–1924)

Revolutionary, founder, and leader of the Bolshevik (Communist) Party, Lenin became the head of the first Soviet government and indispensable Communist leader though the Russian civil war. Born Vladimir Ilich Ulianov (also transliterated as Ul'ianov, Ulyanov, and Ul'yanov) on April 23, 1870, in Simbirsk (later renamed Ulianovsk), he assumed the revolutionary pseudonym "Lenin" in 1901. His father was of humble origin, but rose through the tsarist educational administration to acquire hereditary title of nobility (nobility could be earned through government service), which later benefited his son. Lenin excelled in school, where, by quirk of fate, his headmaster was the father of Alexander Kerensky. Lenin's older brother, Alexander, was executed in 1887 for participation in an assassination attempt against the emperor, and later that year, Lenin was expelled from Kazan University for political activities. After several years of gradually developing revolutionary interests, Lenin was attracted to Marxism, just then beginning to influence Russian radicals. Arrested in 1895, he was exiled to Siberia.

During exile (reasonably comfortable thanks to his noble status), Lenin began to work out the ideas of revolutionary organization that later developed into Bolshevism. On his release in 1900 he went abroad, joining the

group of emigrés who organized around the newspaper *Iskra* (The Spark) in
an attempt to form a unified Marxist revolutionary party. In 1902, he published *What is to be Done?*, one of the most important books of the twentieth century, in which he argued for the formation of a small party of
professional revolutionaries from the intelligentsia that would both cultivate the necessary revolutionary consciousness among industrial workers
and provide leadership and direction in the revolution. In 1903, the *Iskra*
group organized the Second Congress of the Russian Social Democratic
Labor Party to create such a unified Social Democratic movement (an earlier abortive meeting was accorded the honor of being the "first" congress).
Having formally founded the party, the *Iskra* group immediately split. The
key issue was Lenin's demand for a more restrictive party membership, but
Lenin's own domineering personality was an important factor as well.

In the years after 1903 the split deepened, evolving into two parties, the
Bolsheviks and Mensheviks, each claiming to be the legitimate party. The
terms originated with Lenin, who seized on a temporary majority to claim
for his faction the term Bolsheviks, "Majorityites," while dubbing his opponents the Mensheviks, or "Minorityites." Underlying the specific disagree-
ments between the two parties were fundamentally different outlooks about
party organization and relationship to the workers. Lenin proceeded, following ideas laid down in *What Is to Be Done?*, to create a party emphasizing a higher degree of centralization and discipline and one that exalted the
importance of leadership and distrusted initiative from below. The Mensheviks, in contrast, gave a greater role to the workers themselves and never had
the central organization or single recognized leader that Lenin gave to the
Bolsheviks. The years leading up to 1917 were spent in political and ideological struggles, as Lenin attempted to build a Bolshevik movement under
his own leadership and following his own ideas.

Still living abroad at the outbreak of World War I, Lenin became one of
the most extreme antiwar spokesmen, calling for transformation of the
world war into civil war and arguing that Russia's defeat was the lesser evil.
Therefore, he found it difficult to return to Russia when news came of the
February Revolution. Living in Switzerland, he was blocked by the surrounding Allied countries, who were reluctant to see the antiwar socialists
return to Petrograd, where they could only be a problem for the Provisional
Government and the war effort. Frustrated, he accepted an arrangement by
which he (and others) would travel across Germany in a "sealed" train, that
is, one in which their car was off limits to all Germans, official and nonoffi-
cial, and all necessary dealings would be via Swiss intermediaries. Realizing that this would provoke charges of being a German agent, Lenin
nonetheless felt that the need to return to Russia outweighed the negatives.

For the Germans, it was simply part of a larger program of aiding the activities of those hostile to Russia's government and war effort. Lenin arrived in Petrograd on April 3, 1917, via Sweden.

Lenin immediately, during the welcoming ceremonies, attacked the Provisional Government and the moderate socialist leadership of the Petrograd Soviet, calling for the swift movement to a new, radical stage of the revolution. His "April Theses," as these ideas immediately became known, were out of step with the optimistic mood of the time. Even many of the Bolshevik leaders rejected them. However, he quickly brought the Bolshevik Party (in which there was no other leader of equal status) into line and positioned his party to be the beneficiary of discontent when the government failed to fulfill popular aspirations. By June, that was beginning to happen. The early optimism faded, social-economic problems persisted, and the government and moderate socialists failed to find a way out of the war. By the end of June, the Bolsheviks were the most prominent of several radical left groups riding a tide of popular discontent summed up in the slogan of "All Power to the Soviets," i.e., a demand for a new, more radical government. When popular discontents erupted in the demonstration of the "July Days," the Bolsheviks, who had been stoking the unrest, found themselves in a difficult situation. Neither Lenin nor the top party leadership had sanctioned any attempt to seize power, but they were being besieged by workers, soldiers, and sailors demanding that they take leadership of the demonstration for "Soviet power" that had effectively taken over the city. Lenin was not even in Petrograd, but resting in nearby Finland. By the time the Bolshevik leaders cautiously endorsed continued demonstrations and Lenin returned, the demonstrations were on the verge of collapse. The government published documents (falsely) accusing Lenin of being a German agent, and Lenin and some other Bolshevik leaders were forced to flee into hiding, while others were arrested (although soon released).

Lenin spent the entire period from July 5 to October 25 in hiding, mostly in Finland. Thus, his ability to influence the course of events was limited. However, growing popular discontents fueled a steady growth in the rise of the popularity of the radical left, including the Bolsheviks. After the Kornilov Affair in late August, their popularity soared and Bolshevik-led radical left coalitions took over the Petrograd, Moscow, and other city soviets. From his hiding place in Finland, Lenin urged the party to seize power before the forthcoming Second Congress of Soviets. His call for a violent seizure of power split the party leadership. Grigorii Zinoviev and Lev Kamenev led the opposition to Lenin, while Leon Trotsky followed a third path. Despite the persistent myth of Lenin's plan for and direction of the October Revolution, the party's general leadership had in fact bypassed Lenin's demand for a violent seizure of power and was looking at the forthcoming Congress of Soviets to declare the transfer of power to a multiparty, all-socialist, Soviet-based government. No concrete plans had been made for a seizure of power before the congress. Kerensky's move against Bolshevik newspapers on October 24 upset this, however, and began the struggle for power before the congress met, sparking what turned out to be the October Revolution. By October 25, pro-Soviet forces, called out to defend the Soviet and the revolution, controlled Petrograd. Lenin, appearing at Bolshevik headquarters for the first time since July, took advantage of this late on the morning of the October 25 to proclaim the overthrow of the Provisional Government, and thus was able to present the Congress of Soviets with an accomplished fact. The congress, meeting the night of October 25–26, confirmed the transfer of power. Lenin unexpectedly had his revolution.

Lenin's real leadership came not so much in seizing power as in retaining it, and in turning the revolution in the name of "All Power to the Soviets" into a Bolshevik revolution and government. Unexpectedly finding himself the head of an all-Bolshevik government that no one had foreseen, Lenin struggled mightily over the next days and weeks to avoid efforts to force him to share power. The decision to disband the Constituent Assembly, along with other repressive measures such as the establishment of the Cheka, the political police (both policies pushed by Lenin), finished the first stage of the consolidation of power. It also made civil war unavoidable. In the cauldron of civil war, Lenin's grip on the party leadership and policy tightened. He provided the essential leadership and direction of the party and state throughout the civil war years: he forced reluctant Bolshevik militants to accept Trotsky's use of military specialists and traditional discipline and hierarchy in the building of the Red Army; he mediated disputes among party leaders, central and local; he forced the acceptance of the Brest-Litovsk peace treaty; his insistence on the seriousness of the "nationality question" both helped win support among many minorities during the civil war and laid the foundation for the federal structure of the future Union of Soviet Socialist Republics; he became the popular symbol of the new state (the cult of Lenin had already begun by 1920); and in other ways he was central to the success of the Bolshevik Party (renamed at his insistence, the Communist Party). In 1921, he pulled the party and country back from the brink of disaster by a timely retreat, the New Economic Policy, a reversal that only his enormous prestige could force through the Tenth Party Congress. This was his last great political victory, however, for the next year he suffered the first of a series of strokes that by 1923 effectively removed him from active leadership, and killed him on January 21, 1924.

Lenin was the founder of the Bolshevik (Communist) Party and the Soviet Union. He was also, perhaps, the originator of the modern one-party
dictatorial state. It was implicit in his earliest ideas about party organization
and leadership, and developed further as he led the party into increasingly
dictatorial practices as he struggled to ensure that the party retained control
of the government after October and that he kept control of the party. At the
Tenth Party Congress in 1921, he introduced the resolution "On Unity,"
which forbade factionalism within the party; in the short run it provided a
way for him to gag bothersome critics, but it later became an essential tool
in Stalin's rise to power and ruthless dictatorship. His beliefs and actions
shaped the Communist Party, and through it the Soviet state. Moreover,
through the Communist International and the prestige of the successful
Bolshevik Revolution among leftists in Europe and the world, Lenin had a
global impact that made him one of the most important people of the twentieth century, and his legacy continues into the present century.

Lvov (L'vov), Prince Georgii Evgenievich (1861–1925)

A prominent landowner of liberal tendencies, Lvov became known for
his humanitarian activities and then, in 1917, was the Minister-President of
the Provisional Government after the February Revolution. Born to an old
noble family on August 11, 1861, Lvov spent his childhood and early adult
years on his provincial estate, where he acquired an easy familiarity with
the peasantry and knowledge of agrarian issues. He was drawn to work that
promoted improvement of the peasants' condition, becoming chairman of
the Tula province zemstvo in 1902. He developed a strong faith in "the people" and their natural goodness, attitudes that carried over not only into his
humanitarian work, but also into his later role as Minister-President in
1917. During the Russo-Japanese War of 1904–1905, Lvov personally appealed to Nicholas II to allow the provincial zemstvos to organize relief for
the war sick and wounded. Working with the Russian Red Cross, he raised
funds for famine relief after the war. These activities established his reputation as a humanitarian.

Lvov entered political life reluctantly. He was a member of the zemstvo
delegation that appealed to Nicholas (unsuccessfully) in May 1905 to establish a Duma (legislature) to help resolve the Revolution of 1905. Elected in
1906 and 1907 to the short-lived first and second Dumas as a Kadet, he did
not play an active leadership role. After the second Duma was dismissed in
1907, Lvov returned to humanitarian and zemstvo activity, including a leading role in relief work during the famine of 1911. He was elected mayor of
Moscow in 1913, but his critical attitude toward the government led the lat-

ter to void the election. With the outbreak of war in 1914, he became president of the All-Russia Union of Zemstvos for the Relief of Sick and Wounded Soldiers. Obstructionism from government officials led him to conclude that the government was incapable of managing the war and the needs of Russia and had to be replaced. This brought him into closer ties with opposition political groups. By 1916, his name was widely circulated as a potential member, perhaps even head, of a reformed government if Nicholas could be forced to make concessions or be replaced. Then, during the February Revolution, the Duma Committee, at Paul Miliukov's urging, chose him to be Minister-President rather than the more conservative chairman of the Duma, Michael Rodzianko.

As head of the Provisional Government, Lvov shared the general liberal view that the February Revolution was primarily a political act, and that the main task of the new government was to consolidate political liberty, prosecute the war more effectively, and lead Russia to a freely elected Constituent Assembly that would determine the political future of Russia as well as important social and economic issues. Lvov was central to the political realignment that took place among political parties and leaders during the first weeks of the revolution. The Provisional Government became divided between a group around Paul Miliukov and Alexander Guchkov and another around Lvov and Alexander Kerensky. The former opposed the Soviet's continuing influence, insisting on the government's "plentitude of power" and on prosecution of the war to victory as the government's main objective. The Lvov-Kerensky group accepted the need to cooperate with the Soviet and, given the popularity of its slogan of "peace without annexation or indemnities," pressured Miliukov to accept modification of Russia's foreign policy. After the April Crisis, Lvov became committed to bringing leaders of the Petrograd Soviet into the government, threatening resignation if they refused. This led to the reconstitution of the Provisional Government on May 5, creating the "coalition government" of socialists and nonsocialists, with Irakli Tsereteli, Victor Chernov, and other socialist leaders entering the Provisional Government, while Miliukov and Guchkov resigned. Lvov remained Minister-President.

During the coalition Provisional Government of May–June, Lvov increasingly was at odds with the socialist ministers. The conflict came to a head over Victor Chernov's land program, which the government endorsed but Lvov repudiated as exceeding the authority of the government (he felt that only the Constituent Assembly had such authority). After the July Crisis, frustrated and worn out, Lvov resigned, recommending Kerensky as his successor. Exhausted (he aged noticeably during his four months in office) and disillusioned, he ceased to play a significant role in the revolution. After the October Revolution, Lvov was arrested by the Bolsheviks, but escaped and made his way abroad. Based in Paris, he participated in efforts to establish a Russian government in exile. He died in Paris on March 7, 1925.

Miliukov, Paul (Pavel) Nikolaevich (1859–1943)

Miliukov was a prominent Russian historian, leader of the Constitutional Democratic (Kadet) Party, and one of the leaders of the February Revolution and first Provisional Government. Born in Moscow on January 15, 1859, Miliukov's brilliance as a student at Moscow University attracted the attention of some of Russia's leading academics, who urged him to pursue a scholarly career. Later, as a teacher there, he published several important historical works. His increasing involvement in social issues, historical and contemporary, led to clashes with government authorities. Miliukov's defense of a group of expelled students in 1895 led to his dismissal from his teaching post and his exile from Moscow.

After a period of teaching and research abroad, Miliukov returned to Russia in 1899 and involved himself in political and journalistic activities. He began to develop his political stance as a liberal, rejecting both the Marxist and populist revolutionary traditions. For Miliukov and most educated Russians, liberalism meant overthrow of the autocracy and its replacement by some form of constitutionalism and parliamentary democracy, civil rights, equality before the law, and freedom of press, speech, and association. He tended to look to the British system as a model for Russia. His problems with the government led him to accept an offer to deliver a series of lectures on Russian history at the University of Chicago. To be able to deliver them in English, he quickly learned English. His lectures in 1903 were among the first academic courses on Russia taught in the United States.

When the Revolution of 1905 broke out, Miliukov returned to Russia in April. He resumed his political activity and participated in the founding of the main liberal party, the Constitutional Democrats (Kadets), and edited its newspaper. Initially opposed to cooperation with the government until it made further concessions on the question of Duma authority and constitutional government, after 1907 he moved toward cooperation in an attempt to preserve even the limited parliamentary government that the Duma represented. As chief liberal spokesman in the third and fourth Dumas, he committed the Kadets to reform within the system. During World War I, he believed that Russia's long-term interests demanded the defeat of Germany. By 1915, convinced that Nicholas's government's incompetence was harming the war effort, he helped organize the Progressive Bloc in the Duma, which demanded government reform and an increased role for the Duma.

Faced with government intransigence and incompetence, in November 1916 he attacked the government's failures in his famous "is this treason, or stupidity?" speech in the Duma.

As street demonstrations reached their climax on February 27, 1917, Miliukov shifted from trying to reform the existing government to consolidating, and limiting, the revolution that was upon them. He was instrumental in the Duma leaders' decision to form a Temporary Committee to take over governmental functions and in the various actions that secured the support of the army commanders and then the abdication of Nicholas. Miliukov played a leading role in the formation of the Provisional Government after the February Revolution. He became foreign minister and was expected to assume a dominant role in the new government. His commitment to continuation of the war to victory—he firmly believed that the revolution did not alter Russia's international interests, that her interests as a state remained the same regardless of political regimes—brought him into conflict with the Petrograd Soviet, which demanded a negotiated peace. His attempts to evade the pressure on him to revise Russia's foreign policy sparked the April Crisis, the first serious political crisis of the new era, and led to his resignation and the restructuring of the government. Miliukov continued, however, as the acknowledged leader of the Kadets and the most important nonsocialist politician in Russia in 1917.

After the Bolshevik Revolution, Miliukov escaped Bolshevik repression (several Kadet leaders were killed or arrested) by fleeing south. He tried, unsuccessfully, to provide political leadership for the newly formed anti-Bolshevik Volunteer Army. In early 1918, Miliukov urged Allied intervention to squash the Bolshevik regime. Then, in the summer of 1918, in a complete change of everything he had fought for regarding foreign policy, he called for German help. This, unfortunately, and inaccurately, left him tarred as pro-German and ended his effective political career. Following the civil war, Miliukov emigrated to western Europe, where he was active in emigré politics and as editor of the largest emigré newspaper. He died March 3, 1943, a staunch opponent of both the Stalin and Hitler dictatorships.

Nicholas II and Alexandra (1868–1918 and 1872–1918)

Emperor and Empress of Russia at the time of the Russian Revolution, Nicholas and Alexandra's shortcomings contributed significantly to the coming of the revolution and to their own unhappy fates. Nicholas II (born May 5, 1868) came to the throne in 1894 at the unexpectedly early death of his father, Alexander III. With a limited education and narrow range of experience and interests, he was poorly prepared for the tasks ahead. He appears to have had little in the way of political ideas beyond preserving the institution of autocracy. To this, however, he was passionately committed, and it became the one consistent principle of his reign. He also had an almost mystical faith in "the people," and practically to the end retained a belief that they in turn loved him and supported the institution of absolute monarchy. Such unrealistic views of the world in which he lived contributed to his ultimate destruction.

Nicholas's commitment to autocracy and his misguided vision of the common people were reinforced by his wife, Empress Alexandra. Born a German princess (Princess Alix of Hesse-Darmstadt) and grandchild of Queen Victoria of Great Britain on June 6, 1872 (May 25 by the Russian calendar), Alexandra was shy and uncomfortable in most public functions. The royal couple preferred, as much as possible, to isolate the royal family at the palace at Tsarskoe Selo, outside the capital. Nonetheless, Alexandra became a fierce defender of her husband's autocratic rights: "Never forget that you are and must remain authocratic [sic] emperor." Her defense of autocracy increased after the long-awaited birth of Alexis, the heir. She believed that Nicholas must preserve intact the autocratic prerogatives for "baby." Her opposition to any yielding of authority, hysterical at times, was perhaps reinforced by her knowledge—never made public—that Alexis suffered from hemophilia, a fatal blood disease inherited through her. Her advice to Nicholas, although its exact influence is unknowable, certainly reinforced Nicholas's own political attitudes.

Yet, no amount of exhortations from Alexandra could make Nicholas a decisive or effective ruler. A personally kind man and loving husband and father, Nicholas failed as a ruler. Under his direction, government drifted, problems went unsolved, and Russia suffered two unsuccessful wars and two revolutions in his slightly over two decades of rule. Despite his personal affection for his family, his policies made him "Nicholas the Bloody" to his subjects. Between them, Nicholas and Alexandra became major obstacles to timely and meaningful political and social reform, and thereby contributed significantly to the coming of the Russian Revolution, its nature, and their own tragic fates.

Despite his beliefs, and a wife and advisors who reinforced them, Nicholas was ill equipped to be an autocrat. Mild-mannered, of limited ability, narrowly educated, disliking governance, and drawn more to the trivia of administration than to major policy questions, Nicholas never mastered the skills of leadership nor understood the issues of the age. Russia was going through a vast social and economic upheaval fueled by industrialization, urbanization, and expanded education. Most classes of society were deeply dissatisfied. Political movements ranging from demands for liberal constitutionalism to radical socialism emerged to challenge Nicholas's authority. The future political structure of Russia became one of the key issues of his reign, but it is not clear whether he realized that. It would have required great skill, and more than a little luck, to steer Russia thorough the troubled times. Nicholas lacked such abilities, and, it appeared, even luck.

Nicholas's personal role in formulating the policies of his reign are difficult to determine. To what extent he initiated or simply endorsed polices presented to him cannot be known. What is clear, however, is that he bears significant responsibility for them because he jealously guarded his autocratic rights against ambitious officials and blocked calls for political reform, so that all government policies had at least his approval, and often more. Thus. he bears a responsibility for all the major negative developments of his reign: "Russification" (imposition of requirements to use Russian, limitations on the use of native languages and cultural practices, etc.) against some minority peoples and anti-Semitic policies, official indifference to the suffering and discontents of the new industrial working class, economic policies that contributed to rural famine, and many others, including the two wars of his reign. Indeed, he took a special interest in foreign affairs and was an exponent of the reckless expansionist policies in the Far East that sparked the war with Japan in 1904–1905.

The Russo-Japanese War, added to domestic discontents, led to the Revolution of 1905. This began on "Bloody Sunday," January 9 (23), 1905, when workers in St. Petersburg marched to the Winter Palace, carrying icons (religious paintings) and portraits of Nicholas. They called on Nicholas to intercede with the officialdom and industrialists on their behalf. Instead, government police and soldiers fired on the packed mass of men, women, and children, killing and wounding hundreds. Nicholas was not even in the city, but at the nearby Tsarskoe Selo palace. Nonetheless, Bloody Sunday more than any other event discredited Nicholas in the eyes of his subjects, earning him the sobriquet of "Nicholas the Bloody." Only after disorders had continued for several months and threatened the regime's survival did he finally yield to advice to offer major concessions. These, embodied in the "October Manifesto," involved especially expanded civil rights and the establishment of a broadly and freely elected legislature, the Duma.

The details of the Duma, spelled out in the Fundamental Laws issued in April 1906, disappointed almost everyone. Liberals found that they left too much power with the monarch and gave too little to the Duma, while Nicholas and his advisors resented what they had given up. Indeed, Nicholas continued to think of himself as an autocrat and steadfastly refused to recognize that he was now a constitutional monarch with limits, however small, on his authority. The result was immediate conflict with the Duma over relative authority, leading Nicholas and his new Minister-President, Peter Stolypin, to a kind of coup d'etat from above in 1907. The Duma was dismissed and the electoral laws revised so as effectively to disenfranchise the bulk of the population, giving electoral control to a small wealthy minority. This produced conservative third and fourth Dumas and contributed to Nicholas's illusion that he was still an autocrat. It also set the stage for renewed revolution and thus was a Pyrrhic victory for Nicholas.

After 1912, the political and social conditions worsened. Growing social unrest and revived activity by revolutionary parties threatened the regime, as did growing dissatisfaction with Nicholas's government, even among conservatives. At the same time, the caliber of government leadership deteriorated, with men of lesser ability increasingly appointed as ministers of state. Alexandra's expanding role in political affairs, for which she was even less fitted than Nicholas, worsened the general situation. Moreover, this coincided with the growing influence over her of Gregorii Rasputin, a disreputable "holy man" who she believed could save her son from his illness. Wild rumors circulated of Rasputin's dissolute life (partly true) and even of supposed sexual adventures with the royal family (Alexandra and her four daughters—not true). These tarnished the royal family's personal reputation among all classes of society, even aristocratic.

The outbreak of World War I brought Nicholas a brief respite, as patriotic fervor swept the land. Disastrous defeats soon changed that. Then, against the advice of his ministers, Nicholas decided to go to the front to take personal command of the army. This unwise act had several negative consequences. First, Nicholas now bore personal responsibility for defeats, even though his presence at front headquarters could not really affect the military situation (however much it addressed Nicholas's own psychological need for this symbolic sharing of the rigors of war with his soldiers). Second, it allowed Alexandra, and thus Rasputin, to play an even larger role in government affairs. Third, it deprived the government of its key member at the very time that even Nicholas's limited ability to lead and deal with issues was more needed than ever. Fourth, it contributed, via the disastrous management of the war effort and discontent over the German-born and incompetent Alexandra's involvement, to a growing belief among the upper classes that either Alexandra had to be exiled or Nicholas himself removed. By 1916, this gained fairly widespread currency among political leaders in the Duma, some generals, and even some of Nicholas' own relatives, and there were several conspiracies afoot at the time the February Revolution broke out. This paved the way for the rapidity with which even conservatives and his generals abandoned Nicholas during the February Revolution.

Nicholas's immediate contribution to the February Revolution was his ill-considered order on February 25 to officials in Petrograd that they immediately suppress the disorders there. This led to the use of armed force on February 26, which broke the fragile discipline of the troops on the twenty-seventh and guaranteed the transformation of demonstrations into successful revolution. After ordering that troops from the front be sent to suppress the Petrograd uprising, Nicholas then left military headquarters to go to his family at Tsarskoe Selo. Railway workers supporting the revolution shunted his train around, so that during a key period on February 28–March 1, Nicholas was largely isolated. March 2 found him at a railway siding in the city of Pskov. There, senior generals advised him of the need to give in to demands from the Duma for a government based on the Duma. After he had agreed, fresh news from Petrograd showed the demand for his resignation. At his generals' recommendation, he abdicated.

After his abdication, Nicholas and his family were held under house arrest at Tsarskoe Selo. Plans to send them to England (King George was a cousin) failed, partly because of opposition in Russia (where popular opinion wanted him tried for "crimes"), and partly because of popular opposition in Britain. Fear of either mob violence or escape plans led the Provisional Government to send the family to the distant provincial city of Tobolsk. In April 1918, after the Bolshevik Revolution, harsher jailers moved them to Ekaterinburg, in the Ural Mountains. There, in the early hours of July 17, 1918, as anti-Bolshevik armies approached, the entire family was hastily executed in the cellar of the house where they lived. This apparently was done with the knowledge or even orders of Lenin. The reasons remain obscure, and were probably a combination of factors: fear that a free Nicholas might become a monarchist rallying point, the intense hatred toward Nicholas and the Romanovs, growing class warfare, and the brutality of the times. Several other Romanovs were killed at about the same time. The bodies of Nicholas and his family were burned and buried in a mine shaft. Little was made of Nicholas's execution at the time, by either Reds or Whites, a reflection of the degree to which Nicholas was discredited even among conservatives, of how irrelevant he had become to the revolution, and what a secondary event it was in the struggle of the times. Despite claims that the heir, Alexis, or one of the daughters (most commonly Anastasia), survived, no credible evidence supports those romantic legends.

Ironically, Nicholas and Alexandra played a revived, if minor, role in post-Soviet Russia. A romantic interest in the royal family, about whom little information was available during the Soviet era, fascinated public taste, fed by television specials and printed materials (often of the most sensational and unhistorical kind). The question of reburying Nicholas's bones alongside his ancestors in St. Petersburg stirred a small political tempest for a time.

Trotsky, Leon (1879–1940)

Trotsky was a leading Russian Marxist and revolutionary, chairman of the Petrograd Soviet during the October Revolution, People's Commissar of War, and chief architect of the Red Army. His role in the revolution and civil war was enormous.

Trotsky was born Lev Davidovich Bronshtein in a southern Ukrainian village on October 26, 1879. Arrested in 1898 for radical activities, he spent his prison time studying radical, especially Marxist, literature. Escaping Siberian exile in 1902, he made his way to western Europe under the false passport name of Trotsky. There, he joined the Marxist group around *Iskra* and worked closely with Lenin. At the Social Democratic (SD) Party split in 1903, Trotsky sided with the Mensheviks against Lenin's definition of the party. He soon cut his formal ties to the Mensheviks, but continued to be at odds with Lenin, remaining an independent SD until July 1917. In 1905, Trotsky returned to Russia, then in revolution, where he got the opportunity to display his talents as an orator, political organizer, and newspaper writer and editor. One of the leading figures of the St. Petersburg Soviet of Workers' Deputies, he edited its newspaper and became its vice-chairman and then chairman from November 27–December 3, 1905, when he was arrested.

His year of imprisonment in 1906 was again put to good use reading and thinking, and he developed what was perhaps his most important theoretical contribution to Marxism, the theory of "permanent revolution." This argued that Russia's peculiar combination of backwardness and modernity created a situation whereby a revolution, once begun by the industrial workers of a relatively backwards country such as Russia, could find support first from peasants and then from revolution in the more advanced western European countries. In this way, it would be possible to move swiftly, by a permanent, or uninterrupted, revolutionary process, from tsarism through the bourgeois stage to the socialist (proletarian) stage. This theory opened up prospects for a socialist revolution in Russia, but also made its ultimate success dependent on Western revolutions. This theory became important to his and the Bolsheviks success in 1917–18, and to Trotsky's ultimate defeat in the power struggle of the 1920s.

Hearing of the February Revolution, Trotsky made his way back to Russia from New York, where he was working as a correspondent for Russian newspapers. Arriving in May, he immediately joined the Interdistrictites (Mezhraiontsy). Trotsky was extremely active as orator, writer, and organizer. As a speaker, he became as popular and as effective in the second half of 1917 as Kerensky had been in the first half. Similarities between Trotsky's theory of permanent revolution and Lenin's program laid out in the April Thesis, plus Trotsky's criticisms of the Provisional Government and the moderate socialist leadership of the Petrograd Soviet, brought the two men close in 1917. Old personal animosities delayed Trotsky's joining the Bolsheviks. In July, however, Trotsky led the Interdistrictites into the Bolshevik Party, and he soon was taken into the Bolshevik Central Committee. He quickly became the leading Bolshevik spokesman in the Petrograd Soviet and one of the party's most important leaders (Lenin was still in hiding in Finland). The tide of popular support for the radical left swept him into the chairmanship of the Petrograd Soviet on September 25. From that position, he constantly advocated and worked for the transfer of power to the soviets.

Trotsky played a key role in the debates of October over what course of action the Bolsheviks should take. He guided the Petrograd Soviet and, it appears, most Bolsheviks toward the goal of having the Second Congress of Soviets assume power, fending off both Lenin's impatient demands for a seizure of power before the Congress and the cautiousness of Grigorii Zinoviev and Lev Kamenev. Trotsky played an essential role in preparing for the Soviet assumption of power. On October 24, Trotsky led the defense of the revolution and Soviet in the confrontation with Kerensky's government that rallied popular support and put the Soviet and Bolsheviks in the position to seize power the next day.

After the October Revolution, Trotsky, now closely allied with Lenin on basic issues, played a crucial role in consolidating the new regime and winning the civil war. He supported Lenin's hard line, insisting on an all-Bolshevik government and rejecting a broad socialist coalition. He also became a leading defender of the new Bolshevik-imposed censorship and the use of terror against opponents. He initially took the post of People's Commissar for Foreign Affairs in the new government. Applying his long-held theory that the success of the Russian Revolution depended on revolution in western Europe, but also accepting that a quick peace was essential, he pushed for an armistice with Germany, but then strung out the actual peace negotiations, treating them as a propaganda opportunity while awaiting revolution in Germany and Austria-Hungary. Confronted by German demands for a harsh peace treaty, he countered with "no war, no peace," whereby Russia would neither sign the peace treaty nor continue the war. When this failed—Germany simply launched an offensive—Trotsky gave in to Lenin's insistence that they must sign whatever peace Germany put before them.

Moving to the post of People's Commissar of War, Trotsky played a central role in the Red victory. He replaced the assorted volunteer force of Red Guards, soldiers, sailors, and elected commanders with an army based on traditional practices of discipline, appointed officers, hierarchy, and conscription. Professional officers ("specialists") were recruited from the old army, but under the watchful eyes of reliable party men. From his mobile headquarters in an armored train, he raced around the country to direct the construction of the Red Army and its main fronts in the civil war. In the popular imagination his role was second only to Lenin's in the new regime.

Despite some later glorification of Trotsky as an alternative to Stalin, he was in fact a harsh leader, as arrogant and vain as he was talented, and quite ready to spill blood and resort to repression. During the civil war, he both practiced and wrote ideological justifications for mass terror against those declared "enemies," whether military or civilians. He instituted concentration camps, labor armies, militarization of labor, and other ruthless measures. Nor were these merely driven by the civil war—some of his harshest proposals and measures came after the Red victory was assured.

When Lenin fell ill in 1922 and his condition worsened in 1923, an open struggle for power developed. Zinoviev, Kamenev, and Stalin organized the "triumvirate" to take control of the party, while Trotsky appeared incapable of or indifferent to the basics of power accumulation. He failed to translate his great personal popularity as a war hero into a political machine, as the other leaders did. He seemed to disdain both his party colleagues and the prosaic work of the post–civil war era, and alienated many by his refusal to compromise on issues and by his arrogance. Instead, he challenged the triumvirate on several losing issues, which led to his condemnation for "factionalism" (outlawed since the Tenth Party Congress in 1921). In late 1924 Trotsky published an essay, "Lessons of October," which not only criticized Zinoviev and Kamenev for their behavior in October 1917 and emphasized his own leading role, but suggested that because of his behavior at the time of the October Revolution, he was the true Leninist and thus the person best qualified to lead the party. His opponents responded with a series of attacks on him and a war of recriminations followed. Both they and Trotsky used, and abused, history in assailing each other. In January 1925, he was forced to resign as commissar of war. In progressive steps he was expelled from his Communist Party offices and finally, in 1927, from the party. In 1929 he was driven out of the country.

In foreign exile he wrote widely, including his highly influential *History of the Russian Revolution* (1932–1933), which not only glorified his own role, but strongly influenced the writing of the history of the revolution in the West and the world, although professional historians today treat it with significant reservations. He carried on a bitter polemic against Stalin and became central to efforts to build an anti-Stalin communist movement. "Trotskyism" became an important political movement among leftist intellectuals in the West in the 1930s, and still survives today as a small fringe movement. Trotsky and "Trotskyism" were prominent targets of the Moscow show trials of the "Great Terror" of the 1930s. Finally, on August 20, 1940, a Soviet agent murdered Trotsky in Mexico by driving an ice axe into his skull.

Tsereteli, Irakli (1881–1959)

Irakli Tsereteli was the undisputed leader of the Petrograd Soviet during the critical first months of the revolution. His theory of Revolutionary Defensism spoke to the sentiments and hopes of the broad mass of the population as well as to the political elite, and became not only the policy of the Soviet, but also underpinned the Provisional Government in the spring, summer, and early fall of 1917. Tsereteli was, with the historically much better known Kerensky, Lenin, and Trotsky, one of the quartet of political leaders who struggled for the fate of the revolution, and thus was perhaps one of the four most important figures of 1917.

Tsereteli was born November 21, 1881, into a prominent Georgian intellectual and noble family, but one that was extensively Russianized and even Westernized. As a result, he focused on all-Russia issues rather than narrowly Georgian issues, even to the extent of underestimating the importance of nationalist sentiments in 1917. He became involved in radical politics while a student at Moscow University and, during a several-year period of arrests, political activity in Georgia, and Siberian and German exile, adopted Menshevism. Elected to the second Duma in 1907, he quickly made a name as an orator and leader of the Social Democratic faction. When the second Duma was dissolved, Tsereteli was arrested and exiled to Siberia, where he remained until 1917. After the outbreak of World War I, Tsereteli led a multiparty group of socialists in developing both the theoretical position on the war and the core of the cross-party coalition of socialists that in turn laid the basis for Revolutionary Defensism and the "moderate socialist" alliance of 1917, and of Tsereteli's leadership.

Tsereteli returned to Petrograd on March 20, and was greeted with bands and speeches at the train station. He immediately plunged into the debate about war that was going on in the Petrograd Soviet Executive Committee. In speeches on March 21–22, he laid out the basic doctrine of what quickly was dubbed "Revolutionary Defensism." Building on ideas developed in Siberia, he argued that the revolution changed the defense issue for socialists. No longer was it a war in defense of Nicholas's government, but rather a war in defense of the Russian Revolution against Imperial Germany. This was not a mere continuation of the war, he argued, because the Soviet and government would begin an energetic effort to end the war through a negotiated peace. The combination of defense of the country and revolution with the program for a negotiated peace and end to the war struck just the right note among both the war-weary but still patriotic soldiers and the socialist intellectuals. It catapulted Tsereteli into the leadership of the Petrograd Soviet. Although he never became the titular head (his close friend and fellow Georgian Menshevik, Nikolai Chkheidze, remained chairman), he was generally recognized as the leader of the Soviet. Around him coalesced a leadership group of Mensheviks, SRs, former Bolsheviks, and others. At the same time, Tsereteli changed the way the Soviet dealt with the government. He had long believed in the importance of a broad working alliance of socialists and liberals to advance the cause of democracy. He now sought to replace the confrontation politics favored by many of the early Soviet leaders with negotiation with the Provisional Government through a special Liaison Commission.

Tsereteli and the Soviet quickly put pressure on the Provisional Government, especially Paul Miliukov (the foreign minister), to accept the Soviet's program for a negotiated peace based on the slogan, "peace without annexations or indemnities, self-determination of peoples." As a first step, the Provisional Government would get its allies to agree to renounce all territorial ambitions from the war and the secret treaties that spelled them out. At the same time, the Soviet would work with socialist parties in Europe to generate popular support for such a negotiated peace. Miliukov's resistance sparked the "April Crisis," the first serious and open clash between the Provisional Government and the Soviet. The outcome demonstrated, for any doubters, the Soviet's predominant power and led to a growing demand that the government be restructured by the addition of some Soviet leaders. Tsereteli resisted this, arguing that to enter the government now would create expectations among their supporters that could not be fulfilled, leading to a loss of popular support. Nonetheless, pressure from all sides forced him to give in, and on May 5 the "coalition government" was formed, with prominent Soviet leaders, including Tsereteli, entering the government. The Revolutionary Defensists now took a direct responsibility for government actions, with the dire consequences that Tsereteli had worried about.

From May to the July Days, Tsereteli, along with Kerensky, became the embodiment of the new coalition of moderate socialists and left liberals, and Tsereteli was at the height of his influence. Almost immediately, however, the ground began to erode beneath him and Revolutionary Defensism.

June was critical to this. By then, the early optimism that their peace initiative would yield rapid results proved ill-founded, and thus the very basis of Revolutionary Defensism was endangered. Then, partly as a result, they agreed to support a military offensive. This undermined their support among the soldiers, who defined Revolutionary Defensim as requiring only defensive military actions. Finally, June began to see the effects of the growing economic crisis and the fading of popular optimism about rapid fulfillment of aspirations. All of these led to increased criticism from both left and right, eroding Revolutionary Defensism's base of support in army and factory committees, trade unions, soviets, and other popular institutions, while the political right talked of counterrevolution. Even the Menshevik and SR party organizations became restive with the Tsereteli group's leadership. The Kornilov Affair in late August further undermined Tsereteli, who had acquiesced in Kornilov's appointment. While Tsereteli continued to argue for—and claimed that Kornilov's failure demonstrated the value of—a broad socialist-liberal coalition, many of his previous supporters among the Menshevik and SR Party leaders began to search for a formula for some sort of all-socialist government based on the Soviet. Tsereteli fought tenaciously against this throughout September, and blocking it was his last major political victory. In doing so, however, he may have prevented formation of a government that might have appeased popular opinion a while longer, until the Constituent Assembly and perhaps the end of the war. Thus, his action may have inadvertently aided his archrival, Lenin, and made the Bolshevik Revolution possible.

After the October Revolution (he was away from Petrograd during the revolution itself), Tsereteli joined in efforts to create a broad-based government and head off civil war. He spoke for the Mensheviks at the Constituent Assembly on January 5, 1918. After its dispersal, he returned to Georgia, where he played an active, but secondary role in the politics of independent Georgia. He represented Georgia at the Paris peace conference. Tsereteli participated in emigre politics during the 1920s, but gradually broke with most of his Menshevik and Georgian comrades and withdrew from politics. He lived in Paris until 1948, when he moved to New York, where he died on May 21, 1959.

Tsereteli was, without a doubt, not only one of the most important figures of the revolution, but also one of the personally most attractive. Like many leaders of 1917, he was young, only thirty-five at the time of his return to Petrograd in March. He had a deep personal integrity that commanded respect even from political rivals. Not as flamboyant as Kerensky or Trotsky, Tsereteli succeeded through integrity, clear and forceful political thinking, and the ability to define precisely his objectives and then work purposefully to fulfill them. Although an effective public orator (in a period of exceptional orators), he was most effective in direct conversations, where his personal charm, personal magnetism, and reasoned arguments could work to their best effect.

Zinoviev, Grigorii (1883–1936)

Zinoviev had the peculiar paradox of being one of Lenin's closest collaborators and personal friends before 1917, and yet was in basic disagreement with him over tactics in 1917. After the October Revolution, he rallied to the defense of the new state and became one of its top leaders before losing to Stalin in the power struggles of the 1920s, and losing his life in 1936. In all this, he was similar to Lev Kamenev, with whom he is closely linked in the history of the revolution.

Born Ovsei Radomysl'skii on November 20, 1883, to a Jewish dairy farmer in southern Ukraine, he gained sufficient education to obtain a clerical job. In 1900 he joined radical circles and, in 1901, the Russian Social Democratic Labor Party. He went abroad, where he allied with Lenin's Bolshevik faction in 1903. In and out of Russia over the next few years, he became active in both legal and illegal party activities. In 1908, he went abroad for good (until 1917), becoming one of Lenin's prize proteges and then collaborator. From 1912 through 1916, he worked closely with Lenin in rebuilding the Bolshevik Party, and the two families lived close together most of the time (often with Kamenev as well).

Zinoviev returned to Petrograd with Lenin on April 3. Now, however, he began to dissent from his leader's policies. He felt that the April Theses were too extreme, but supported the slogan of "All Power to the Soviets." During the rising tensions of June and the outbreak of popular demonstrations in the July Days, he urged caution and restraint and was an important voice among the Bolsheviks for limiting the direct challenge to the government. Nonetheless, in the aftermath he was forced, with Lenin, to flee into hiding to avoid arrest. In September, he joined Kamenev in resisting Lenin's call for a violent seizure of power. He preferred a more cautious policy of allowing the growing popular support of the Bolsheviks and radical left to grow, pointing toward the Constituent Assembly to create a multiparty, all socialist, perhaps radical left, government. After the October Revolution, he continued to press for forming a multiparty socialist government, and in November resigned from the Bolshevik Central Committee over this issue and freedom of the press. He quickly returned, however, and resumed his position as one of Lenin's closest collaborators. In December 1917, he became chairman of the Petrograd Soviet, a powerful position he continued to hold until the power struggles of the mid 1920s.

Although a top party leader and thus involved in many facets of policy during the civil war, Zinoviev devoted much of his energies to the international revolution in his capacity as chairman of the Communist International (Comintern), founded in March 1919. He directed the work of the Comintern as it strove to ignite world revolution and to build communist parties abroad, including editing its newspaper.

With Lenin's illness, he became a potential successor to party leadership, giving Lenin's customary keynote speech to the Party Congress in 1923. Initially, many saw him as the leading member of the triumvirate with Kamenev and Stalin. In the struggle to isolate Trotsky, then seen as the most dangerous rival claimant to Lenin's mantle of leadership, Zinoviev took the role of chief public debater with Trotsky. Even as Trotsky was defeated, however, Zinoviev's own position began to slip. In 1925–26, Stalin managed to undermine Zinoviev's control of the Petrograd party apparatus and of the Comintern. In 1926–27, Zinoviev attempted to form an alliance with Trotsky against Stalin, but the latter quickly defeated them and they were expelled from the party's Central Committee and then from the party. Zinoviev's power and influence swiftly ebbed away and he was forced to make humiliating confessions of errors. In 1935, at the beginning of the Great Terror, Zinoviev was among the former party leaders charged with (obviously false) counterrevolutionary and treasonous activities. After a partial confession, he was sentenced to prison. In 1936, he had an unwilling star role in the second great show trial of former party leaders (including Kamenev), confessed to the farfetched charges of treason and espionage, and was executed in August (exact date unknown).

Primary Documents of the Revolution and Civil War

FORMATION OF THE PROVISIONAL GOVERNMENT

The first cabinet of the Provisional Government was established by negotiation between the Temporary Committee of the State Duma (the Duma was the popularly elected part of the legislative body of Imperial Russia, but elected on a restricted franchise) and the leaders of the newly established Petrograd Soviet of Workers' and Soldiers' Deputies. The former were liberals and conservatives, the latter socialists. The document somewhat misrepresents the reality of the situation when it says that the government was "appointed" by the Temporary Committee. The statement of principles also was agreed upon by the two groups. It stressed basic civil rights and promised the convening of a Constituent Assembly elected on a universal franchise. Conspicuously missing are two issues that would immediately become major and contentious questions: the war, and land distribution. The composition of the government and this statement were agreed upon on March 2, and immediately circulated as posters and published the next morning in the only functioning "newspaper" (newspapers had ceased publication during the revolution and the only source of printed news was a temporary broadsheet published by a committee of journalists). At the same time, a statement from the Petrograd Soviet leaders expressing support for the new Provisional Government was distributed along with the government's announcement.

Document 1
"FROM THE PROVISIONAL GOVERNMENT"

The Temporary Committee of the members of the State Duma, with the assistance and the sympathy of the army and the inhabitants of the capital, has now attained such a large measure of success over the dark forces of the old regime that it is possible for the Committee to undertake the organization of a more stable executive power.

With this end in mind, the Temporary Committee of the State Duma has appointed the following persons as ministers of the first cabinet representing the public; their past political and public activities assure them the confidence of the country:

Minister-President and Minister of the Interior—Price G. E. Lvov

Minister of Foreign Affairs—P. N. Miliukov

Minister of War and Navy—A. I. Guchkov

Minister of Transport—N. V. Nekrasov

Minister of Trade and Industry—A. I. Konovalov

Minister of Finance—M. I. Tereschchenko

Minister of Education—M. I. Manuilov

Ober-Procurator of the Holy Synod—V. Lvov

Minister of Agriculture—A. I. Shingarev

Minister of Justice—A. F. Kerensky

The actual work of the cabinet will be guided by the following principles:

1. An immediate and complete amnesty in all cases of a political and religious nature, including terrorist acts, military revolts, and agrarian offenses, etc.

2. Freedom of speech, press, and assembly, and the right to unionize and strike with the extension of political freedom to persons serving in the armed forces as limited by the exigencies of military and technical circumstances.

3. The abolition of all restrictions based on class, religion, and nationality.

4. The immediate preparation for the convocation of the Constituent Assembly on the basis of universal, equal, direct suffrage and secret ballot, which will determine the form of government and the constitution of the country.

5. The substitution of a people's militia for the police, with elective officers responsible to the organs of self-government.

6. Elections to the organs of self-government are to be held on the basis of universal, direct, equal suffrage and secret ballot.

7. Those military units which took part in the revolutionary movement shall be neither disarmed nor withdrawn from Petrograd.

8. While preserving strict military discipline on duty and during military service, the soldiers are to be freed from all restrictions in the exercise of those civil rights to which all other citizens are entitled.

The Provisional Government considers it its duty to add that it has not the slightest intention of taking advantage of the military situation to delay in any way the realization of the reforms and the measures outlined above.

President of the State Duma, M. RODZIANKO

Minister-President of the Council of Ministers, PRICE LVOV

Ministers: MILIUKOV, NEKRASOV, MANUILOV, KONOVALOV,
TERESCHCHENKO, V. LVOV, SHINGAREV, KERENSKY

Source: Robert Paul Browder and Alexander F. Kerensky, eds., *The Russian Provisional Government, 1917*, vol. I (Stanford, CA: Stanford University Press, 1961) 135–36.

THE PETROGRAD SOVIET'S STATEMENT OF SUPPORT OF THE NEW PROVISIONAL GOVERNMENT

This announcement of support for the new government by the Soviet was issued along with the preceding "From the Provisional Government," often being pasted up on walls alongside it. The phrase that the Soviet would support the government "in so far as" it followed policies of which the Soviet approved, however, underscored the tentative nature of the cooperation between the two bodies, and itself became a subject of political controversy.

Document 2
"FROM THE EXECUTIVE COMMITTEE OF THE SOVIET OF WORKERS' AND SOLDIERS' DEPUTIES"

Comrades and citizens!

The new government, which was created from socially moderate elements of society, today has announced all the reforms which it pledges to carry out, partly in the process of struggling with the old regime, partly upon conclusion of this struggle. These reforms include some which should be welcomed by wide democratic circles: the political amnesty, the commitment to make preparations for the Constituent Assembly, the realizations of civil liberties, and the abolition of nationality restrictions. And we believe that, in so far as the emergent government acts in the direction of realizing these obligations and of struggling resolutely against the old regime, the democracy must lend its support.

Comrade citizens. The complete victory of the Russian people over the old regime is approaching. But enormous efforts, exceptional endurance and steadfastness are still required to [attain] this victory. Disunity and anarchy cannot be tolerated. All excesses, looting, breaking into private lodgings, plundering and destroying property of any kind, [and] aimless seizures of public establishments, must be stopped at once. A breakdown of discipline and anarchy will ruin the revolution and the freedom of the people.

The danger of an armed movement against the revolution has not been eliminated. In order to avert this danger it is very important to assure the harmonious, coordinated work of soldiers and officers. Officers who value freedom and the progressive development of the country must exert every effort to adjust their joint activities with the soldiers. They will respect the personal and civil dignity of the soldier, they will be sensitive to the soldier's sense of honor. The soldiers, on their part, will remember that an army is strong only in so far as there is a union between soldiers and officers, that one cannot stigmatize the entire officers' corps for the bad conduct of individual officers. For the sake of the successes of the revolutionary struggle, one must show tolerance and forget the insignificant misdemeanors against the democracy on the part of the officers who have joined the decisive and final struggle which you are now waging against the old regime.

Source: Robert Paul Browder and Alexander F. Kerensky, eds., *The Russian Provisional Government*, 1917, vol. I (Stanford, CA: Stanford University Press, 1961), 136.

DECLARATION OF THE
FIRST "COALITION" GOVERNMENT

Following the "April Crisis" over the war and Russia's foreign policy, and the obvious political instability which it revealed, the Provisional Government was restructured to bring in leading members of the Soviet. This was referred to as a "coalition" government, meaning that it contained socialists and nonsocialists. Several leaders of the Petrograd Soviet entered the government, including Irakli Tsereteli. Their policy of Revolutionary Defensism is reflected in the declaration's emphasis on a negotiated peace without annexations or indemnities and based on self-determination of peoples, coupled with assurances that they would continue to defend the country and revolution against Germany. The changed situation since the Provisional Government issued its first declaration (document 1) just two months earlier, is reflected also in the emphasis on economic and land issues in points 3–6. It is worth taking time to compare the two documents, both in tenor and in the issues raised.

Document 3
DECLARATION OF THE REORGANIZED
PROVISIONAL GOVERNMENT, MAY 5, 1917

The Provisional Government, reorganized by representatives of the revolutionary democracy, declares that it will energetically carry into effect the ideas of liberty, equality, and fraternity, beneath the standards of which the great Russian revolution came to birth.

The Provisional Government is particularly united as to the fundamental lines of future action, as follows:

(1) In its foreign policy the Provisional Government, rejecting, in concert with all the people, all thought of a separate peace, adopts openly as its aim the re-establishment of a general peace which shall not tend toward either domination over other nations, or the seizure of their national possessions, or the violent usurpation of their territories—a peace without annexations or indemnities, and based on the rights of nations to decide their own affairs.

In the firm conviction that the fall of the regime of tsarism in Russia and the consolidation of democratic principles in our internal and external policy will create in the Allied democracies new aspirations toward a stable peace and the brotherhood of nations, the Provisional Government will take steps toward bringing about an agreement with the Allies on the basis of its declaration of March 27.

(2) Convinced that the defeat of Russia and her allies not only would be a source of the greatest calamities to the people, but would postpone or make impossible the conclusion of a world-wide peace on the basis indicated above, the Provisional Government believes firmly that the Russian revolutionary army will not permit the German troops to destroy our Western Allies and then throw themselves upon us with the full force of their arms.

The strengthening of the principles of democratization in the army and the development of its military power, both offensive and defensive, will constitute the most important task of the Provisional Government.

(3) The Provisional Government will fight resolutely and inflexibly against the economic disorganization of the country by the further systematic establishment of governmental control of the production, transportation, exchange, and distribution of commodities, and in necessary cases it will have recourse also to the organization of production.

(4) Measures for the protection of labor in every possible way will continue to be promoted further with energy.

(5) Leaving it to the Constituent Assembly to deal with the question of transferring land to the toilers, and proceeding with preparatory measures

relative thereto, the Provisional Government will take all necessary steps toward ensuring the greatest possible production of grain required by the country and toward furthering the systematic utilization of the land in the interests of the national economy and of the toiling population.

(6) Looking forward to the introduction of a series of reforms of the financial system upon a democratic basis, the Provisional Government will devote particular attention to the increasing of direct taxes on the wealthy classes (inheritance taxes, taxes on excessive war profits, a property tax, etc.).

(7) Efforts to introduce and develop democratic institutions of self-government will be continued with all possible speed and assiduity.

(8) The Provisional Government will also make all possible efforts to bring about, at the earliest date practicable, the convocation of a Constituent Assembly at Petrograd.

Resolutely adopting as its aim the realization of the program indicated above, the Provisional Government declares categorically that fruitful work is possible only if it has the full and absolute confidence of all the revolutionary people and the opportunity to exercise fully the power essential to the confirmation of the victories of the revolution and to their further development.

Addressing to all citizens a firm and pressing appeal for the safeguarding of the unity of power in the hands of the Provisional Government, the latter declares that, for the safety of the fatherland, it will take the most energetic measures against all attempts at a counterrevolution, as well as against all anarchical, illegal, or violent acts calculated to disorganize the country and to prepare the ground for a counterrevolution.

The Provisional Government believes that, in so proceeding, it will have the firm support of all those to whom the freedom of Russia is dear.

Source: Robert Paul Browder and Alexander F. Kerensky, eds., *The Russian Provisional Government, 1917*, vol. III (Stanford, CA: Stanford University Press, 1961), 1277–78.

LENIN DENOUNCES THE PROVISIONAL GOVERNMENT, THE SOVIET LEADERS, AND CALLS FOR A RADICAL REVOLUTION: THE "APRIL THESES"

Lenin's "April Theses" was first delivered as a speech immediately after his arrival in Petrograd on April 3, 1917, and then embodied in a newspaper article ("The Tasks of the Proletariat in the Present Revolution") on April 7. In it, he attacked the Provisional Government, the Petrograd Soviet leadership's policy of Revolutionary Defensism, and the latter's cooperation with the Provisional Government. It went on to declare that the soviets should be the basis for a new, revolutionary, government. This latter position soon aligned the Bolsheviks with popular sentiment, which by summer was demanding "All Power to the Soviets," i.e., a government based on the Petrograd and other soviets. Lenin's call for immediate radical social, economic, and land reforms also struck a responsive cord. Although Lenin's theses were too radical for the optimistic and cooperative mood of early April, they positioned the Bolsheviks to be the recipients of the discontented and disillusioned in the summer and fall, as the Provisional Government failed to solve the war, economic, and other issues. Ironically, when *Pravda*, the Bolshevik newspaper, published the theses on April 7, the editors attached a note stating that the ideas expressed were those of "Comrade Lenin" and not necessarily those of the party. Lenin soon brought the Bolshevik Party into line, and a party conference sanctioned the theses as party policy. The "April Theses" was one of the most influential and important documents of the revolution. Lenin signed it "N. Lenin," one of the pseudonyms he had used in exile, instead of the more familiar V. I. Lenin. "Petty-bourgeois" elements or party is Lenin's derogatory term for the moderate socialists, the Mensheviks and SRs.

Document 4
THESES

1) In our attitude towards the war, which under the new government of Lvov and Co. unquestionably remains on Russia's part a predatory imperialist war owing to the capitalist nature of that government, not the slightest concession to "revolutionary defensism" is permissible.

The class-conscious proletariat can give its consent to a revolutionary war, which would really justify revolutionary defensism, only on condition: (a) that the power pass to the proletariat and the poorest sections of the peasants aligned with the proletariat; (b) that all annexations be renounced in deed and not in word; (c) that a complete break be effected in actual fact with all capitalist interests.

In view of the undoubted honesty of those broad sections of the mass believers in revolutionary defensism who accept the war only as a necessity, and not as a means of conquest, in view of the fact that they are being deceived by the bourgeoisie, it is necessary with particular thoroughness, persistence and patience to explain their error to them, to explain the inseparable connection existing between capital and the imperialist war, and to prove that without overthrowing capital *it is impossible* to end the war by a truly democratic peace, a peace not imposed by violence.

The most widespread campaign for this view must be organized in the army at the front.

Fraternization.

2) The specific feature of the present situation in Russia is that the country is *passing* from the first stage of the revolution—which, owing to the insufficient class-consciousness and organization of the proletariat, placed power in the hands of the bourgeoisie—to its *second* stage, which must place power in the hands of the proletariat and the poorest sections of the peasants.

This transition is characterized, on the one hand, by a maximum of legally recognized rights (Russia is *now* the freest of all the belligerent countries in the world); on the other, by the absence of violence towards the masses, and, finally by their unreasoning trust in the government of capitalists, those worst enemies of peace and socialism.

This peculiar situation demands of us an ability to adapt ourselves to the *special* conditions of Party work among unprecedentedly large masses of proletarians who have just awakened to political life.

3) No support for the Provisional Government; the utter falsity of all its promises should be made clear, particularly of those relating to the renunciation of annexations. Exposure in place of the impermissible, illusion-breeding "demand" that *this* government, a government of capitalists, should *cease* to be an imperialist government.

4) Recognition of the fact that in most of the Soviets of Workers' Deputies our Party is in a minority, so far a small minority, as against *a bloc of all* the petty-bourgeois opportunist elements, from the Popular Socialists and the Socialist-Revolutionaries down to the Organizing Committee (Chkheidze, Tsereteli, etc.), Steklov, etc., etc., who have yielded to the influence of the bourgeoisie and spread that influence among the proletariat.

The masses must be made to see that the Soviets of Workers' Deputies are the *only possible* form of revolutionary government, and that therefore our task is, as long as *this* government yields to the influence of the bourgeoisie, to present a patient, systematic and persistent *explanation* of the errors of their tactics, an explanation especially adapted to the practical needs of the masses.

As long as we are in the minority we carry on the work of criticizing and exposing errors and at the same time we preach the necessity of transferring the entire state power to the Soviets of Workers' Deputies, so that the people may overcome their mistakes by experience.

5) Not a parliamentary republic—to return to a parliamentary republic from the Soviets of Workers' Deputies would be a retrograde step—but a republic of Soviets of Workers,' Agricultural Laborers' and Peasants' Deputies throughout the country, from top to bottom.

Abolition of the police, the army and the bureaucracy. [In the original, a footnote at this point stated: "I.e., the standing army must be replaced by the arming of the whole people."]

The salaries of all officials, all of whom are elective and displaceable at any time, not to exceed the average wage of a competent worker.

6) The weight of emphasis in the agrarian programme to be shifted to the Soviets of Agricultural Laborers' Deputies.

Confiscation of all landed estates.

Nationalization of *all* lands in the country, the land to be disposed of by the local Soviets of Agricultural Laborers' and Peasants' Deputies. The organization of separate Soviets of Deputies of Poor Peasants. The setting up of a model farm on each of the large estates (ranging in size from 100 to 300 dessiatines, according to local and other conditions, and to the decisions of the local bodies) under the control of Agricultural Laborers' Deputies and for the public account.

7) The immediate amalgamation of all banks in the country into a single national bank, and the institution of control over it by the Soviet of Workers' Deputies.

8) It is not our *immediate* task to "introduce" socialism, but only to bring social production and the distribution of products at once under the *control* of the Soviets of Workers' Deputies.

9) Party tasks:
   (a) Immediate convocation of a Party congress:
   (b) Alteration of the Party Programme, mainly:
       (1) On the question of imperialism and the imperialist war;
       (2) On our attitude towards the state and *our* demand for a "commune state";
       (3) Amendment of our out-of-date minimum programme.
   (c) Change of the Party's name. [Lenin added a note proposing that it be changed to "Communist Party."]

10) A new International.

We must take the initiative in creating a revolutionary International.

Source: V. I. Lenin, *Collected Works*, vol. 34 (Moscow: Progress Publishers, 1964), 21–24.

THE UKRAINIAN RADA ASSERTS ITS AUTHORITY AS THE GOVERNMENT OF UKRAINE AND CALLS FOR AUTONOMY, JUNE 10

Nationalism unexpectedly exploded in 1917 as a major issue. Nationalist movements in particular demanded (1) the restructuring of the Russian state as a federal state based on national-territorial autonomy

for large groups (such as Ukrainians), (2) recognition of local organizations such as the Rada as speaking for the population of the region, and
(3) the use of the local language in administration and education, staffing of government positions by people of the local nationality, and formation of nationality-based military units. The Rada took an early role
in this, and because of the number of Ukrainians (second in population
only to the Russians), its activities were especially important. The
Rada's initial demands, summarized herein, were rejected by both the
Provisional Government and the Petrograd Soviet leaders. Most of
the government and Soviet leaders were committed to a much more
centralized form of government than the decentralized federal system
called for by nationalists, and also simply failed to realize the importance of the issue. The government's rejection of the Rada's demands
led to the issuing of this proclamation (called a "Universal"). The demands of the larger nationality groups increased as 1917 wore on and
central political authority disintegrated.

Document 5
FIRST UNIVERSAL OF THE UKRAINIAN CENTRAL
RADA TO ALL UKRAINIAN PEOPLE WHETHER
RESIDING IN THE UKRAINE OR BEYOND
ITS BORDERS

Ukrainian people! Nation of peasants, workers, toilers!

By your will you have placed us, *the Ukrainian Central Rada*, to guard
the rights and freedoms of the Ukrainian land.

Your finest sons, those who represent villages, factories, military barracks, all Ukrainian communities and associations, have elected us, *the
Ukrainian Central Rada*, and ordered us to stand firm and defend these
rights and freedoms.

Your elected representatives, nation, have expressed their will thus:

Let the Ukraine be free! Without separating from all of Russia, without
breaking with the Russian state, let the Ukrainian people have the right to
manage its own life on its own soil. Let a National Ukrainian Assembly
(*Soim*), elected by universal, equal, direct, and secret balloting, establish order and harmony in the Ukraine. Only our *Ukrainian Assembly* has the right
to establish all laws which can provide that order among us here in the
Ukraine.

Those laws which would govern the entire Russian state should be pro-
mulgated in the All-Russian Parliament.

No one can know better than we what we need and which laws are best
for us.

No one can know better than our peasants how to manage their own land, therefore we desire that after all the lands throughout Russia held by the nobility, the state, the monasteries, and the tsar have been confiscated and have become the property of the people, and after a law concerning this has been enacted by the All-Russian Constituent Assembly, the right to administer the Ukrainian lands shall belong to us, to our Ukrainian Assembly (*Soim*).

Thus spoke the electors from the entire Ukrainian land.

Having so resolved, they elected us, *the Ukrainian Central Rada*, from amongst their midst and commanded us to be at the head of our people, to stand for its rights, and to create a new order in a free *autonomous Ukraine*.

And so, we, *the Ukrainian Central Rada*, have fulfilled the will of our people, we took upon ourselves the heavy burden of building a new life, and have now begun this great task.

We thought that the Central Russian Government would extend its hands to us in this task, that in agreement with it, we, *the Ukrainian Central Rada*, would be able to provide order for our land.

But the Provisional Russian Government rejected all our demands, it pushed aside the outstretched hand of the Ukrainian people. We have sent our delegates (envoys) to Petrograd so that they might present our demands to the Russian Provisional Government.

Our major demands were the following:

That the Russian government publicly, by a special act, declare that it does not oppose the national will of the Ukraine, the right of our people to *autonomy*.

That the Central Russian Government have accredited to it our *Commissar on Ukrainian affairs* for all matters concerning the Ukraine.

That local power in the Ukraine be united under one representative from the Central Russian Government, that is, by a *Commissar in the Ukraine*, chosen by us.

That a definite *portion of the monies* which are collected for the Central Treasury from our people be turned over to us, the representatives of this people, for its own national-cultural needs.

The Russian Central Government *rejected* all of these demands.

It was not willing to say whether or not it recognizes the right of our people to autonomy and the right to manage its own life. It evaded an answer, and referred us to the future All-Russian Constituent Assembly.

The Russian Central Government did not wish to include our Commissar; *it did not want to join us in the establishment of a new order*. Likewise, *it did not wish to recognize a Commissar for all the* Ukraine with whom we might bring the land to order and accord.

It also refused to return the monies collected from our own land for the needs of our schools, education and organizations.

And now, Ukrainian people, we are forced to *create our own destiny*. We cannot permit our land to fall into lawlessness. Since the Russian Provisional Government *cannot* provide order for us, since it does *not want* to join us in this great task, then we must take it upon ourselves. This is our duty to our land and to the peoples who live on our land.

That is why we, *the Ukrainian Central Rada*, issue this Universal to our entire nation and proclaim: from this day forth we shall build our life.

Source: Taras Hunczak, ed., *The Ukraine, 1917–1921: A Study in Revolution* (Cambridge, MA: Harvard University Press for the Harvard Ukrainian Research Institute, 1977), 382–84.

RESPONSE OF THE SOVIET LEADERS TO THE UKRAINIAN RADA'S DEMANDS

The Soviet and government leaders failed to comprehend the power of the new nationalist upsurge. The liberals, and many socialists, were staunch defenders of the territorial integrity of the Russian state and hostile to the decentralized, federal vision put forward by the nationalists. Many socialists, in addition, believed that national identity was not an important issue and would fade away once political freedom, civil rights, and social and economic reforms were implemented. Ironically, the Rada was led by moderate socialists similar to those who dominated the Petrograd Soviet and the Provisional Government in Petrograd. *Izvestiia* was the newspaper of the Petrograd Soviet and reflected the views of its leaders.

Document 6
IZVESTIIA EDITORIAL ON THE FIRST UNIVERSAL

By a special manifesto, the Central Ukrainian Rada proclaimed the broad autonomy of the Ukraine. This autonomy is established in defiance of the Provisional Government's demands to postpone the question of the scope and form of Ukrainian autonomy pending the decision of the All-Russian Constituent Assembly.

The revolutionary democracy of Russia stands for the indivisibility of the State. To split up a great state, created by a thousand years of historical development, means taking a big step backward. Splitting up a large state into a series of small [ones], each with its own peculiar laws, would retard the development of industry, disunite the great workers' army, and thereby worsen the conditions of the worker's struggle for economic and political emancipation.

Regardless of the language the workers speak, [or] their ethic affiliations, once they become aware of their interests they cannot [help] but stand for the indivisibility of the State. As their awareness increases, they necessarily free themselves from the powerful hold of nationalism which the bourgeoisie readily implants [in their minds] in order to weaken their power of resistance to exploitation.

But a stand for the indivisibility of a country does not signify a stand for barracks-like centralization, as the nationalists assure us. On the contrary. The workers are demanding the most extensive regional and national autonomy. Their party is the socialist party—they inscribe this demand on their banner, because they know well that the great national yoke only binds more strongly the exploited by the illusion of a "common" national cause.

From this point of view, no objections in principles can be raised to the demands of autonomy, advanced by the Rada. . . .

But the question as to whether it is timely, right now, to carry out a unilateral decision on autonomy, as the Central Rada wants to do, is an entirely different matter.

To this question we answer categorically in the negative.

In the first place, it has not been proved that the opinion of the Rada is, in reality, the opinion of the majority of the Ukrainian people. It has not been proved that the plans of the Rada are, in reality, the plans of the Ukrainian workers and peasants and not only of its ruling classes.

And in the second place—and this is the most important—the Rada wants to proceed to the establishment of Ukrainian autonomy at a time when the very foundation of revolutionary law and order has not as yet been made secure.

Source: Robert Paul Browder and Alexander F. Kerensky, eds., *The Russian Provisional Government, 1917*, vol. I (Stanford, CA: Stanford University Press, 1961), 388–89.

THE BOLSHEVIKS CALL FOR A DEMONSTRATION ON JUNE 10, 1917

In late May and early June, the Provisional Government and Petrograd Soviet leaders tried to stimulate enthusiasm for a military offensive, which began June 18. This was enormously unpopular. The Bolsheviks and other radicals responded to popular opposition to the offensive as well as to growing dissatisfaction over economic and other problems, calling for a great antiwar and antigovernment demonstration in Petrograd on June 10. While written in the inflammatory style and carelessness with facts typical of the Bolsheviks (the tsarist State Council and the "June 3 Duma," for example, no longer functioned, but the resolution talks as if they did), the resolution nonetheless summarizes many of the discontents of the population. The demonstration was called off at the last minute, at the demand of the Soviet leaders, leaving large numbers of workers and soldiers angry and frustrated. The Petrograd Soviet leaders decided to call a great demonstration for June 18 to show support of the Soviet's policies. It backfired terribly. The massed columns of marching soldiers and workers overwhelmingly carried banners opposing the offensive and coalition government and calling for radical social and economic reforms and for "all power to the soviets." In other words, they supported the positions the Bolsheviks had advocated for the demonstration on June 10, not those the Soviet leaders had hoped for.

Document 7
BOLSHEVIK CALL FOR A DEMONSTRATION, JUNE 9, 1917

To all toilers, to all workers and soldiers of Petrograd!
Comrades!

Russia is experiencing heavy trials.

The war, which carries off millions of victims, continues. It is deliberately prolonged by millionaire bankers who grow rich from war.

The industrial collapse brought about by the war leads to the shutdown of factories and to unemployment. The lockout capitalists in their greed for fantastic profits deliberately encourage unemployment.

Shortages of bread and other foodstuffs are felt ever more. High prices strangle the population. And prices continue to rise at the whim of pillagers-speculators.

The sinister specter of famine and ruin hovers over us . . .

At the same time dark clouds of counterrevolution are gathering.

The June 3 Duma which helped the Tsar to strangle the people now demands an offensive at the front—what for? In order to drown in blood the freedom that has been gained.

The State Council which supplied the Tsar with ministers-hangman is quietly weaving a treacherous noose in the name of the law—what for? In order to emerge at the auspicious moment and tighten it around the people's neck.

The Provisional Government, placed between the tsarist Duma and the Soviet of Deputies, with ten bourgeois members, is clearly falling under the influence of *pomeshchiki* [noble landlords] and capitalists.

Instead of guaranteeing the rights of the soldiers, the "Declaration" of Kerensky violates these rights at a number of very important points. Instead of ratifying the freedoms gained by the soldiers in the days of the revolution, new "orders" threaten penal servitude at hard labor.

Instead of combating counterrevolution, there is a tolerance of revelry and bacchanalia by counterrevolution.

And the ruin grows ever more and no steps are taken against it.

And the war continues and no effective steps are taken to stop it.

And famine is ever closer and no effective steps are taken against it.

Small wonder that the counterrevolutionaries are getting ever more insolent, inciting the Government to repression against soldiers, sailors, workers, and peasants.

Comrades!

We must not continue to endure such things in silence! To be silent after what has been happening is criminal!

Protest is already beginning in the heart of the working masses.

We are free citizens; we have the right to protest, and we must take advantage of this right while it is not too late.

We reserve the right of peaceful demonstration. Let us then stage a peaceful demonstration and make our needs and wishes known!

May the victorious banner rise in the air to frighten the enemies of liberty and socialism!

May our call, the call of the sons of revolution, be heard by all Russia, to the joy of all who are oppressed and enslaved!

Workers! Join the soldiers and support their just demands. Don't you remember how they supported you in the days of the revolution?

All out in the street, comrades!

Soldiers! Stretch your hand to the workers and support them in their just demands. In the union of the workers and the soldiers is the strength of the revolution. Today not one regiment, not one division should remain in the barracks!

All out in the street, comrades!

March through the streets of the capital in fine order.

State your wishes calmly and with confidence, as befits those who are strong.

Down with the tsarist Duma!

Down with the State Council!

Down with the ten capitalist ministers!

All power to the All-Russian Soviet of Workers,' Soldiers,' and Peasants' Deputies!

Re-examine the "Declaration of the rights of the soldier!"

Abolish the "orders" against soldiers and sailors!

Down with anarchy in industry and the lockout capitalists!

Hail the control and organization of industry!

Time to end the war! Let the Soviet of Deputies declare just conditions of peace!

Neither separate peace with Wilhelm, nor secret treaties with the French and English capitalists!

Bread! Peace! Liberty!

[Follows the names of the various Bolshevik Party organizations in Petrograd.]

Source: Robert Paul Browder and Alexander F. Kerensky, eds., *The Russian Provisional Government, 1917*, vol. III (Stanford, CA: Stanford University Press, 1961), 1311–13.

THE FAILURE OF THE RUSSIAN OFFENSIVE, JUNE–JULY 1917

The Provisional Government decided on a military offensive, which the Petrograd Soviet leaders supported. It was extremely unpopular. The government devoted enormous efforts to building enthusiasm among the troops. Alexander Kerensky, now Minister of War, made long tours of the front. His speeches usually were greeted with cheers, but that mood evaporated as his car disappeared down the road. Meetings of regiment and other army committees debated everything from the whole offensive to specific military commands. Nonetheless, the offensive opened June 18, on the Austrian front, and made significant advances. However, many units soon refused to go further, some withdrew, and others refused to move up to replace front-line troops. When the German army reinforced the Austrians and launched a counteroffensive, the Russian army collapsed. This telegram, from a group of government and Soviet officials and pro-offensive soldiers' committeemen at the front, describes the situation in the demoralized army. The telegram itself became a major political controversy. The offensive proved conclusively that the Russian soldiers no longer believed any offensive operations were justified and wanted the war ended promptly.

Document 8
TELEGRAM REGARDING THE ROUT OF THE ELEVENTH ARMY, SOUTHWESTERN FRONT

The German offensive, which began on July 6 on the front of the 11th Army, is assuming the character of a disaster which threatens a catastrophe to revolutionary Russia. A fatal crisis has occurred in the morale of the troops recently sent forward against the enemy by the heroic efforts of the conscientious minority. Most of the military units are in a state of complete disorganization, their enthusiasm for an offensive has rapidly disappeared, and they no longer listen to the orders of their leaders and neglect all the exhortations of their comrades, even replying to them with threats and shots. Some elements voluntarily evacuated their positions without even waiting for the approach of the enemy. Cases are on record in which an order given to proceed with all haste to such-and-such a spot, to assist comrades in distress, has been discussed for several hours at meetings, and the reinforcements were consequently delayed for 24 hours. These elements abandon their positions at the first shots fired by the enemy.

For a distance of several hundred versts long files of deserters, both armed and unarmed, men who are in good health and robust, who have lost all shame and feel that they can act altogether with impunity, are proceeding to the rear of the army. Frequently entire units desert in this manner.

Source: Robert Paul Browder and Alexander F. Kerensky, eds., *The Russian Provisional Government, 1917*, vol. II (Stanford, CA: Stanford University Press, 1961), 967–68.

PEASANTS' ACTIONS AGAINST LANDOWNERS

During 1917, the peasantry began to take action to dispossess nonpeasant landowners. This took various forms: seizure of land and property, taking over use of land and resources, destruction of noble and other estates, and various pressures intended to force nonpeasant owners from the countryside. Typically, the peasant village decided as a unit on the action to be taken and all participated in it, so that responsibility was collectively shared. The following description comes from a newspaper account in 1917, by the property owner's daughter, of the concluding action by a village against a landowner, confiscating the land and movable property and destroying the rest. The length of time this took underscores how powerless officials were to stop this kind of activity. The article does not explicitly state, but the landowner was probably a noble of middling means, neither one of the poorer nor richer landowners. The destruction of the house and its furnishing was in part practical—destroying the house and other property forced the landowner to leave and made it more difficult for him or her to return—and in part symbolic, the destruction of the physical symbols of an alien lifestyle (Western style furniture and gardens, pianos, etc.) and revenge for past oppression.

Document 9
DESTRUCTION OF AN ESTATE

At mid-day the village assembly met to decide the fate of our property, which was large and well equipped. The question to be decided was posed with stark simplicity; should they burn the house or not? At first they decided just to take all our belongings and to leave the building. But this decision did not satisfy some of those present, and another resolution was passed; to burn everything except the house, which was to be kept as a school. At once the whole crowd moved off to the estate, took the keys from the manager, and commandeered all the cattle, farm machinery, carriages, stores etc. For two days they carried off whatever they could. Then they split into groups of 20, divided up the loot into heaps, one for each group, and cast lots which group should get which. In the middle of this redistribution a sailor appeared, a local lad who had been on active service. He insisted that they should burn down the house as well. The peasants got clever. They went off to inspect the house a second time. One of them said: 'What sort of a school would this make? Our children would get lost in it.' Thereupon they decided to burn it down [the next day]. They went home quietly leaving a guard of 20 men, who had a regular feast: they heated the oven, butchered a sheep, some geese, ducks and hens, and ate their fill until dawn. . . . Thus the night passed. The whole village assembled and once again the axes began to strike. . . . They chopped out the windows, doors and floors, smashed the mirrors and divided up the pieces, and so on. At three o'clock in the afternoon they set light to the house from all sides. . . .

Source: John L. H. Keep, *The Russian Revolution: A Study in Mass Mobilization* (London: Weidenfeld and Nicolson, 1976), 211–12.

GROWING ANARCHY AND SOCIAL BREAKDOWN

This editorial on September 20 in *Volia naroda*, a newspaper reflecting moderate socialist views, summarized the problem of social and political breakdown facing Russia by fall. It reflects the growing sense of a society falling apart and a government powerless to deal with problems.

Document 10
EDITORIAL IN *VOLIA NARODA* ON THE GROWING ANARCHY

Against the background of merciless foreign war and defeats of the armies of the Republic, internally the country has entered upon a period of anarchy and, virtually, a period of civil war.

National class animosity has flared up everywhere—in the north and in the south, in the west and in the east in Turkestan, near Moscow, in Finland, in the Urals, in Siberia, and in the Caucasus. From words people passed to action, and the singular devastation of Russian life is further complicated by strikes, revolts, upheavals, and outright robberies.

In a few more weeks, perhaps a few days, all of Russia will be swept by the fire of dissension, mutual discord, and the complete paralysis of all life.

An open revolt flares up in Tashkent, and the Government sends armies and bullets to suppress it.

A mutiny in Orel. Armies are sent there.

In Rostov the town hall is dynamited.

In Tambovsk guberniya [province] there are agrarian pogroms; experimental fields are destroyed, also pedigreed cattle, etc.

In Novgorod-Voynsk uyezd [district] zemstvo storehouses are looted.

Grain reserve stores in Perm guberniya are looted.

Gangs of robbers appear on the roads in Pskov guberniya.

In the Caucasus there is slaughter in a number of places.

Along the Volga, near Kamyshin, soldiers loot trains.

In Finland the army and the fleet disassociated themselves completely from the Provisional Government.

Russia is threatened by a railway employee's strike . . .

Unbridled, merciless anarchy is growing. Any cause is used.

Events of colossal importance take place throughout the country. The Russian state collapses. Whole regions secede . . .

How much further can one go . . .

Source: Robert Paul Browder and Alexander F. Kerensky, eds., *The Russian Provisional Government, 1917*, vol. III (Stanford, CA: Stanford University Press, 1961), 1641–42.

LENIN DEMANDS THAT THE BOLSHEVIKS SEIZE POWER

In early September, Lenin began an insistent call for the Bolsheviks to seize power, sending a series of letters to the Bolshevik leaders in Petrograd from his hiding place in Finland, where he had been since the July Days. Two considerations drove him. First, a recognition of the growing popularity of the call for all power to the soviets, along with the Bolshevik-led radical majorities in the Petrograd and Moscow soviets (and elsewhere), led him to resume his insistence, first expressed in the April Theses, that the revolution must move on to the next stage, a Soviet-based government. Second, he feared that the Menshevik and SRs might change their opposition to a Soviet-based government, as growing numbers of both parties demanded, and lead the formation of a broad-based, multiparty, all-socialist government, thereby undercutting the Bolshevik's most popular campaign demand. He realized that the moment was ripe for a radical transformation of politics, led by the Bolsheviks, and that if it was not seized now it might not occur again. This letter was written September 12–14, but not made public (published) until 1921. All italics are as in the original—Lenin wrote with extensive use of stressed words and phrases. The separation into sections by three asterisks is as in the original.

Document 11
THE BOLSHEVIKS MUST ASSUME POWER

A LETTER TO THE CENTRAL COMMITTEE AND THE PETROGRAD AND MOSCOW COMMITTEES OF THE R.S.D.L.P.(B.)

The Bolsheviks, having obtained a majority in the Soviet of Workers' and Soldiers' Deputies of both capitals, can and *must* take state power into their own hands.

They can because the active majority of revolutionary elements in the two chief cities is large enough to carry the people with it, to overcome the opponent's resistance, to smash him, and to gain and retain power. For the Bolsheviks, by immediately proposing a democratic peace, by immediately giving the land to the peasants and by reestablishing the democratic institutions and liberties which have been mangled and shattered by Kerensky, will form a government which *nobody* will be able to overthrow.

The majority of people are *on our side*. This was proved by the long and painful course of events from May 6 to August 31 and to September 12. The majority gained in the Soviets of the metropolitan cities *resulted* from the people coming over *to our side*. The wavering of the Socialist-Revolutionaries and Mensheviks and the increase in the number of internationalists within their ranks prove the same thing. . . .

* * *

Why must the Bolsheviks assume power *at this very moment*?

Because the impending surrender of Petrograd will make our chances a hundred times less favorable.

And it is *not in our power* to prevent the surrender of Petrograd while the army is headed by Kerensky and Co.

Nor can we "wait" for the Constituent Assembly, for by surrendering Petrograd Kerensky and Co. *can* always *frustrate* its convocation. Our Party alone, on taking power, can secure the Constituent Assembly's convocation; it will then accuse the other parties of procrastination and will be able to substantiate its accusations.

A separate peace between the British and German imperialists must and can be prevented, but only by quick action.

The people are tired of the waverings of the Mensheviks and Social-ist-Revolutionaries. It is only our victory in the metropolitan cities that will carry the peasants with us.

* * *

We are concerned now not with the "day" or "moment" of insurrection in the narrow sense of the word. That will be only decided by the common voice of those who are *in contact* with the workers and soldiers, with *the masses*. The point is that now, at the Democratic Conference, our Party has virtually *its own congress*, and this congress (whether it wishes to or not) must decide the *fate of the revolution*.

The point is to make the *task* clear to the Party. The present task must be an *armed uprising* in Petrograd and Moscow (with its region), the seizing of power and the overthrow of the government. We must consider *how* to agitate for this without saying as much in the press.

We must remember and weigh Marx's words about insurrection, *"Insurrection is an art,"* etc.

* * *

It would be naive to wait for a "formal" majority for the Bolsheviks. No revolution ever waits for *that*. Kerensky and Co. are not waiting either and are preparing to surrender Petrograd. It is the wretched waverings of the Democratic Conference that are bound to exhaust the patience of the workers of Petrograd and Moscow! History will not forgive us if we do not assume power now.

There is no apparatus? There is an apparatus—the Soviets and the democratic organizations. The international situation *right* now, on *the eve* of the conclusion of a separate peace between the British and Germans, is *in our favor*. To propose peace to the nations right now means *to win*.

By taking power in Moscow and in Petrograd *at once* (it doesn't matter which comes first, Moscow may possibly begin), we shall win *absolutely and unquestionably*.

Source: V. I. Lenin, *Collected Works*, vol. 26 (Moscow: Progress Publishers, 1964), 19–21.

THE BOLSHEVIK RESOLUTION OF OCTOBER 10 ON POWER

This resolution is central to the myth of the October Revolution as something carefully planned and directed by Lenin. Many of the "events" referred to in the resolution were either untrue or misrepresented (a peace by imperialists at Russia's expense; preparation for a "second Kornilov revolt"; a decision to surrender Petrograd to the Germans). The popular swing toward the Bolsheviks in elections was true.

Document 12
RESOLUTION

The Central Committee recognises that the international position of the Russian revolution (the revolt in the German navy which is an extreme manifestation of the growth throughout Europe of the world socialist revolution; the threat of peace by the imperialists with the object of strangling the revolution in Russia) as well as the military situation (the indubitable decision of the Russian bourgeoisie and Kerensky and Co. to surrender Petrograd to the Germans), and the fact that the proletarian party has gained a majority in the Soviets—all this, taken in conjunction with the peasant revolt and the swing of popular confidence toward our Party (the elections in Moscow), and, finally, the obvious preparations being made for a second Kornilov revolt (the withdrawal of troops from Petrograd, the dispatch of Cossacks to Petrograd, the encircling of Minsk by Cossacks, etc.)—all this places the armed uprising on the order of the day.

Considering therefore that an armed uprising is inevitable, and that the time for it is fully ripe, the Central Committee instructs all Party organisations to be guided accordingly, and to discuss and decide all practical questions (the Congress of Soviets of the Northern Region, the withdrawal of troops from Petrograd, the action of our people in Moscow and Minsk, etc.) from this point of view.

Source: V. I. Lenin, *Collected Works*, vol. 26 (Moscow: Progress Publishers, 1964), 190.

KAMENEV AND ZINOVIEV OPPOSE A BOLSHEVIK UPRISING, OCTOBER 11

Grigorii Zinoviev and Lev Kamenev, two of Lenin's oldest and closest collaborators, were also in 1917 among the staunchest opponents within the Bolshevik Party of Lenin's ideas about a seizure of power. They argued against Lenin at the October 10 meeting and continued to do so right down to the October Revolution. They argued that Bolshevik support was continuing to grow, but that the masses were not in such a desperate mood as to desire a street uprising at this time. Therefore, to risk everything on an unnecessary uprising was foolish and would endanger the continued growth of the revolutionary mood and the long-term prospects for a new revolution. Even after the October Revolution, they, especially Kamenev, continued to argue for transforming the Soviet government into a more broadly based, multi-party government.

Document 13
ABOUT THE PRESENT SITUATION

As regards the whole political situation, the Bolshevik walk-out from the pre-parliament presented our party with the question: *what will happen next?*

A current is forming and growing in workers' groups which sees the only way out in an immediate declaration of an armed uprising. Now all the time scales have coincided so that if one is to speak of such an uprising, one has plainly to fix a date and moreover for the immediate future. This question is already being debated in one form or another in all the periodical press, in workers' meetings and is occupying the minds of a wide circle of party workers. We, in our turn, regard it as our duty and our right to speak out on this question with full frankness.

We are most profoundly convinced that to declare at once an armed uprising would mean to stake not only the fate of our party, but also the fate of the Russian and the international revolution. There is no doubt that there are such historical situations that an oppressed class has to acknowledge that it is better to join battle and lose than to surrender without a fight. Is the Russian working class in such a position now? *No, and a thousand times no.* . . .

It is said that: (1) the majority of the people in Russia are already for us and (2) the majority of the international proletariat are for us. Alas! Neither the one nor the other is true, and this is the crux of the matter.

A majority of workers and a significant part of the army in Russia are for us. But all the rest are in question. We are all convinced, for example, that if it now comes to elections to the Constituent Assembly, then the majority of peasants will vote for the SRs. What is this, chance? The mass of soldiers supports us not because of our war slogan but because of our peace slogan. This is an extremely important circumstance which if we do not take account of it we risk basing all our calculations on false premises. If we take power now alone and are forced (as a consequence of the whole world situation) to wage a revolutionary war, the mass of soldiers will flee from us. . . .

And now we come to the second assertion, that supposedly, the majority of the international proletariat are already on our side. This, unfortunately, is not true. . . . It is extremely harmful to overrate one's forces. We have doubtless been given much and much will be required from us. But if we now lose the battle, having staked everything, we shall inflict a cruel blow also to the international proletarian revolution. . . .

But everyone who does not wish only to speak of an uprising is obliged to assess also its chances soberly. And here we regard it as our duty to say that at present to underestimate the strength of our adversary and overestimate our own strength would be the most harmful thing of all. The strength of our adversary is greater than it appears. . . .

The strength of the proletarian party, of course, is very considerable, but the decisive question is, is the mood among the workers and soldiers of the capital really such, that they themselves see salvation already only in street fighting and are bursting to go on to the streets. No. This mood does not exist. . . .

No! The party of the proletariat [Bolsheviks] will grow, its program will become clearer to even wider masses. It will have the opportunity of continuing its merciless unmasking of the policy, on a yet greater scale, of the Mensheviks and SRs, who have ceased to advance on the path leading to a real transfer of power to the majority of the people. And there is only one way that it can nullify its successes in present circumstances, and that is by taking the initiative for an uprising itself and in so doing subjecting the proletariat to the blows of the whole united counterrevolution, supported by petty-bourgeois democracy.

We raise a warning voice against this ruinous policy.

Source: Martin McCauley, ed., *The Russian Revolution and the Soviet State 1917–1921* (London and Basingstoke: Macmillan Press Ltd., 1975), 115–17.

TROTSKY DENIES A BOLSHEVIK PLAN TO SEIZE POWER BEFORE THE CONGRESS OF SOVIETS

As the date for the Second All-Russia Congress of Soviets neared, Petrograd was filled with rumors and discussions of what would happen, and especially what the Bolsheviks were planning. Leon Trotsky here specifically denies plans for a demonstration, but acknowledges that the Congress of Soviets would resolve to transfer power to itself, which would be a revolutionary act of sorts. Both parts of the statement correspond to the historical record, and there is no evidence that Trotsky was trying to mislead people about what was planned, as has often been asserted. Ironically, Trotsky's last sentence is quite close to what actually happened.

Document 14
TROTSKY'S DENIAL

Comrades, during the past days all the press has been full of reports of rumors and articles concerning the coming alleged demonstrations attributed to the Bolsheviks, sometimes to the Petrograd Soviet.

I must make the following statement on behalf of the Petrograd Soviet:

"The decisions of the Petrograd Soviet are published for public information. The Soviet is an elective institution; every deputy is responsible to his electors. This revolutionary parliament cannot adopt decisions that would be withheld from the knowledge of all the workers and soldiers.

"All those persons from the bourgeoisie who consider that they have the right to question us regarding our political plans we can refer to our political decisions, which are known to all.

"If the Petrograd Soviet finds it necessary to call a demonstration, then it will do so.

"But I do not know where and when these demonstrations were decided upon. The bourgeoisie press says that a demonstration has been set for October 22. But October 22 was unanimously set by the Executive Committee as a day of propaganda, of agitation, and for raising funds.

"It was also pointed out that I, as President of the Soviet, had signed an order for 5,000 rifles. By virtue of the decision of the Committee for the People's Struggle Against Counterrevolution, even back in the Kornilov days, it was decided to form a workers' militia and arm it. It was in execution of this decision that I ordered 5,000 rifles from the Sestroretskii factory.

"Another important question concerns the convocation of the Congress. They [the bourgeoisie] want at this time to clear Petrograd of its garrison. This is perfectly understandable, because they know that the Congress will definitely pass a resolution on transferring the power to the All-Russian Congress of Soviets, for the immediate conclusion of truces on all fronts and for the transfer of all land to the peasants. The bourgeoisie knows this and therefore wants to arm all the forces that are subordinate to it against us.

"This lie and slander is, in fact, the preparation for an attack against the Congress.

"It is known to all honest people that the Petrograd Soviet has not set a date for armed demonstration, but if it does so, the entire Petrograd Garrison and the proletariat will follow under its banner. At the same time, we declare to the workers and soldiers that the attack in the bourgeoisie press is in preparation for conflict, a mobilization of all the forces against the workers and soldiers.

"We have still not set a date for the attack. But the opposing side has, evidently, already set it. We will meet it, we will repel it duly, and we will declare that at the first counterrevolutionary attempt to hamper the work of the Congress we will answer with a counteroffensive which will be ruthless and which we will carry out to the end."

Source: Robert Paul Browder and Alexander F. Kerensky, eds., *The Russian Provisional Government, 1917*, vol. III (Stanford, CA: Stanford University Press, 1961), 1767–68.

ANNOUNCEMENT OF THE OVERTHROW OF THE PROVISIONAL GOVERNMENT AND ESTABLISHMENT OF SOVIET POWER

By the morning of October 25, it was obvious that the pro-Soviet forces were winning the struggle for control of the city, and the Soviet shifted from a defensive to an offensive posture. Key to that was the arrival of Lenin at Soviet headquarters just after midnight. Around mid-morning Lenin hastily wrote out this declaration that the Provisional Government was overthrown and the popular demand for a Soviet-based government fulfilled. The declaration was quickly printed and distributed throughout the city. This was followed that night, at the Second All-Russia Congress of Workers' and Soldiers' Deputies, by a proclamation taking power in the name of the Congress. Congresses of Soviets thereafter became the main legislative and legitimizing bodies of the new Soviet state.

Document 15
TO THE CITIZENS OF RUSSIA!

The Provisional Government has been deposed. State power has passed into the hands of the Military Revolutionary Committee, the organ of the Petrograd Soviet of Workers' and Soldiers' Deputies—which stands at the head of the Petrograd proletariat and the garrison.

The cause for which the people have fought: the immediate offer of a democratic peace, the abolition of landed proprietorship, workers' control over production, and the establishment of Soviet power—this cause has been secured.

LONG LIVE THE REVOLUTION OF WORKERS,
SOLDIERS AND PEASANTS!
Military Revolutionary Committee of the Petrograd
Soviet of Workers' and Soldiers' Deputies

Source: Rex A. Wade, ed., *Documents of Soviet History*, vol. 1, *The Triumph of Bolshevism, 1917–1919* (Gulf Breeze, FL: Academic International Press, 1991), 1.

DECREE ON PEACE

The popular desire for an end to the war was perhaps the most pressing problem facing the new Soviet government, which was well aware of the role it had played in the downfall of its predecessor. Therefore, the Bolsheviks put an appeal for peace before the second session of the Second All-Russia Congress of Soviets the night of October 26–27. This appeal to all belligerents for an immediate peace was written by Lenin and read to the Congress by him, with introductory and concluding remarks (not included).

Document 16
DECREE ON PEACE

The workers' and peasants' government, created by the Revolution of October 24–25 and basing itself on the Soviets of Workers,' Soldiers' and Peasants' Deputies, calls upon all the belligerent peoples and their governments to start immediate negotiations for a just, democratic peace.

By a just or democratic peace, for which the overwhelming majority of the working people of all the belligerent countries, exhausted, tormented and racked by the war, are craving—a peace that has been most definitely and insistently demanded by the Russian workers and peasants ever since the overthrow of the tsarist monarchy—by such a peace the government means an immediate peace without annexations (i.e., without the seizure of foreign lands, without the forcible incorporation of foreign nations) and without indemnities.

The Government of Russia proposes that this kind of peace be immediately concluded by all the belligerent nations, and expresses its readiness to take all the resolute measures now, without the least delay, pending the final ratification of all the terms of such a peace by authoritative assemblies of the people's representatives of all countries and all nations. . . .

Proposing to the governments and peoples of all countries immediately to begin open negotiations for peace, the [Soviet] government, for its part, expresses its readiness to conduct these negotiations in writing, by telegraph, and by negotiations between representatives of the various countries, or at a conference of such representatives. In order to facilitate such negotiations, the government is appointing its plenipotentiary representative to neutral countries.

The government proposes an immediate armistice to the governments and peoples of all the belligerent countries, and, for its part, considers it desirable that this armistice should be concluded for a period of not less than three months, i.e., a period long enough to permit the completion of negotiations for peace with the participation of the representatives of all people or nations, without exception, involved in or compelled to take part in the war, and the summoning of authoritative assemblies of the representatives of the peoples of all countries for the final ratification of the peace terms.

Source: V. I. Lenin, *Collected Works*, vol. 26 (Moscow: Progress Publishers, 1964), 249–53, as reprinted in Rex A. Wade, ed., *Documents of Soviet History*, vol. 1, *The Triumph of Bolshevism, 1917–1919* (Gulf Breeze, FL: Academic International Press, 1991), 6–7.

DECREE ON LAND

Land distribution was, along with peace, the other most pressing problem facing the new Soviet government. Therefore, the Bolsheviks also put a decree on land distribution before the second meeting of the Congress, just after the decree on peace, during the night of October 26–27. Lenin presented and defended the decree, which he had just written. Included in the decree was a "mandate" which had been compiled from 242 local peasant mandates in midsummer 1917, and published in the newspaper of the All-Russia Congress of Peasants' Deputies (the Congress was SR-controlled and opposed the Bolshevik Revolution). The "mandate" (not included here) spelled out a few more details of the land transfer and reflected peasant beliefs, in particular that "All land ... shall be confiscated without compensation and become the property of the whole people, and pass into the use of those who cultivate it."

Document 17
DECREE ON LAND

(1) Landed proprietorship is abolished forthwith without any compensation.

(2) The landed estates, as also all crown, monastery, and church lands, with all their livestock, implements, buildings and everything pertaining thereto, shall be placed at the disposal of the *volost* [subdistrict] land committees and the *uyezd* [district] Soviet of Peasants' Deputies pending the convocation of the Constituent Assembly.

(3) All damage to confiscated property, which henceforth belongs to the whole people, is proclaimed a grave crime to be punished by the revolutionary courts. The *uyezd* Soviets of Peasants' Deputies shall take all necessary measures to assure the observance of the strictest order during the confiscation of the landed estates, to determine the size of estates, and the particular estates subject to confiscation, to draw up exact inventories of all property confiscated and to protect in the strictest revolutionary way all agricultural enterprises transferred to the people, with all buildings, implements, livestock, stocks of produce, etc.

(4) [The peasant mandate, which contained many details of minor significance for understanding events and is excluded for reasons of length, was given here.]

(5) The land of ordinary peasants and ordinary Cossacks shall not be confiscated.

Source: V. I. Lenin, *Collected Works*, vol. 26 (Moscow: Progress Publishers, 1964), 257–61, as reprinted in Rex A. Wade, ed., *Documents of Soviet History*, vol. 1, *The Triumph of Bolshevism, 1917–1919* (Gulf Breeze, FL: Academic International Press, 1991), 9–11.

CENSORSHIP OF THE PRESS

The first law issued by the new Council of People's Commissars, on October 27, was a decree instituting and justifying censorship of the press (some papers already had been closed). The decree touched sensitive nerves among revolutionaries who had long struggled against such restrictions on freedom of expression. It provoked stormy controversy within the Bolshevik Party and also between the Bolsheviks and allies such as the Left SRs over what weapons the government could legitimately use to combat its critics and enemies. It marks the beginning of press control in Soviet Russia.

Document 18
DECREE ON THE PRESS

In the serious decisive hour of the revolution and the days immediately following it the Provisional Revolutionary Committee was compelled to adopt a whole series of measures against the counter-revolutionary press of all shades.

Immediately on all sides cries arose that the new socialistic authority was violating in this way the essential principles of its program by an attempt against the freedom of the press.

The Workers' and Soldiers' Government draws the attention of the population to the fact that, in our country, behind this liberal shield there is actually hidden the liberty for the richer class to seize into their hands the lion's share of the whole press and by this means to poison the minds and bring confusion into the consciousness of the masses.

Everyone knows that the bourgeois press is one of the most powerful weapons of the bourgeoisie. Especially in this critical moment when the new authority, that of the workers and peasants, is in process of consolidation, it was impossible to leave this weapon in the hands of the enemy at a time when it is not less dangerous than bombs and machine guns. This is why temporary and extraordinary measures have been adopted for the purpose of cutting off the stream of mire and calumny in which the yellow and green press would be glad to drown the young victory of the people.

As soon as the new order is consolidated, all administrative measures against the press will be suspended; full liberty will be given it within the limits of responsibility before the laws, in accordance with the broadest and most progressive regulations in this respect.

Bearing in mind, however, the fact that any restrictions of the freedom of the press, even critical moments, are admissible only within the bounds of necessity, the Council of People's Commissaries decrees as follows:

General rules on the press:

1. The following organs of the press shall be subject to be closed: (a) Those inciting to open resistance or disobedience towards the Workers' and Peasants' Government; (b) those sowing confusion by means of an obviously-calumniatory perversion of facts; (c) those inciting to acts of a criminal character punishable by the penal laws.

2. The temporary or permanent closing of any organ of the press shall be carried out by a resolution of the Council of People's Commissars.

3. The present decree is of a temporary nature and will be revoked by special decree when the normal conditions of public life are reestablished.

> Chairman of the Council of People's Commissaries
> Vladimir Ulianov (Lenin)

Source: James H. Meisel and Edward Kozera, eds, *Materials for the Study of the Soviet System* (Ann Arbor, MI: G. Wahr Publishing, 1950) 23–24, with minor changes.

THE BOLSHEVIK CENTRAL COMMITTEE REJECTS A BROAD-BASED SOCIALIST GOVERNMENT

The new Soviet government turned out, to everyone's surprise, to be composed of only one party, the Bolsheviks, rather than the multiparty government that had generally been meant by the slogan of "All Power to the Soviets." Therefore, discussions for reforming the government began immediately. Central to this was *Vikzhel*, the All-Russian Union of Railway Workers, which was Left SR-dominated. Because of *Vikzhel*'s ability to control railway, and thus troop, movement, and because of the Bolsheviks' tenuous position, the latter agreed to participate in the talks. Some Bolshevik leaders, such as Kamenev, also favored such talks and such a government on principle. The Bolshevik Party's Central Committee debated the issue on October 29, apparently in the absence of Lenin and Trotsky. Not only did they agree to continue discussion of broadening the government, but also considered the possible exclusion of Lenin and Trotsky, which was being demanded by some other parties. On November 1, an angry Lenin attacked the very idea of continuing the talks. By November 2, Lenin and Trotsky managed to defeat those Bolsheviks favoring continued compromise, in which they probably were helped by the failure of Kerensky's military efforts to retake the city, thus lessening the immediate threat to the regime, and news from Moscow that the Bolshevik side had prevailed in fighting there. The Central Committee meeting that day passed this resolution, written by Lenin, which firmly reasserted his principle of a Bolshevik-only government and rejected compromise, especially with those socialists who had walked out of the Congress of Soviets.

Document 19
RESOLUTION OF THE CENTRAL COMMITTEE OF
THE R.S.D.L.P.(B.) ON THE OPPOSITION WITHIN THE
CENTRAL COMMITTEE

The Central Committee considers that the present meeting is of historic importance and that it is therefore necessary to record the two positions which have been revealed here.

1. The Central Committee considers that the opposition formed within the Central Committee has departed completely from all the fundamental positions of Bolshevism. . . .

3. The Central Committee affirms that the purely Bolshevik government cannot be renounced without betraying the slogan of Soviet power, since the majority at the Second All-Russia Congress of Soviets, without excluding anybody from the Congress, entrusted power to this government.

4. The Central Committee affirms that, without betraying the slogan of the power of the Soviets of Workers,' Soldiers' and Peasants' Deputies, there can be no entering into petty bargaining over the affiliation to the Soviets of organizations of a non-Soviet type, i.e., organizations which are not voluntary associations of the revolutionary vanguard of the people who are fighting for the overthrow of the landowners and capitalists.

5. The Central Committee affirms that to yield to the ultimatums and threats of the minority of the Soviets would be tantamount to complete renunciation not only of Soviet power but of democracy, for such yielding would be tantamount to the majority's fear to make use of its majority, it would be tantamount to submitting to anarchy and inviting the repetition of ultimatums on the part of any minority.

6. The Central Committee affirms that, not having excluded anybody from the Second All-Russia Congress of Soviets, it is even now fully prepared to permit the return of those who walked out and to agree to a coalition within the Soviets with those who walked out, and that, consequently, all talk about the Bolsheviks refusing to share power with anybody is absolutely false.

7. The Central Committee affirms that on the day the present government was formed, a few hours before its formation, the Central Committee invited three representatives of the Left Socialist-Revolutionaries to attend its meeting and formally proposed that they should join the government. The refusal of the Left Socialist-Revolutionaries, although it was provisional and conditional, places on these Left Socialist-Revolutionaries the entire responsibility for the fact that an agreement with them was not reached. . . .

9. The Central Committee affirms, finally, that despite all difficulties, the victory of socialism both in Russia and in Europe can only be ensured by the unswerving continuation of the present government's policy. The Central Committee expresses its firm belief in the victory of this socialist revolution and calls upon all skeptics and waverers to abandon their waverings and whole-heartedly and with supreme energy support the actions of this government.

Source: V. I. Lenin, *Collected Works*, vol. 26 (Moscow: Progress Publishers, 1964) 277–79, as reprinted in Rex A. Wade, ed., *Documents of Soviet History*, Vol. 1, *The Triumph of Bolshevism, 1917–1919* (Gulf Breeze, FL: Academic International Press, 1991), 23–24.

DECLARATION OF THE RIGHTS OF THE PEOPLES OF RUSSIA

Equality of all nationalities within the Russian state had been generally accepted by liberals and socialists throughout 1917. The right of self-determination, and especially of autonomy or independence, was more controversial. The Bolsheviks now took the extreme position, allowing even for secession, at least in theory. This brought, as intended, some support for the Bolsheviks from various nationality groups, or at least helped prevent their support for the Whites during the Civil War. It also brought serious problems in applying it to specific cases, and required reinterpretation as the new government battled national independence movements, as document 23 (below) demonstrates. Issued November 2, 1917.

Document 20
DECLARATION OF THE RIGHTS OF THE PEOPLES OF RUSSIA

The October revolution of the workmen and peasants began under the common banner of emancipation.

The peasants are being emancipated from the power of the landowners, for there is no longer the landowner's property right in the land—it has been abolished. The soldiers and sailors are being emancipated from the power of autocratic generals, for generals will henceforth be elective and subject to recall. The workingmen are being emancipated from the whims and arbitrary will of the capitalists, for henceforth there will be established the control of the workers over mills and factories. Everything living and capable of life is being emancipated from the hateful shackles.

There remain only the peoples of Russia, who have suffered and are suffering oppression and arbitrariness, and whose emancipation must immediately be begun, whose liberation must be effected resolutely and definitely.

During the period of tsarism the peoples of Russia were systematically incited against one another. The results of such a policy are known: massacres and pogroms on the one hand, slavery of peoples on the other.

There can be and there must be no return to this disgraceful policy of instigation. Henceforth the policy of a voluntary and honest union of the peoples of Russia must be substituted. . . .

[The] Council of People's Commissars resolves to base its actions concerning the nationality question in Russia according to the following principles:

1. The equality and sovereignty of the peoples of Russia.

2. The right of the peoples of Russia to free self-determination, even to the point of separation and the formation of an independent state.

3. The abolition of any and all national and national-religious privileges and disabilities.

4. The free development of national minorities and ethnographic groups inhabiting the territory of Russia.

The concrete decrees that follow from these principles will be immediately elaborated after the setting up of a Commission on Nationality Affairs.

Source: James H. Meisel and Edward Kozera, eds, *Materials for the Study of the Soviet System* (Ann Arbor, MI: G. Wahr Publishing, 1950), 25–26, with modification by this author.

ESTABLISHMENT OF THE CHEKA, THE POLITICAL POLICE

Among the early acts of the new Soviet government was the revival of a secret, or political, police, but one that went far beyond its tsarist predecessor in its actions. This grew out of a combination of factors: continued opposition to the new Soviet government, Lenin's intolerance of opposition, and a tendency to view the world in somewhat apocalyptic terms of inevitable conflict. On December 6, 1917, Lenin wrote a letter to Feliks Dzerzhinski, a Polish Bolshevik, proposing a decree establishing an organization "for fighting saboteurs and counterrevolutionaries." The next day, December 7, the government created the All-Russian Extraordinary Commission for the Struggle with Counter-Revolution and Sabotage, generally known as the "Cheka." It quickly evolved far beyond the modest activities outlined here. It was the origins of the secret police which, in various names (including the NKVD of the 1930s and the KGB of the late Soviet Union), was a major feature of the Soviet system throughout its history and the main vehicle for repression and terror. Dzerzhinski became the first head of the Cheka. Apparently it was established not by any formal published government decree, but via approval of this report from Dzerzhinski to the Council of People's Commissars, which Lenin had requested.

Document 21
ESTABLISHMENT OF THE CHEKA: ACTION OF THE COUNCIL OF PEOPLE's COMMISSARS

The Commission is to be called the All-Russian Extraordinary Commission for the Struggle with Counter-Revolution and Sabotage and is to be attached to the Council of People's Commissars.

The duties of the Commission are to be as follows:

1. To investigate and nullify all acts of counter-revolution and sabotage throughout Russia, irrespective of origin.

2. To bring before the Revolutionary Tribunal all counter-revolutionaries and saboteurs and to work out measures to combat them.

3. The Commission is to conduct the preliminary investigation only, sufficient to suppress (the counter-revolutionary act). The Commission is to be divided into sections: (1) the information (section) (2) The organization section (in charge of organizing the struggle with counter-revolution throughout Russia) with branches, and (3) the fighting section.

The Commission shall be set up finally tomorrow. Then the fighting section of the All-Russian Commission shall start its activities. The Commission shall keep an eye on the press, saboteurs, right Socialist Revolutionaries and strikers. Measures to be taken are confiscation, imprisonment, confiscation of cards, publication of the names of the enemies of the people, etc.

Chairman of the Council of People's Commissars,
V. Ulyanov (Lenin)

Source: Martin McCauley, ed., *The Russian Revolution and the Soviet State, 1917–1921* (London and Basingstoke: Macmillan Press, 1975), 181–82.

DISSOLUTION OF THE CONSTITUENT ASSEMBLY

A universally elected Constituent Assembly, which had been the goal for socialists and liberals for decades, finally convened on January 5, 1918. The Bolsheviks and their allies were in a minority, and various Bolshevik statements since the elections in November had pointed toward possible suppression of the assembly. Ironically, in light of this act, the Bolsheviks had criticized the Provisional Government for delay in convening the assembly and argued that only a Soviet government could guarantee its convocation (see, for example, Lenin's letter of September 12, document 12). The meeting opened with the spectators' gallery packed with a selected hostile crowd, many of them drunk, and confronted with Bolshevik appointed "guards." Nonetheless, under SR leadership, the assembly refused a Bolshevik motion to in effect limit itself to recognizing Lenin's government. The Bolsheviks and Left SRs then walked out. The assembly proceeded to pass a land law and take other measures, before pressure from the guards forced them to recess for the night. When the deputies attempted to reconvene the next day, January 6, they were blocked by armed force. This decree of dissolution (which had been written by Lenin) was posted. By announcing that the government could not be changed through elections, the dissolution of the Constituent Assembly made civil war unavoidable.

Document 22
DECREE DISSOLVING
THE CONSTITUENT ASSEMBLY

The Russian revolution at its outset brought the Soviets of Workers,' Soldiers' and Peasants' Deputies into the foreground as the mass organization of all the working and exploited classes. They alone are capable of leading these classes in their struggle for complete political and economic freedom.

As the first period of the Russian revolution proceeded the Soviets increased, grew and won strength, abandoning, as the result of their own experience, the illusion of an understanding with the bourgeoisie, with the deceitful forms of bourgeois democratic Parliamentarism and from practical experience coming to the conclusion that freedom for the oppressed classes is impossible without making a break with these forms and with all kind of compromise. The October revolution made such a break—the transference of all power into the hands of the Soviets.

The Constituent Assembly elected from lists presented before the October revolution was the expression of the former political class relationships of the time when the compromisers and the Cadets were at the helm.

The people, when they voted for the candidates of the Social Revolutionary Party, were not then in a position to make their choice between the Right Social Revolutionaries, the adherents of the bourgeoisie, and the Left Social Revolutionaries, the adherents of socialism. Thus this Constituent Assembly, which should have been the crown of the bourgeois parliamentary Republic, could not but thwart the designs of the October revolution and the Soviet Power. In that the October revolution gave power to the Soviets and through the Soviets to the working and exploited classes it roused the desperate resistance of the exploiters and in overcoming this resistance, showed itself to be the beginning of the socialist revolution.

The working classes must be convinced, as the result of their own experience, that the old, bourgeois parliamentary system has outlived itself, that it is absolutely inconsistent with the realization of socialism, that not common-national institutions but only class institutions (such as the Soviets) are able to overcome the resistance of the possessing classes and to lay the foundations of a socialist social order.

Any retreat from the complete sovereignty of the Soviets, any going back upon the Soviet Republic won by the people, in favor of a bourgeois parliamentarism and consequently in favor of the Constituent Assembly, would now be a step backwards and lead to the destruction of the whole October revolution of the workers and peasants.

The Constituent Assembly, opened on January 5th, gave, as a result of circumstances known to all, a majority to the Party of the Right Social Revolutionaries, i.e., to the Party of Kerensky, Avksentiev and Chernov. It was to be expected that this party should refuse to put on the Agenda the absolutely exact, clear immutable resolution of the highest Soviet organizations for the recognition of the "Declaration of the Rights of the Toiling and Exploited People," of the October revolution and of the Soviet Power. In doing this the Constituent Assembly cut all ties between itself and the Russian Soviet Republic. It was inevitable that the fraction of the Bolsheviks and Left Social Revolutionaries—which at this moment are known to have an overwhelming majority in the Soviets and enjoy the confidence of the workers and most of the peasants—should leave such a Constituent Assembly.

And outside the walls of the Constituent Assembly, the Parties which hold a majority in the Constituent Assembly, the Right Socialist Revolutionaries and the Mensheviks are waging open war against the Soviet Power by calling for the overthrow of the latter in their journals and thereby objectively supporting the exploiters in their resistance to the transfer of the land and of the factories to those who labor. It is clear that the remaining section of the Constituent Assembly can, in these circumstances, but serve as a cloak for the struggle of the bourgeois counter-revolution to overthrow the Soviet Power.

Consequently the Central Executive Committee resolves: *The Constituent Assembly shall be dissolved.*

Source: Rex A. Wade, ed., *Documents of Soviet History*, vol. 1, *The Triumph of Bolshevism, 1917–1919* (Gulf Breeze, FL: Academic International Press, 1991), 82–83.

BOLSHEVIK POLICY ON THE NATIONALITY QUESTION

By the time the Bolsheviks took power, the nationality question had become a major issue. After the dispersal of the Constituent Assembly, several nationalities moved toward independence. Under Lenin's prodding, the Bolsheviks in 1917 had supported the calls of nationality groups for self-determination, whether autonomy or independence. Once in power, however, they were unwilling to see the breakup of the state they now governed and policy had to be adjusted. The new policy stressed proletarian class unity and downplayed national identity. Joseph Stalin, People's Commissar for Nationalities, now made clearer the distinction between "genuine" autonomy or independence movements, which were based on the interests of the working class, and other nationalist movements that were declared to be the handiwork of the "bourgeoisie" and mere cloaks for counterrevolution. Stalin expressed this first in an article on December 12, 1917, and then restated it as a general principle at the Third All-Russia Congress of Soviets on January 15, 1918, thus giving it greater authority as party and state policy. Note especially the last paragraph.

Document 23
NEWSPAPER REPORT OF STALIN'S SPEECH ON THE NATIONAL QUESTION

One of the questions that was particularly agitating Russia just now, the speaker said, was the national question. Its importance was enhanced by the fact that the Great Russians did not constitute an absolute majority of the population of Russia and were surrounded by a ring of other, "non-sovereign" peoples, the inhabitants of the border regions.

The tsarist government realized the importance of the national question and tried to handle the affairs of the nationalities with a rod of iron. It carried out a policy of forcible Russification of the border peoples, and its method of action was the banning of native languages, pogroms and other forms of persecution.

Kerensky's coalition government abolished these national disabilities, but, because of its class character, it was incapable of a full solution of the national question. The government of the early period of the revolution not only did not adopt the course of completely emancipating the nations, but in many instances it did not hesitate to resort to repressive measures to crush the national movement, as was the case with the Ukraine and Finland.

The Soviet Government alone publicly proclaimed the right of all nations to self-determination, including complete secession from Russia. The new government proved to be more radical in this respect than even the national groups within some of the nations.

Nevertheless, a series of conflicts arose between the Council of People's Commissars and the border regions. They arose, however, not over issues of a national character, but over the question of power. The speaker cited a number of examples of how the bourgeois nationalist governments, hastily formed in the border regions and composed of representatives of the upper sections of the propertied classes, endeavored, under the guise of settling their national problems, to carry on a definite struggle against the Soviet and other revolutionary organizations. All these conflicts between the border regions and the central Soviet Government were rooted in the question of power. And if the bourgeois elements of this or that region sought to lend a national coloring to these conflicts, it was only because it was advantageous to them to do so, since it was convenient for them to conceal behind a national cloak the fight against the power of the laboring masses within their region.

As an illustration, the speaker dwelt in detail on the Rada, convincingly showing how the principle of self-determination was being exploited by the bourgeois chauvinist elements in the Ukraine in their imperialist class interests.

All this pointed to the necessity of interpreting the principle of self-determination as the right to self-determination not of the bourgeoisie, but of the laboring masses of the given nation. The principle of self-determination should be a means in the struggle for socialism and should be subordinated to principles of socialism.

Source: Joseph Stalin, *Works*, vol. 4 (Moscow: Foreign Languages Publishing House, 1952), 30–32, as reprinted in Rex A. Wade, ed., *Documents of Soviet History*, *The Triumph of Bolshevism, 1917–1919* (Gulf Breeze, FL: Academic International Press, 1991), 93–94.

THE ROLE OF MILITARY COMMISSARS, APRIL 6, 1918

The building of a new Red Army faced a serious problem in the shortage of experienced military officers. Trotsky solved this by enlisting (or drafting) officers of the old army, termed "military specialists." To deal with their expected political unreliability, the institution of political commissars, perhaps the greatest innovation of the new Red Army, was created. The commissars would watch over the military commanders, be on the alert for betrayal, and carry on political education work among the troops. They remained a key feature of the Red Army and later Soviet army throughout the history of the Soviet Union.

Document 24
ON MILITARY COMMISSARS AND MEMBERS
OF MILITARY COUNCILS

The military commissar is the direct political agent of Soviet power within the army. His post is of the highest importance. Commissars are appointed from the ranks of exemplary revolutionaries, capable of remaining the embodiments of revolutionary duty at the most critical moments and under the most difficult circumstances.

The person of a commissar is inviolable. Interference with a commissar in the performance of his duties and, all the more, assault on a commissar, is deemed an extremely serious crime against the Soviet state. The military commissar ensures that the army does not become isolated from the Soviet system as a whole and that individual military institutions do not become breeding grounds for conspiracy or weapons that are turned against the workers and peasants. The commissar participates in all the activities of the military commanders and along with them receives reports and dispatches and countersigns orders. The orders of Military Councils are valid only if they are signed not only by the military members (commanders) of the Councils, but by at least one commissar.

All work must be carried out in the presence of the commissar, but the primary command responsibility for specialized military decisions belongs not to the commissar, but to the military specialist who works closely with him.

The commissar is not responsible for the success of purely military operational or battle orders. This is totally the responsibility of the military commander. The commissar's signature on an operational order indicates that he vouches for the fact that it was dictated by operational and not some other (counterrevolutionary) considerations. If he is dissatisfied with a purely military instruction, the commissar does not countermand it, but merely reports his dissatisfaction to the superior Military Council. A commissar can countermand an operational order only if he has grounds for believing that it was dictated by counterrevolutionary motives.

If an order has been signed by a commissar it has the force of law and must be obeyed at any cost. It is the duty of the commissar to ensure that the order is obeyed to the letter and, in performing this duty, he has all the authority and all the resources of the Soviet State at his disposal. The military commissar who connives at noncompliance with orders is subject to immediate dismissal and prosecution.

The commissars provide a link between the institutions of the Red Army and central and local institutions of the Soviet State and facilitate the latter's support of the Red Army.

The commissars on the Supreme Military Council are appointed by the Council of People's Commissars.

Commissars of the *okrug* [area] or *raion* [regional] Soviets are appointed through agreement between the Highest Military Councils and the leadership of the Council of Deputies of the given *okrug* or *raion*.

An All-Russian Bureau of Military Commissars has been established under the auspices of the Supreme Military Council.

This Bureau coordinates the activity of the Commissars, responds to their requests, develops instructions for them, and, if necessary, convenes congresses of the commissars.

Signed by the People's Commissar of Military Affairs,
Chairman of the Supreme Military Council, L. Trotsky.

Source: *Izvestiia*, April 6, 1918, as translated in Rex A. Wade, ed., *Documents of Soviet History*, vol. 1, *The Triumph of Bolshevism, 1917–1919* (Gulf Breeze, FL: Academic International Press, 1991), 119–20.

DECREE ON FOOD PROCUREMENT

The food supply, especially for the large northern industrial cities and for the army, already a problem in 1917, became critical in 1918. This, plus the Bolsheviks' ideological hostility toward the peasants and toward private trade, led to various schemes for forced food procurement and requisitioning from the peasantry. This decree of May 13, 1918, established a virtual food dictatorship. It was based on the false assumption, derived from Bolshevik ideology, that there was a large class of wealthy peasants and "rural bourgeoisie" who were hoarding large amounts of grain—note especially the second and third paragraphs. It marked the beginning of requisitioning and the virtual civil war of the regime against the peasants. Indeed, this had to be followed up with other decrees, including instructions to food requisitioning detachments on August 20 that began with the sentence: "Each food detachment is to consist of not less than seventy-five men, with two or three machine guns." The reason, of course, was bitter peasant resistance to requisitioning.

Document 25
DECREE OF THE ALL-RUSSIAN CENTRAL
EXECUTIVE COMMITTEE

A ruinous process of disintegration of the food procurement of the country—the heavy legacy of a four-year war—continues to extend and aggravate the existing distress.

While the consuming provinces are starving, great stocks of cereals, including the 1916 harvest and the 1917 harvest which has not yet been threshed, lie, as habitually, in the producing provinces. These stocks are in the hands of rural kulaks [wealthy peasants] and wealthy people, in the hands of the rural bourgeoisie. Replete and satisfied, having accumulated an enormous mass of money earned in the years of war, this rural bourgeoisie remains deaf and unresponsive in the face of the moanings of starving workers and poor peasants; it refuses to dispatch cereals to the state station points with the aim of forcing the state to increase again and again the price of cereals, while at the same time it sells for its own benefit cereals in the provinces at fabulous prices to speculators and bagmen.

The obstinacy of the greedy kulaks and wealthy peasants must be brought to an end. The food procurement experience of the last years has shown that the failure to apply fixed prices on cereals and a grain monopoly facilitates the feeding of a small group of our capitalists by making food inaccessible to several millions of toiling people and exposing them to the inevitability of death by starvation.

The reply to the violence of grain holders upon the rural poor must be violence upon the bourgeoisie.

Not one single pud [36.1 pounds] of grain must remain in the hands of the grain holders, except the quantity needed for sowing and subsistence of the household until the next harvest.

And it is necessary to implement all this immediately, especially after the occupation of the Ukraine by the Germans, as we must content ourselves with the resources of cereals which are barely sufficient for sowing and survival.

Taking into account this situation and considering that only by rigorous accounting and even distribution of all grain stocks of Russia is it possible to get out of the food provision crisis, the All-Russian Central Executive Committee has decreed:

1. By keeping firmly the grain monopoly and fixed prices and also carrying out a merciless struggle against grain speculators and bagmen, to compel each grain holder to declare the surrender of all surpluses, except the quantity needed for consumption on established norms until the next harvest, in one week after the notification of this decree in each *volost* [subdistrict]. The rules applying to the orders [of delivery] will be defined by the local food procurement organs of Narkomprod [People's Commissariat of Food Procurement].

2. To invite all toiling people and propertyless peasants to unite immediately in a merciless struggle against the kulaks.

3. To declare enemies of the nation all people having surpluses of grain and not handing them over to the station points and even dissipating the stocks of cereals for their own home brew instead of delivering them to the collecting stations; to bring them before the Revolutionary Courts, put them in jail for not less than ten years, confiscate all their belongings, banish them out of the *obshchina* [village communal structure] and condemn the holders of home brew to forced labor in public works.

4. In the case of discovery of any surplus grain which had not been declared for delivery, according to point 1, grain will be requisitioned without payment, and half of the value which was due at fixed prices for the undeclared surplus will be paid to the people who took part in discovering the surpluses, after they have been in fact received in the collecting stations, and the other half to the Agricultural Community. Information about discovery of surpluses has to be reported to the local food procurement organs.

Source: Silvana Malle, *The Economic Organization of War Communism, 1918–1921* (Cambridge: Cambridge University Press, 1985), 359–61.

INTENSIFICATION OF THE RED TERROR, SEPTEMBER 4, 1918

Both sides executed opponents during the summer of 1918. However, the attempted assassination of Lenin on August 30 and attacks on other Bolshevik leaders led to demands for more widespread use of terror by the Bolsheviks. On September 4, the Commissar for Internal Affairs sent the following order to local officials. The next day, the Council of People's Commissars passed a resolution officially approving more extensive use of terror. There followed a wave of executions of people totally unconnected with the assassination attempt but who were members of the "bourgeoisie" or other ideologically targeted groups. Authorities announced 512 executions in Petrograd alone on September 7.

Document 26
ORDER FOR INTENSIFIED RED TERROR, SEPTEMBER 4

The murder of Volodarsky, the murder of Uritsky, the attempt to murder and the wounding of the President of the Council of People's Commissars, Vladimir Ilyitch Lenin, the mass shooting of tens of thousands of our comrades in Finland, in Ukraina, on the Don, and in Czecho-Slavia [sic], the constant discovery of plots in the rear of our army, the open implication of Right Socialist Revolutionaries and other counterrevolutionary scoundrels in these plots, and at the same time the extremely negligible number of serious repressions and mass shootings of the White Guards and the bourgeoisie by the Soviets, all this shows that, notwithstanding constant words about mass terror against the Socialist Revolutionaries, the White Guards and the bourgeoisie, this terror really does not exist.

There must emphatically be an end to such a situation. There must be an immediate end of looseness and tenderness. All Right Socialist Revolutionaries who are known to local Soviets must be arrested immediately. Considerable numbers of hostages must be taken from among the bourgeoisie and the officers. At the least attempt at resistance or the least movement among the White Guards mass shooting must be inflicted without hesitation. The local Provincial Executive Committees must display special initiative in this direction.

The departments of administration, through the militia, and the Extraordinary Commissions must take all measures to detect and arrest all persons who are hiding under assumed names and must shoot without fail all who are implicated in White Guard activity.

All the above mentioned measures must be carried out immediately.

The heads of the departments of administration are bound to report immediately to the People's Commissariat for Internal Affairs any actions in this connection of organs of the local soviets which are indecisive.

The rear of our armies must, at last, be finally cleared of all White Guard activity and of all vile plotters against the power of the working class and of the poorest peasantry. Not the least wavering, not the least indecision in the application of mass terror.

Confirm the receipt of this telegram.

Communicate it to the county Soviets.

People's Commissar for Internal Affairs, Petrovsky

Source: William Henry Chamberlin, *The Russian Revolution*, vol. II (New York: Macmillan, 1935), 475–76.

KOLCHAK ON THE FUTURE OF RUSSIA, APRIL 19, 1919

In the late winter and early spring of 1919, Admiral Kolchak's White Army made impressive gains from the east against the Red Army. Here, in the flush of victory, Kolchak addressed a supportive audience of local officials in Ekaterinburg. His speech reflects the tendency of the Whites to focus on defeat of the Bolsheviks and then convening a constituent assembly (presumably conservative), and their failure to address social and economic issues which might have developed a broader base of support. Support for "autonomous development of the nationalities" was quite circumscribed.

Document 27
THE WHITES' HOPE FOR A DEMOCRATIC RUSSIA

Omsk, April 19—Admiral Kolchak, the head of the Omsk Government and Commander-in-Chief of the Russian Armies, attended in Ekaterinburg a joint session of the Municipal Council and of the Zemstvo Assembly....

[In response to speeches] Admiral Kolchak answered: "During my tour to the front I often met representatives of Municipalities, Zemstvos, professional, workingmen and Socialist organizations. I am happy to state that there is complete unity of purpose and action between the Government and the representatives of the people. The time has gone forever when the Government and public opinion in Russia are two different factors opposed to each other. A new free Russia must be built upon complete union between the Government and the people.

"The program of the Government is to reestablish the economic and political life of the country in close cooperation with the organs of local self-government—Municipalities and Zemstvos. The first task of the Government is to reestablish the rule of law and order, the rule destroyed by Bolshevism from the Left and the Right. The Government will fight, without any possibility of compromise, the Bolsheviki of the Left and of the Right, with the purpose of establishing a great, free, democratic Russia.

"The future Russia will be a democratic Russia. The Government, of which I have the honor to be the head, believes in universal suffrage, in the autonomous development of the nationalities comprising Russia, in a democratic solution of the main Russian problems: the land problem and the labor problem.

"With regard to the international relations, the Government will endeavor to continue the relations established between Russia and the rest of the world at the moment of Russia's entrance into the war, in 1914. The Government will do its best to strengthen the bonds between Russia and the Allies. It is evident that no conciliation is possible with the Bolsheviki, and those of the Allied leaders who recently supported the idea of the Prinkipo Conference are now repudiating the Bolsheviki and call them by their proper name: murderers of humanity.

"This is the program of the Government, the program for the realization of which it calls upon the country to be ready for sacrifices. The Government considers the people of Russia the supreme authority in all problems pertaining to Russia's life. After the menace of Bolshevism is destroyed, the people of Russia, through a freely chosen Constituent Assembly, will express their supreme will and will define the structure of the State, will solve the main political, social and national problems. The Government and myself will consider it our duty to transfer to the Constituent Assembly all the power which now belongs to the Government."

Source: *Struggling Russia*, May 3, 1919, p. 106, as reprinted in Rex A. Wade, ed., *Documents of Soviet History*, vol. 1, *The Triumph of Bolshevism, 1917–1919* (Gulf Breeze, FL: Academic International Press, 1991), 348–49.

CIVIL WAR CONDITIONS IN THE UKRAINE, DECEMBER 1, 1919

During 1919, civil war, foreign invasion, economic and social disintegration, political mismanagement, and other problems left many areas of Russia in chaos and brutalized. Henry Alsberg, an American journalist, wrote a remarkable account of the situation in Ukraine. He had little patience for the brutalities committed by the White armies, but neither did he excuse the excesses of the Bolsheviks. His sympathy was with the suffering people caught up in the turmoil, and he did not reduce them to ideological abstractions, as for example Trotsky did in his defense of terror. At the time he wrote General Denikin's army had just passed its high point of success and was beginning its retreat. The Volunteer Army was a key component of Denikin's army.

Document 28
HENRY G. ALSBERG, "IN THE WAKE OF DENIKIN"

Practically every train from Odessa to Kiev, except the one I traveled in, was held up, looted, and robbed. We went through free because we had an armored car and locomotive hitched to either end of our train. . . . And, armored train notwithstanding, we were delayed for hours until the road ahead of us could be cleared. . . . We had to avoid Kursk on account of the proximity of the Bolsheviki. We could not go by way of Poltava, because Makhno had been there and looted the town and was still athwart the railway. So we dodged in and out by way of devious branch lines till we arrived at Kharkov. We could not travel by night for fear of being derailed. In passing through every considerable forest, those of us that had them unlimbered our shooting irons in expectation of a hold-up. . . .

Denikin's troops are to a large extent ex-Bolshevik soldiers. The explanation is that after every battle—and this holds good of Bolsheviks and

Denikin as well—all the captured officers are killed, and those of the soldiers whose papers show that they were volunteers meet a similar fate. The balance of the prisoners is given the choice of enlisting with its captors' army or being shot. . . .

You on the other side of the water have heard of Bolshevik excesses. Excesses have taken place. During their last three days' stay in Kiev the Bolshevik Cheka (extraordinary commission) made a pyramid of 250 dead in the courtyard of their buildings. Indignant Volunteer Army officers showed me where the brains of the victims had been spattered against the walls. But these indignant officers will not tell of the 250 Jews killed by the Volunteer Army on their occupation of Kiev, nor will they tell of the 150 young girls violated, or of the Jews hacked to pieces by wanton soldiery. I have the complete reports of the Kiev Committee for the Regeneration of Russia, a Jewish organization. It makes the most terrible reading.

Source: *The Nation*, January 10, 1920, pp. 38–40.

RUSSIA's CURRENCY
AND ECONOMIC SITUATION, 1919

By late 1919, the Russian economy was in shambles and lacked a stable currency (which some Bolsheviks gladly accepted as marking the end of a money economy, part of their utopian schemes). The following was written in late 1919, as part of a larger review of worldwide post-war currency issues prepared for the opening of the League of Nations. It suggests the economic chaos in Russia by this time. Indeed, money had become largely worthless and the money economy was being replaced by a barter economy. A "milliard" equals a thousand million.

Document 29
SUMMARY

At least eight different sorts of paper currency now circulate in Russian proper. Each of these is differently valued in different places, and none of them has any fixed or determinate value abroad. . . .

It may be useful here to give a list of the various forms of paper money now in circulation in Russian, amounting in the autumn of 1919 to perhaps 100 milliards of roubles:

(a) "Tsar" or Romanov notes, about 9 milliards genuine and an unknown quantity forged; this is an issue of the State Bank and beautifully printed.

(b) "Duma" notes of 1,000 and 250 roubles, also a note of the State Bank, issued between March and November, 1917, and well printed. About 8 milliards genuine and an unknown quantity forged.

(c) "Kerenskis," called by the populace 'beer labels,' issued first by the Kerensky and now by the Bolshevik Governments. Small pieces of bad paper, khaki or green, inscribed in red with the statement that they represent 20 or 40 roubles.

(d) The new notes of the Bolshevik Government.

(e) Stamps, bearing on the back, in place of the gum, the legend that they are legal tender.

(f) Treasury bonds of the Omsk and Archangel Governments, bearing interest, used as legal tender in the areas controlled by these Governments. Also a currency printed at Tiflis.

(g) Local issues made by branches of the State Bank on the instructions of local Soviets (e.g., the Archangel 'walrus' notes issued before North Russia disowned the Bolsheviks).

(h) The North Russian currency, based on a reserve at the Bank of England, and referred to below.

Source: Rex A. Wade, *Documents of Soviet History*, vol. 1, *The Triumph of Bolshevism, 1917–1919* (Gulf Breeze, FL: Academic International Press, 1991), 419–20.

TROTSKY IN DEFENSE OF TERRORISM

The Bolshevik Revolution divided European socialism, with many prominent socialist leaders critical of the new regime, especially its repressive policies. They saw these as contrary to both socialism and democracy. The Red Terror especially drew their condemnation. Karl Kautsky, an Austrian socialist and one of the leading figures of European socialism, was particularly critical. A book by Kautsky prompted Trotsky to write a lengthy defense of Bolshevik policies, from the seizure of power through the civil war and Red Terror. The following summarizes his general defense of the use of terror. It was dated May 29, 1920.

Document 30
TERRORISM

The chief theme of Kautsky's book is terrorism. The view that terrorism is of the essence of revolution Kautsky proclaims to be a widespread delusion. It is untrue that he who desires revolution must put up with terrorism. As far as he, Kautsky, is concerned, he is, generally speaking, for revolution, but decidedly against terrorism. From there, however, complications begin. . . .

The problem of revolution, as of war, consists in breaking the will of the foe, forcing him to capitulate and to accept the conditions of the conqueror. The will, of course, is a fact of the physical world, but in contradistinction for a meeting, a dispute, or a congress, the revolution carries out its object by means of the employment of material resources—though to a less degree than war. The bourgeoisie itself conquered power by means of revolts, and consolidated it by civil war. In the peaceful period, it retains power by means of a system of repression. As long as class society, founded on the most deep-rooted antagonisms, continues to exist, repression remains a necessary means of breaking the will of the opposing side.

Even if, in one country or another, the dictatorship of the proletariat grew up within the external framework of democracy, this would by no means avert the civil war. The question as to who is to rule the country, i.e., of the life or death of the bourgeoisie, will be decided on either side, not by references to the paragraphs of the constitution, but by the employment of all forms of violence. However deeply Kautsky goes into the question of the food of the anthropopithecus (see page 122 et seq. of his book) and other immediate and remote conditions which determine the cause of human cruelty, he will find in history no other way of breaking the class will of the enemy except the systematic and energetic use of violence.

The degree of ferocity of the struggle depends on a series of internal and international circumstances. The more ferocious and dangerous is the resistance of the class enemy who have been overthrown, the more inevitably does the system of repression take the form of a system of terror. . . .

The working class, which seized power in battle, had as its object and its duty to establish that power unshakeably, to guarantee its own supremacy beyond question, to destroy its enemies' hankering for a new revolution, and thereby to make sure of carrying out Socialist reforms. Otherwise there would be no point in seizing power.

The revolution "logically" does not demand terrorism, just as "logically" it does not demand an armed insurrection. What a profound commonplace! But the revolution does require of the revolutionary class that it should attain its end by all methods at its disposal—if necessary, by an armed rising: if required, by terrorism. A revolutionary class which has conquered power with arms in its hands is bound to, and will, suppress, rifle in hand, all attempts to tear the power out of its hands. Where it has against it a hostile army, it will oppose to it its own army. Where it is confronted with armed conspiracy, attempt at murder, or rising, it will hurl at the heads of its enemies an unsparing penalty. . . .

The question of the form of repression, or its degree, of course, is not one of "principle." It is a question of expediency. . . .

. . . Intimidation is a powerful weapon of policy, both internationally and internally. War, like revolution, is founded upon intimidation. A victorious war, generally speaking, destroys only an insignificant part of the conquered army, intimidating the remainder and breaking their will. The revolution works in the same way: it kills individuals, and intimidates thousands. In this sense, the Red Terror is not distinguishable from the armed insurrection, the direct continuation of which it represents. The State terror of a revolutionary class can be condemned "morally" only by a man who, as a principle, rejects (in words) every form of violence whatsoever—consequently, every war and every rising. For this one has to be merely and simply a hypocritical Quaker.

"But, in that case, in what do your tactics differ from the tactics of Tsarism?" we are asked, by the high priests of Liberalism and Kautskianism.

You do not understand this, holy men? We shall explain to you. The terror of Tsarism was directed against the proletariat. The gendarmerie of Tsarism throttled the workers who were fighting for the Socialist order. Our Extraordinary Commissions shoot landlords, capitalist, and generals who are striving to restore the capitalist order. Do you grasp this distinction? Yes? For us Communists it is quite sufficient.

Source: Leon Trotsky, *The Defense of Terrorism (Terror and Communism), A Reply to Karl Kautsky* (London, 1921), as reprinted in Rex A. Wade, ed., *Documents of Soviet History*, vol. 2, *Triumph and Retreat, 1920–1922* (Gulf Breeze, FL: Academic International Press, 1993), 85– 87.

RESOLUTION OF THE KRONSTADT SAILORS, MARCH 1, 1921

The winter of 1920–21 saw widespread discontent, peasant rebellions and worker unrest. These grew out of the shortage of food, hard living conditions, and resentment of the forced labor policies, among other factors. The immediate spark for the Kronstadt uprising was a strike movement in Petrograd, with anticommunist as well as economic demands, to which the government responded with force. In reaction to the events in the city, the sailors of the Kronstadt naval base, in the harbor of Petrograd, sent a delegation to investigate. The Kronstadt sailors had a long history of turbulence, had been among the most radical elements in 1917, and were among the most reliable forces the Bolsheviks had during the civil war. Trotsky had called them the pride of the revolution. Therefore, their actions had special significance for the regime. The combination of their growing disillusionment with the Soviet government and the strike activities in Petrograd produced this resolution, which reflected widespread discontent. The Bolshevik leaders rejected it because the nature of the demands of the

Kronstadters were a threat to the monopoly of power held by the Communist Party. Instead of compromise, the Communist leaders reacted with a furious assault, both propaganda and military, against Kronstadt. This sparked a several-day revolt before a concentrated assault, across the still frozen water surrounding the island fortress, overwhelmed the defenders and occupied the base by July 18. Just under half of the 14,000-man garrison perished, either in the assault, executed immediately afterwards, or in labor camps, while the rest escaped across the ice to Finland. Red Army casualties were heavier.

Document 31
RESOLUTION OF THE GENERAL MEETING OF THE 1ST AND 2ND SQUADRONS, HELD ON MARCH 1, 1921

Having heard the report of the representatives sent by the general meeting of ships' crews to Petrograd to investigate the situation there, we resolve:

1. In view of the fact that the present soviets do not express the will of the workers and peasants, immediately to hold new elections by secret ballot, with freedom to carry on agitation beforehand for all workers and peasants;

2. To give freedom of speech and press to workers and peasants, to anarchists and left socialist parties;

3. To secure freedom of assembly for trade unions and peasant organizations;

4. To call a nonparty conference of the workers, Red Army soldiers, and sailors of Petrograd, Kronstadt, and Petrograd province, no later than March 10, 1921;

5. To liberate all political prisoners of socialist parties, as well as all workers, peasants, soldiers, and sailors imprisoned in connection with the labor and peasant movements;

6. To elect a commission to review the cases of those being held in prisons and concentration camps;

7. To abolish all political departments because no party should be given special privileges in the propagation of its ideas or receive the financial support of the state for such purposes. Instead, there should be established cultural and educational commissions, locally elected and financed by the state;

8. To remove immediately all roadblock detachments;

9. To equalize the rations of all working people, with the exception of those employed in trades detrimental to health;

10. To abolish the Communist fighting detachments in all branches of the army, as well as the Communist guards kept on duty in factories and

mills. Should such guards or detachments be found necessary, they are to be appointed in the army from the ranks and in the factories and mills at the discretion of the workers;

11. To give the peasants full freedom of action in regard to the land, and also the right to keep cattle, on condition that the peasants manage with their own means, that is, without employing hired labor;

12. To request all branches of the army, as well as our comrades the military cadets (kursanty), to endorse our resolution;

13. To demand that the press give all our resolutions wide publicity;

14. To appoint an itinerant bureau of control;

15. To permit free handicrafts production by one's own labor.

PETRICHENKO, Chairman of the Squadron Meeting

PEREPELKIN, Secretary

Sources: Paul Avrich, *Kronstadt, 1921* (Princeton, NJ: Princeton University Press, 1970), 73–74, and *Pravda o Kronstadte* (Prague, 1921), 9–10.

THE NEW ECONOMIC POLICY

With the economy in shambles, the peasants in revolt, and faced with the implications of the still ongoing Kronstadt revolt, Lenin moved to change fundamentally the economic policies of the Communist Party and Soviet state, introducing what came to be known as The New Economic Policy, or NEP. Key to the fundamental economic reform—and retreat—was the new agricultural tax in kind, which replaced the requisitioning of the War Communism era. The intent was to calm popular discontent and to get the economy functioning again. Lenin introduced the basic principles and rationale for the policy in a lengthy speech at the Tenth Party Congress on March 15, 1921. The Congress's resolution was translated into law by an act of the Central Executive Committee on March 21.

Document 32a
V. I. LENIN: REPORT ON THE SUBSTITUTION OF A TAX IN KIND FOR THE SURPLUS-GRAIN APPROPRIATION SYSTEM

Comrades, the question of substituting a tax for surplus-grain appropriation is primarily and mainly a political question, for it is essentially a question of the attitude of the working class to the peasantry. We are raising it because we must subject relations of these two main classes, whose struggle or agreement determines the fate of our revolution as a whole, to a new or, I should perhaps say, a more careful and correct re-examination and some revision. There is no need for me to dwell in detail on the reasons for it. You all know very well of course what totality of causes, especially those due to the extreme want arising out of the war, ruin, demobilization, and the disastrous crop failure—you know about the totality of circumstances that has made the condition of the peasantry especially precarious. . . .

Why must we replace surplus appropriation by a tax? Surplus appropriation implied confiscation of all surpluses and establishment of a compulsory state monopoly. We could not do otherwise, for our need was extreme. Theoretically speaking, state monopoly is not necessarily the best system from the standpoint of the interests of socialism. A system of taxation and free exchange can be employed as a transitional measure in a peasant country possessing an industry—if this industry is running—and if there is a certain quantity of goods available.

The exchange is an incentive, a spur to the peasant. The proprietor can and will surely make an effort in his own interest when he knows that all his surplus produce will not be taken away from him and that he will only have to pay a tax, which should whenever possible be fixed in advance. The basic thing is to give the small farmer an incentive and a spur to till the soil. We must adapt our state economy to the economy of the middle peasant, which we have not managed to remake in three years, and will not be able to remake in another ten.

Document 32b
ON THE REPLACEMENT OF THE REQUISITIONING
OF FOOD AND RAW MATERIALS BY A TAX IN KIND

1. In order to assure an efficient and stable economic life on the basis of a freer disposition by the farmer of the products of his labor and of his economic resources, in order to strengthen the peasant economy and raise its productivity and also in order to calculate precisely the obligation to the state which falls on the peasants, requisitioning, as a means of state collection of food supplies, raw material and fodder, is to be replaced by a tax in kind.

2. This tax must be less than what the peasant has paid up to this time through requisitions. The sum of the tax must be calculated so as to cover the most essential needs of the Army, the city workers, the non-agricultural population. The general sum of the tax must be decreased inasmuch as the reestablishment of transportation and industry will permit the Soviet Government to receive agricultural products in exchange for factory and handicraft products.

3. The tax is to be taken in the form of the percentage or partial deduction from the products raised in the peasant holding, taking into account the

harvest, the number of consumers in the holding and the number of cattle on hand.

4. The tax must be progressive; the percentage deducted must be lower for the holdings of the middle-class and poorer peasants and of town workers. The holdings of the poorest peasants may be exempted from some and, in exceptional cases, from all forms of the tax in kind.

The industrious peasants who increase the sown-areas and the number of cattle in their holdings and those who increase the general productivity of their holdings on the whole, receive benefits when paying the tax in kind.

Source: Rex A. Wade, ed., *Documents of Soviet History*, vol. 2, *Triumph and Retreat, 1920–1922* (Gulf Breeze, FL: Academic International Press, 1993), 218–26, 237–38. No. 1 as quoted in John L. H. Keep, *The Russian Revolution: A Study in Mass Mobilization* (London: Weidenfeld and Nicolson, 1976), 211–12.

Glossary of Selected Terms

CEC (TsIK): Central Executive Committee (executive of the Congress of Soviets).

Cheka (Vcheka): Common name for the All-Russia Extraordinary Commission for Combating Counter-Revolution and Sabotage, the secret, or political, police. Established by the Bolsheviks in December 1917; forerunner of later secret police under different names (GPU, OGPU, NKVD, KGB) during the Soviet Union.

Comintern: The Communist, or Third, International, founded in 1919.

Commissar: Term used to designate revolutionary officials, especially agents of the soviets, in 1917. After the October Revolution, it was incorporated into the official name for the main government ministers (i.e., people's commissar for foreign affairs, etc.), the equivalent for secretary in the American government and minister in European governments (including Russia before 1917 and after 1946).

Constituent Assembly: The assembly to be elected by a universal, free, secret, and direct ballot after the overthrow of Nicholas II, and which was to establish the future basic political structure and principles for Russia; dispersed by Bolsheviks after one meeting.

Constitutional Democrats (Kadets): The main liberal party in Russia, based on a program of civil liberties and constitutional and parliamentary government.

Council of People's Commissars (Sovnarkom, CPC, SNK): Formal name for the government formed by the Bolsheviks after the October Revolution, and used until 1946, when the name of the government was changed to Council of Ministers.

Duma: Usually means, especially if capitalized, the State Duma, the lower house of the legislature established after the Revolution of 1905, which lasted from 1906 to 1917. Also name of city councils before and during the revolution.

Guberniia (Guberniya): A province, the main administrative subdivision of the Russian state.

Kadets: See *Constitutional Democrats*.

Komuch: Committee of Members of the Constituent Assembly. Created by SRs in June 1918, at Samara, claiming to be the legitimate government of Russia; an important center of opposition to the Bolsheviks in the summer and fall of 1918.

Kulak: Term used to describe the wealthier peasants, but also used by Bolsheviks to describe any peasant who opposed their policies.

Left SRs: Radical wing of the Socialist Revolutionary Party, cooperated with the Bolsheviks in the radical left coalitions of the fall of 1917; became a separate party after the October Revolution and participated in the Soviet government until March 1918.

Mensheviks: The more moderate branch (in opposition to the Bolsheviks) of the Russian Social Democratic Labor Party, the Russian Marxist revolutionary party; by 1917, effectively a separate party. After the October Revolution, they attempted, unsuccessfully, to find a role as a "loyal opposition" to the Bolsheviks during the civil war, and were outlawed afterwards.

Menshevik-Internationalists: Left wing of the Mensheviks in 1917, opposed Revolutionary Defensism and often cooperated with the Bolsheviks and Left SRs in the radical left bloc in 1917, but opposed the October Revolution.

MRC: The Military Revolutionary Committee, formed by the Petrograd Soviet in October and played a key role in the October Revolution and in maintaining the new Soviet government for a few weeks thereafter.

NEP (New Economic Policy): Policy instituted by Lenin at the Tenth Party Congress in March 1921, to call a halt to the radical socializing economic policies of the civil war era, especially grain requisitioning. It imposed instead a 10 percent tax on the peasants and allowed limited private entrepreneurial activity, in an effort to encourage recovery of the economy. Seen by Bolshevik leaders as temporary.

Obshchina: The traditional village commune, the village as a political and economic entity.

Octobrists: Members of the Union of 17 October Party, the main moderate conservative party.

Politburo: Political Bureau of the Central Committee of the Bolshevik Party; the party's key decision-making body.

Rada: Literally, the Ukrainian equivalent of the Russian word "soviet," a council. During the revolutionary period, usually refers to the Ukrainian Central Rada in Kiev, which asserted leadership of the Ukrainian national movement and later formed the government of independent Ukraine.

Revolutionary Defensism: Political position, developed by Irakli Tsereteli and others, that dominated the Petrograd Soviet from March–September 1917 and, to a degree, the Provisional Government as well. It stressed the importance of a swift negotiated peace, but with defense of the country and revolution until that could be achieved, and cooperation with the liberals in "coalition" Provisional Government ministries.

RKP(b): Russian Communist Party (Bolsheviks). Official name of the party after the name change in March 1918, until 1925, when it was changed again to CPSU—Communist Party of the Soviet Union.

RSDLP or **RSDWP** or **RSDRP:** Russian Social Democratic Labor (or Workers') Party, the main Russian Marxist revolutionary party; by 1917, it had long since split into Bolshevik and Menshevik wings, although both still claimed and used the formal party title. The Bolsheviks often used the acronym RSDLP(b).

RSFSR: Russian Socialist Federal Soviet Republic; official name of the Russian state from July 1918 to January 1924.

SD, SDs: Social Democrats; see RSDLP.

Socialist Revolutionary Party: Peasant-oriented revolutionary party but with a strong appeal to workers and intelligentsia, it stressed the opposition of "toilers" to oppressors of all kinds. Largest political party in 1917 and in the Constituent Assembly. Tended toward internal divisions, and in 1917 had right, center, and left wings, which weakened its effectiveness. The left wing cooperated with the Bolsheviks before and for a few months after the October Revolution (see Left SRs), while the right wing played a major role in the anti-Bolshevik opposition during the 1918 period of the civil war.

Soviet(s): Literally, "council," the term has come to be used historically to refer to the soviets (councils) of workers,' soldiers,' and peasants' deputies formed in 1917. Capitalized, it refers to the the Petrograd Soviet in 1917 and to the Soviet government formed after the October Revolution.

Sovnarkom: Common abbreviation for the Council of People's Commissars, based on the first syllable of each word in Russian.

SR, SRs: See *Socialist Revolutionary Party.*

Stavka: Front military headquarters of the Russian army in World War I.

Uezd (Uyezd): A rural district, subdivision of a province (guberniia).

Verst: Russian unit of measurement—0.66 miles or 1.0688 kilometers.

Volost: A rural subdistrict, subdivision of a uezd.

Zemstvo: Elected (by nobles and peasants, with former predominating) local rural government institutions with limited authority to deal with health, agriculture, education, and other issues. Some liberals hoped they were the beginning of elective, representative government in Russia. Through their professional employees, they became a major conduit for revolutionary ideas into the countryside. Abolished after the Bolshevik Revolution.

Zimmerwaldists: Antiwar left wing of European (including Russian) socialism during World War I, named for a conference held at Zimmerwald, Switzerland.

Annotated Bibliography

Before 1967, there were only a few serious studies of the revolution and the civil war. From about 1967 and through the 1970s, Russian studies in the West matured and a significant number of valuable works appeared, mostly on political subjects. During the 1980s and 1990s, study of the revolution became more diverse, topically, with more studies on social and cultural themes appearing. The following bibliography is only a part of the enormous body of works available on the revolution and civil war. For a more complete guide, see especially the bibliography by Murray Frame, given below. Readers should be aware that because of the difficulty of classifying books by single topic or time period, they may need to look in several of the categories given below.

DOCUMENT COLLECTIONS

The Bolsheviks and the October Revolution: Minutes of the Central Committee of the Russian Social-Democratic Labour Party (bolsheviks), August 1917–February 1918. Translated by Anne Bone. London: Pluto, 1974. Minutes of the meetings of the Bolshevik Central Committee during a crucial period.

Browder, Robert Paul, and Alexander F. Kerensky, eds. *The Russian Provisional Government, 1917: Documents*. 3 vols. Stanford, CA: Stanford University Press, 1961. Excellent collection of documents on the Provisional Government and 1917.

Bunyan, James, ed. *The Origin of Forced Labor in the Soviet State, 1917–1921*, Baltimore, MD: Johns Hopkins University Press, 1967. Good collection on this theme.

Bunyan, James, and H. H. Fisher, eds. *The Bolshevik Revolution 1917–18, Documents and Materials*. Stanford, CA: Stanford University Press, 1934, reprinted 1961, 1965. Good collection on late 1917 to early 1918; many documents, often in very abbreviated form.

Butt, V. P., A. B. Murphy, N. A. Myshov, and G. R. Swain, eds. *The Russian Civil War: Documents from the Soviet Archives*. New York: St. Martin's Press, 1996. Good selection of documents on a wide range of issues during the civil war.

Golder, Frank Alfred, ed. *Documents of Russian History, 1914–1917*. Gloucester, MA: Peter Smith, 1964 (Reprint of 1927 edition). Covers the war years and the revolution of 1917 down to the October Revolution.

Keep, John L. H., ed. *The Debate on Soviet Power: Minutes of the All-Russian Central Executive Committee of Soviets, Second Convocation, October 1917–January 1918*. Oxford: Clarendon, 1979. Excellent source for the critical first months of Bolshevik rule.

Kowalski, Ronald I. *The Russian Revolution: 1917–1921*. New York: Routledge, 1997. Good selection connected by intelligent commentary that forms a running history of the revolution and civil war.

Lenin, V. I. *Collected Works*. 45 vols. Moscow: Progress Publishers, 1960–70. Important source for any study of this era.

McCauley, Martin. *The Russian Revolution and the Soviet State, 1917–1921. Documents*. London and Basingstoke: Macmillan, 1975. Good collection of documents covering the revolution and civil war.

McNeal, Robert H., ed. *Resolutions and Decisions of the Communist Party of the Soviet Union*, vol. I edited by Ralph C. Elwood; vol. II edited by Richard Gregor. Toronto: Toronto University Press, 1974. An important collection of party documents.

The Nicky-Sunny Letters; Correspondence of the Tsar and Tsaritsa, 1914–1917. (Reprint of *The Letters of the Tsar to the Tsaritsa, 1914–1917* [1929] and *The Letters of the Tsaritsa to the Tsar, 1914–1916* [1923]). Gulf Breeze, FL: Academic International Press, 1970. Letters between Nicholas and Alexandra.

Rosenberg, William G. *Bolshevik Visions. First Phase of the Cultural Revolution in Soviet Russia*. 2nd ed., 2 vols. Ann Arbor: University of Michigan Press, 1990. Valuable collection of early Bolshevik writings about the visions for a new society.

Wade, Rex A. *Documents of Soviet History*. vol. 1, *The Triumph of Bolshevism, 1917–1919*. vol. 2, *Triumph and Retreat, 1920–1922*. vol. 3, *Lenin's Heirs, 1923–1925*. Gulf Breeze, FL: Academic International Press, 1991–95. Extensive collection of documents on the early years of Soviet rule; most documents given in full.

MEMOIRS, DIARIES, PARTICIPANTS' ACCOUNTS

Babine, Alexis. *A Russian Civil War Diary: Alexis Babine in Saratov, 1917–1922*. Edited by Donald J. Raleigh. Durham, NC: Duke University Press,

1988. A good picture of life during the revolution and civil war in a provincial city.

Buchanan, George. *My Mission to Russia and Other Diplomatic Memories*. 2 vols. London: Cassell, 1923. Perceptive account by the British ambassador of war and revolution in Russia.

Chernov, Victor. *The Great Russian Revolution*. New Haven, CT: Yale University Press, 1936. Account of the leader of the SR Party, written more as a "history" than as a memoir.

Denikin, Anton Ivanovich. *The Russian Turmoil: Memoirs Military, Social, and Political*. London: Hutchinson, 1922. The best account by a prominent general of the impact of the revolution on the Russian army.

Denikin, General A. *The White Army*. Gulf Breeze, FL: Academic International Press, 1973. Important account of the most important White leader in the civil war.

Francis, David Rowland. *Russia from the American Embassy, April, 1916–November, 1918*. New York: Scribner, 1921. The American ambassador's account; less perceptive than Buchanan's on politics, but sympathetic to Russia's problems.

Gorky, Maxim. *Untimely Thoughts: Essays on Revolution, Culture and the Bolsheviks, 1917–18*. New York: P. S. Eriksson, 1968 and New Haven, CT: Yale University Press, 1995. Selected newspaper editorials by the famous writer, who, while close to the Bolsheviks, was very critical of the October Revolution and of the Bolsheviks' repressive measures.

Got'e, I. V. *Time of Troubles: The Diary of Iurii Vladimirovich Got'e, Moscow, July 8, 1917 to July 23, 1922*. Translated by T. Emmons. Princeton, NJ: Princeton University Press, 1988. Good diary of a prominent, conservative, but nonpolitical, Moscow intellectual; especially good on the struggles of daily life during the civil war.

Kerensky, Alexander F. *Russia and History's Turning Point*. New York: Duell, Sloan and Pearce, 1965. The last, and perhaps best, of Kerensky's several memoirs, although earlier ones are worth reading also.

Knox, Sir Alfred William Fortescue. *With the Russian Army, 1914–1917*. London: Hutchinson, 1921 (and other editions). Account of the British military attache, often quite informative.

Miliukov, P. N. *The Russian Revolution*. Translated by Richard Stites and Gary Hamburg. 3 vols. Gulf Breeze, FL: Academic International Press, 1978–87. The leader of the Kadet Party, a professional historian, immediately turned to writing his account of the revolution, drawing on both his own experiences and his skill as a historian, producing one of the most important first-person accounts of the revolution.

Mstislavskii, Sergei. *Five Days Which Transformed Russia*. Translated by E. K. Zelensky, London: Hutchinson, 1988. Fragments of important events from a Left SR leader.

Nabokov, Vladimir. *Nabokov and the Russian Provisional Government, 1917.* Edited by Virgil Medlin and Steven Parsons. New Haven, CT: Yale University Press, 1976. Memoirs, written soon after the event, by a prominent Kadet; quite perceptive.

Paleologue, Maurice. *An Ambassador's Memoirs.* 3 vols. 2 ed. Translated by F. A. Holt. London: Hutchinson, 1923. The French ambassador's memoirs, heavily retouched.

Price, Morgan Phillips. *Dispatches from the Revolution: Russia 1915–1918.* Durham, NC: Duke University Press, 1998. Insightful accounts of life and politics by a British correspondent in Russia.

Reed, John. *Ten Days That Shook the World.* New York: Random House, 1960 (and several other editions). Account of the era of the October Revolution by an American radical; very influential in later writing about the revolution (first published in 1919).

Shkhovsky, Viktor. *A Sentimental Journey: Memoirs, 1917–1922.* Ithaca, NY: Cornell University Press, 1970. Fascinating and literary memoir by a noted writer who at that time was serving in the army.

Shulgin, V. V. *Days of the Russian Revolution: Memoirs from the Right, 1905–1917.* Translated by B. F. Adams. Gulf Breeze, FL: Academic International Press, 1990. Impressionistic but useful account from an ultra-conservative member of the Duma.

Steinberg, Isaac. *In the Workshop of the Revolution.* New York: Rinehart, 1953. Account by a Left SR who served briefly in the Soviet government in late 1917–early 1918.

Sukhanov, N. N. *The Russian Revolution, 1917: An Eyewitness Account.* 2 vols. Edited, abridged, and translated by Joel Carmichael. Oxford: Oxford University Press, 1955 (and later editions). One of the most important memoir sources for the revolution, especially the first weeks. Sukhanov was an independent radical socialist who played a prominent role in the formation of the Provisional Government and early leadership of the Petrograd Soviet.

Trotsky, Leon. *The Russian Revolution.* 3 vols. New York: Simon and Schuster, 1933 (and later editions). Written by Trotsky longer after the event than most of the accounts listed here. Must be used with great care. Was very influential in shaping Western interpretations of the revolution from the mid-1930s through the 1960s.

COLLECTIONS OF ARTICLES AND ESSAYS

Acton, Edward, Vladimir I. Cherniaev, and William G. Rosenberg, eds. *Critical Companion to the Russian Revolution, 1914–1921.* Bloomington: Indiana University Press, 1997. Outstanding collection of essays by prominent scholars—one of the best collections.

Clowes, Edith W., Samuel D. Kassow, and James L. West, eds. *Between Tsar and People: Educated Society and the Quest for Public Identity in Late Imperial Russia*. Princeton, NJ: Princeton University Press, 1991. Excellent collection of articles on late Imperial Russia by leading scholars focused on the "middle classes" and educated society.

Davies, R. W., ed. *From Tsarism to the New Economic Policy: Continuity and Change in the Economy of the USSR*. Ithaca, NY: Cornell University Press, 1990. Essays on the economic history of the era, by leading experts.

Elwood, Ralph Carter, ed. *Reconsiderations on the Russian Revolution*. Cambridge, MA: Slavica Publishers, 1976. Somewhat older, but still valuable, collection of articles.

Frankel, Edith Rogovin, Jonathan Frankel, and Baruch Knei-Paz, eds. *Revolution in Russia: Reassessments of 1917*. Cambridge: Cambridge University Press, 1992. Excellent collection of articles by leading experts on the revolution.

Gleason, Abbott, Peter Kenez, and Richard Stites, eds. *Bolshevik Culture: Experimentation and Order in the Russian Revolution*. Bloomington: Indiana University Press, 1985. Very good collection of essays on the early Bolshevik era's efforts at cultural transformation, by prominent scholars.

Hunczak, Taras, ed. *The Ukraine, 1917–1921: A Study in Revolution*. Cambridge, MA: Harvard University Press, 1977. Essays on the revolution and civil war in Ukraine; very good.

Jackson, George, and Robert Devlin, eds. *Dictionary of the Russian Revolution*. New York: Greenwood Press, 1989. Good collection of short essays on many topics by leading scholars.

Kaiser, Daniel H., ed. *The Workers' Revolution in Russia, 1917. The View from Below*. Cambridge: Cambridge University Press, 1987. Six essays on the social history of the revolution, focused on the industrial workers and their relation to the political parties; very good.

Koenker, Diane, William G. Rosenberg, and Ronald G. Suny, eds. *Party, State, and Society in the Russian Civil War*. Bloomington: Indiana University Press, 1989. Excellent collection by foremost specialists, focused on social history and the interaction of politics and society.

Pipes, Richard, ed. *Revolutionary Russia: A Symposium*. Cambridge, MA: Harvard University Press, 1968. An older collection, now somewhat superseded, but still some useful materials.

Service, Robert, ed. *Society and Politics in the Russian Revolution*. Basingstoke and London: Macmillan, 1992. An excellent collection of essays on 1917 by British scholars.

Shukman, Harold, ed. *The Blackwell Encyclopedia of the Russian Revolution*. Oxford: Basil Blackwell, 1988. Good collection of short essays on the revolution and civil war by leading scholars, mostly British.

Suny, Ronald, and Arthur Adams. *The Russian Revolution and Bolshevik Victory: Visions and Revisions*. 3rd ed. Lexington, MA: D. C. Heath, 1990. Articles and selections from books that explore the nature of the Russian Revolution of 1917.

POLITICAL PARTIES, POLITICAL THOUGHT, BIOGRAPHIES

Abraham, Richard. *Alexander Kerensky. The First Love of the Revolution.* New York: Sidgwick and Jackson, 1987. Best biography of Kerensky.

Brovkin, Vladimir N. *The Mensheviks after October: Socialist Opposition and the Rise of the Bolshevik Dictatorship.* Ithaca, NY: Cornell University Press, 1987. Examines the Mensheviks' opposition, and popular support, after the October Revolution; useful for its argument concerning the political complexity of the era, but overstates the case for the Mensheviks.

Clements, Barbara Evans. *Bolshevik Women.* Cambridge: Cambridge University Press, 1997. Comprehensive account of women Bolsheviks, their roles and fates; very good.

Deutscher, Issac. *The Prophet Armed: Trotsky 1879–1921.* Oxford: Oxford University Press, 1954. An older but detailed biography of Trotsky, marred by an uncritical approach to the subject; middle part of three volumes.

Galili, Ziva. *The Menshevik Leaders in the Russian Revolution. Social Realities and Political Strategies.* Princeton, NJ: Princeton University Press, 1989. Good study of the Mensheviks in 1917.

Getzler, Israel. *Martov: A Political Biography of a Russian Social Democrat.* Cambridge: Cambridge University Press, 1967. Best biography of Martov.

Harding, Neil. *Lenin's Political Thought: Theory and Practice in the Democratic Revolution.* 2 vols. New York: St. Martin's Press, 1917, 1981; *Leninism.* Durham, NC: Duke University Press, 1996. Somewhat controversial but stimulating look at Lenin's political thought and its relation to his political activities, stressing the role of ideology in Lenin's actions; compare with Service, below.

Knei-Paz, Baruch. *The Social and Political Thought of Leon Trotsky.* Oxford: Clarendon, 1979. Careful analysis of Trotsky's social and political ideas; an unusually objective study of a subject who has been mostly the object of hero worship or blind condemnation.

Lewin, Moshe. *Lenin's Last Struggle.* London: Faber and Faber, 1969. Looks at Lenin's activities and rethinking of the revolution just before his death.

Lieven, Dominic. *Nicholas II: Twilight of the Empire.* New York: St. Martin's Press, 1994. Excellent biography of Nicholas, exploring his rule in the context of Russian history, institutions and the problems facing Russia at the time.

Radkey, Oliver H. *The Agrarian Foes of Bolshevism. Promise and Default of the Russian Socialist Revolutionaries, February to October 1917*. New York: Columbia University Press, 1958; *The Sickle under the Hammer. The Russian Socialist Revolutionaries in the Early Months of Soviet Rule*. New York: Columbia University Press, 1963. Detailed account of the SR Party during 1917 and early 1918; very critical of the party leadership.

Roobol, W. H. *Tsereteli—A Democrat in the Russian Revolution: A Political Biography*. The Hague: Martinus Nijhoff, 1976. A good biography of Tsereteli.

Rosenberg, William G. *Liberals in the Russian Revolution: the Constitutional Democratic Party, 1917–1921*. Princeton, NJ: Princeton University Press, 1974. The standard—and excellent—study of the Kadets in the revolution and civil war.

Service, Robert. *The Bolshevik Party in Revolution: A Study in Organizational Change, 1917– 1923*. London: Macmillan, 1979. Focuses on the organizational structure and evolution of the Bolshevik Party in response to the demands of revolution, power, and governance.

———. *Lenin: A Political Life*. 3 vols. London: Macmillan, 1985–94. An excellent biography of Lenin, stressing his political activity and pragmatism; compare with Harding, above.

Steinberg, Mark D., and Vladimir Khrustalev. *The Fall of the Romanovs: Political Dreams and Personal Struggles in a Time of Revolution*. New Haven, CT: Yale University Press, 1995. Excellent biographical sketches of Nicholas and Alexandra, coupled with a large section of documents, mainly from 1917–18.

Stockdale, Melissa Kirschke. *Paul Miliukov and the Quest for a Liberal Russia, 1880–1918*. Ithaca, NY: Cornell University Press, 1996. The best biography of Miliukov, the Kadet leader, although focused on the pre-1917 period.

Ulam, Adam. *The Bolsheviks*. New York: Macmillan, 1965 (and later editions). Older, but still a good, and readable, study of Lenin and the Bolshevik Party.

Warth, Robert A. *Nicholas II: the Life and Reign of Russia's Last Monarch*. Westport, CT: Praeger, 1997. A very good biography of Nicholas, stressing his functioning and failures as monarch, especially in relation to government officials and policies.

BEFORE THE REVOLUTION

Hosking, Geoffrey. *The Russian Constitutional Experiment: Government and Duma, 1907– 1914*. Cambridge: Cambridge University Press, 1973. Excellent study of the "Duma monarchy" and the relations between Nicholas's government and the political parties before the war.

Jahn, Hubertus. *Patriotic Culture in Russia During World War I*. Ithaca, NY: Cornell University Press, 1995. Looks at the patriotism and popular culture through art, music, theater, and movies.

Lincoln, W. Bruce. *Passage through Armageddon. The Russians in War and Revolution, 1914–1918*. New York: Simon and Schuster, 1986. Excellent account of Russia at war and during the revolution of 1917; very readable.

McKean, Robert B. *St. Petersburg Between the Revolutions: Workers and Revolutionaries, June 1907–February 1917*. New Haven, CT and London: Yale University Press, 1990. Very good study of the key issue of workers, revolutionaries, the political system, and the roots of the February Revolution.

Pearson, Raymond. The Russian Moderates and the Crisis of Tsarism 1914–1917. London: Macmillan, 1977. A study of behavior of the liberal and moderate conservative political parties and leaders as they confronted the problems of wartime Russia and obstinacy of Nicholas.

Rogger, Hans. *Russia in the Age of Modernization and Revolution 1881–1917*. London: Longman, 1983. Perhaps the best general history of the larger period leading up to the revolution.

Siegelbaum, Lewis. *The Politics of Industrial Mobilization in Russia, 1914–1917: A Study of the War-Industries Committees*. London and New York: Macmillan, 1983. Excellent study of the economic, political, and social dimensions of mobilization during World War I, with emphasis on the War-Industries Committees and their conflict with the government and role in its demise.

Stone, Norman. *The Eastern Front 1914–1917*. New York: Scribners, 1975. Good account of World War I on the Russian front, with emphasis on military matters.

Waldron, Peter. *Between Two Revolutions: Stolypin and the Politics of Renewal in Russia*. DeKalb: Northern Illinois Press, 1998. Examines the last major attempt at political reform by the last significant government leader of Imperial Russia, and why it failed.

THE REVOLUTION AND CIVIL WAR, AND LONGER PERIODS

Atkinson, Dorothy. *The End of the Russian Land Commune 1905–1930*. Stanford, CA: Stanford University Press, 1983. Very good study of peasant Russia over the long revolutionary period.

Carr, E. H. *The Bolshevik Revolution, 1917–1923*. 3 vols. New York: Macmillan, 1951–53. Classic, although somewhat dated, detailed study.

Chamberlin, William Henry. *The Russian Revolution, 1917–1921*. 2 vols. New York: Macmillan, 1935 (and later editions). The classic account of the revolution and civil war, still one of the best, although a bit dated.

Figes, Orlando. *A People's Tragedy: the Russian Revolution*. New York: Viking, 1997. Provocative and readable study of the revolutionary period, with special focus on the people rather than political leaders.

Fitzpatrick, Sheila. *The Russian Revolution, 1917–1932*. 2nd ed. Oxford: Oxford University Press, 1994. Good short history, focused more on the 1920s than on the revolution and civil war.

Frame, Murray, comp. *The Russian Revolution, 1905–1921: A Bibliographic Guide to Works in English*. Westport, CT: Greenwood Press, 1995. A comprehensive listing of articles and books.

Friedgut, Theodore. *Iuzoka and Revolution*. 2 vols. Princeton, NJ: Princeton University Press, 1994. Fascinating, detailed study of an industrial city in southern Russia from the late imperial period through the civil war.

von Geldern, James. *Bolshevik Festivals 1917–1920*. Berkeley, Los Angeles, London: University of California Press, 1993. Looks at how the Bolsheviks and their supporters celebrated their vision of a new world and attempted to legitimize the new regime though public festivals and myths.

Getzler, Israel. *Kronstadt, 1917–1921: The Fate of a Soviet Democracy*. Cambridge: Cambridge University Press, 1983. The story of the Kronstadt sailors, one of the most radical elements of the revolution, whose revolt helps mark the end of the era; focuses especially on 1917–18.

Khalid, Adeeb. *The Politics of Muslim Cultural Reform: Jadidism in Central Asia*. Berkeley: University of California Press, 1998. An excellent study of the revolutionary era in Central Asia, especially Tashkent and the southern part.

Kingston-Mann, Esther. *Lenin and the Problem of Marxist Peasant Revolution*. New York: Oxford University Press, 1983. A penetrating study of Lenin's efforts to grapple with the problems of a Marxist revolution in a primarily peasant country, and the consequences thereof.

Lih, Lars T. *Bread and Authority in Russia, 1914–1921*. Berkeley: University of California Press, 1990. Excellent study of the relationship between the food crises and the broader political and social crises during war, revolution, and civil war.

Read, Christopher. *From Tsar to Soviets: the Russian People and their Revolution, 1917–21*. New York: Oxford University Press, 1996. Perhaps the best modern one-volume account of the revolution and civil war, although not the easiest reading.

Reshetar, John S. *The Ukrainian Revolution, 1917–1920*. Princeton, NJ: Princeton University Press, 1952. Older, but good account of the events in Ukraine.

Stites, Richard. *Revolutionary Dreams: Utopian Vision and Experimental Life in the Russian Revolution*. New York and Oxford: Oxford University Press, 1989. Looks at the visionary aspects of revolutionary Russia, especially 1917 and the civil war.

————. *The Women's Liberation Movement in Russia. Feminism, Nihilism, and Bolshevism, 1860–1930.* Princeton, NJ: Princeton University Press, 1978. The most comprehensive account of the women's movement in Russia over a long period.

Suny, Ronald Grigor. *The Revenge of the Past: Nationalism, Revolution, and the Collapse of the Soviet Union.* Stanford, CA: Stanford University Press, 1993. Outstanding account of the role of nationalism in the revolution and its impact on the end of the Soviet Union, yet brief and readable.

Tirado, Isabela A. *Young Guard: The Communist Youth League, Petrograd 1917–1920.* Westport, CT: Greenwood Press, 1988. Study of the youth movement in revolutionary Russia.

Von Laue, Theodore. *Why Lenin? Why Stalin? A Reappraisal of the Russian Revolution, 1900– 1930.* Philadelphia: J. B. Lippincott, 1964 (and later editions). Masterful short history that sets the revolution, broadly defined, within a world context as well as its place in Russian history; in some ways, the first edition is better than later ones.

White, James D. *The Russian Revolution, 1917–1921: A Short History.* London and New York: Edward Arnold, 1994. A good history, organized in short sections that makes it easy to use for looking up particular aspects of the revolution.

1917 AND EARLY 1918

Acton, Edward. *Rethinking the Russian Revolution.* London: Edward Arnold, 1990. A stimulating overview of the literature on the revolution, offering an interpretation of the history of and trends in writing about the revolution.

Daniels, Robert V. *Red October: The Bolshevik Revolution of 1917.* New York: Scribner's, 1967. A good history of October, with special emphasis upon the day-to-day events, and accidents, leading to the Bolshevik Revolution; a very readable account by an excellent historian.

Ezergailis, Andrew. *The 1917 Revolution in Latvia.* New York: Columbia University Press, 1974. One of the best studies of the revolution in one of the nationality areas.

Ferro, Marc. *The Russian Revolution of February 1917.* Englewood Cliffs, NY: Prentice-Hall, 1972. A translation of his original French language account, provides a provocative look at popular aspirations during the revolution, modeled on studies of the French Revolution.

Figes, Orlando, and Boris Kolonitskii. *Interpreting the Russian Revolution: The Language and Symbols of 1917.* New Haven, CT: Yale University Press, 1999. An intriguing look at the use of language and symbolism in the revolution, especially the cult of Kerensky.

Flenley, Paul. "Industrial Relations and the Economic Crisis of 1917." *Revolutionary Russia* 4, no. 2 (1991): 184–209. The best brief introduction to the relationship between economic conditions and political events.

Gill, Graeme. *Peasants and Government in the Russian Revolution*. London: Macmillan, 1979. Focuses on government policy toward the peasants in 1917, and peasant response.

Hasegawa, Tsuyoshi. *The February Revolution: Petrograd 1917*. Seattle: University of Washington Press, 1981. Best account of the February Revolution, including an extensive section on the coming of the revolution.

Hickey, Michael C. "Local Government and State Authority in the Provinces: Smolensk, February–June 1917." *Slavic Review* 35, no. 1 (1996): 863–81. Excellent essay on the revolution in the provinces.

———. "Revolution on the Jewish Street: Smolensk, 1917." *Journal of Social History* 31, no. 4 (Summer 1998): 823–50. Best account of Jewish response to and activity during the revolution.

Keep, John L. H. *The Russian Revolution: A Study in Mass Mobilisation*. London: Weidenfeld and Nicolson, 1976. One of the best works on the revolution, looks especially at the role of various organizations (soviets, factory committees, etc.) and how the Bolsheviks were able use them to gain and then consolidate power in 1917 and early 1918.

Koenker, Diane. *Moscow Workers and the 1917 Revolution*. Princeton, NJ: Princeton University Press, 1981. Excellent study of the revolution in Moscow, focused on the industrial workers.

Koenker, Diane, and William G. Rosenberg. *Strikes and Revolution in Russia, 1917*. Princeton, NJ: Princeton University Press, 1989. Outstanding, if somewhat difficult, work on strikes and their political and social impact.

Kolonitskii, Boris. "Democracy in the Political Consciousness of the February Revolution." *Slavic Review* 57, no. 1 (1998): 95–106. Fascinating discussion of the idea of democracy and how people used the concept in the early stages of the revolution.

Lincoln, W. Bruce. *Passage through Armageddon. The Russians in War and Revolution, 1914–1918*. New York: Simon and Schuster, 1986. Excellent account of Russia during the war and revolution of 1917; very readable.

Lyandres, Semion. *The Bolsheviks' "German Gold" Revisited. An Inquiry into the 1917 Accusations*. Pittsburgh, PA: Center for Russian and East European Studies, University of Pittsburgh, 1995. Excellent short work on the important question of the commonly asserted German money to the Bolsheviks, and finding it to very different than assumed.

Mawdsley, Evan. *The Russian Revolution and the Baltic Fleet: War and Politics, February 1917–April 1918*. London: Macmillan, 1978. Good study of the important Baltic Fleet.

Melancon, Michael. *The Socialist Revolutionaries and the Russian Anti-War Movement, 1914–1917*. Columbus: Ohio State University Press, 1990. A very good study of the SRs and Russian socialism during the war years and up through the February Revolution.

―――. "The Syntax of Soviet Power: The Resolutions of Local Soviets and Other Institutions, March–October 1917." *Russian Review* 52, no. 4 (1993): 486–505. Good account of the political struggles at the local level.

Munck, J. L. *The Kornilov Revolt: A Critical Examination of the Sources and Research.* Aarhus: Aarhus University Press, 1987. Useful review of the issues around one of the important crises of 1917.

Orlovsky, Daniel. "The Lower Middle Strata in Revolutionary Russia." In *Between Tsar and People: Educated Society and the Quest for Public Identity in Late Imperial Russia.* Edited by Edith W. Clowes, Samuel D. Kassow, and James West, 248–68. Princeton, NJ: Princeton University Press, 1991. A look at an important, but usually ignored, social group.

Pethybridge, Roger W. *The Spread of the Russian Revolution: Essays on 1917.* London: Macmillan, 1972. A series of essays presenting a good study of often neglected subjects such as railways, transportation, communications, and goods distribution.

Rabinowitch, Alexander. *The Bolsheviks Come to Power: The Revolution of 1917 in Petrograd.* New York: Norton, 1976. Continues the story of the following book, focused on the events leading up to and including the October Revolution.

―――. *Prelude to Revolution. The Petrograd Bolsheviks and the July 1917 Uprising.* Bloomington: Indiana University Press, 1968. Outstanding study of the Bolshevik Party in the first part of 1917 and of the July Crisis.

Radkey, Oliver H. *The Election to the Russian Constituent Assembly of 1917.* Updated Edition. Ithaca, NY: Cornell University Press, 1989. The most careful analysis of the elections.

Raleigh, Donald J. *Revolution on the Volga. 1917 in Saratov.* Ithaca, NY and London: Cornell University Press, 1986. Excellent study, and the best book on the revolution in an ethnically Russian province.

Rosenberg, William G. "Russian Labor and Bolshevik Power After October." *Slavic Review* 44, no. 2 (1985): 205–38. Thoughtful exploration of the relationship between industrial workers and the Bolsheviks after the October Revolution; followed by a discussion by other historians of Rosenberg's essay.

Sanders, Jonathan. *Russia 1917: The Unpublished Revolution.* New York: Abbeville Press, 1989. Excellent collection of photographs from 1917, gives a good visual image of the revolution.

Saul, Norman E. *Sailors in Revolt. The Russian Baltic Fleet in 1917.* Lawrence, KS: Regents Press of Kansas, 1978. Very good history of the important Baltic Fleet sailors.

Shkliarevsky, Gennady. *Labor in the Russian Revolution: Factory Committees and Trade Unions, 1917–1918.* New York: St. Martin's Press, 1993. Solid account of these important organizations.

Smith, S. A. *Red Petrograd: Revolution in the Factories, 1917–18*. Cambridge: Cambridge University Press, 1983. Perhaps the best account of the revolution among the industrial workers of Petrograd.

Suny, Ronald Grigor. *The Baku Commune, 1917–1918: Class and Nationality in the Russian Revolution*. Princeton, NJ: Princeton University Press, 1972. Excellent study of the complexities of nationality, class, religion, and politics during the revolution.

Thompson, John H. *Revolutionary Russia, 1917*. 2nd ed. New York: Charles Scribner's Sons, 1989. Good brief history of 1917.

Wade, Rex A. "Irakli Tsereteli and Siberian Zimmerwaldism." *Journal of Modern History* 39, 4 (December 1967): 425–31. The origins of Revolutionary Defensism.

———. *Red Guards and Worker's Militias in the Russian Revolution*. Stanford, CA: Stanford University Press, 1984. Explores worker self-assertiveness through the most militant worker organization of 1917 and their interaction with the political parties.

———. *The Russian Revolution: 1917*. Cambridge: Cambridge University Press, 2000. The most recent general history of the revolution, reflecting the most recent scholarship and stressing the interaction of social and political currents in producing the revolution's outcome by the end of 1917.

———. *The Russian Search for Peace, February–October 1917*. Stanford, CA: Stanford University Press, 1969. A study of the interaction of revolutionary politics and foreign policy in 1917.

Wildman, Allan K. *The End of the Russian Imperial Army: The Old Army and the Soldiers' Revolt (March–April 1917)*. Princeton, NJ: Princeton University Press, 1980; *The End of the Russian Imperial Army: The Road to Soviet Power and Peace*. Princeton, NJ: Princeton University Press, 1987. These two outstanding books provide the best, and detailed, account of the revolution in the army.

THE CIVIL WAR ERA

Avrich, Paul. *Kronstadt, 1921*. Princeton, NJ: Princeton University Press, 1970. Best account of the Kronstadt revolt, with documents.

Benvenuti, Francesco. *The Bolsheviks and the Red Army, 1918–1922*. Cambridge: Cambridge University Press, 1988. Excellent study of the building of the Red Army, focused on the controversies within the Communist Party about the army.

Daniels, Robert V. *The Conscience of the Revolution: Communist Opposition in Soviet Russia*. Cambridge, MA: Harvard University Press, 1960. Excellent study of the controversies within the party after taking power.

David-Fox, Michael. *Revolution of the Mind: Higher Learning Among the Bolsheviks, 1918–1921*. Ithaca, NY: Cornell University Press, 1997. Excellent study of the new Bolshevik institutions of higher learning that attempted to create a new political and intellectual elite for the new state.

Figes, Orlando. *Peasant Russia, Civil War: The Volga Countryside in Revolution, 1917–1921*. Oxford: Clarendon, 1989. Excellent study of the revolution and civil war among the peasantry.

Fitzpatrick, Sheila. *The Commissariat of Enlightenment. Soviet Organization of Education and the Arts under Lunacharsky, October 1917–1921*. Cambridge: Cambridge University Press, 1970. Good exposition of educational and artistic policies and activities, the effort at "enlightenment" of the Russian people, during the optimistic first years, through the most important government agency in that area.

Gerson, Leonard. *The Secret Police in Lenin's Russia*. Philadelphia, PA: Temple University Press, 1976. Origins of the secret police, emphasizing Lenin's role.

Holmes, Larry. *The Kremlin and the Schoolhouse: Reforming Education in Soviet Russia 1917–1931*. Bloomington and Indianapolis: Indiana University Press, 1991. Excellent study of the early educational policy of the Soviet regime, during a time of extensive experimentation with educational methods, in an effort to find ways to use education to transform values and society.

Kenez, Peter. *The Birth of the Propaganda State, Soviet Methods of mass Mobilization 1917–1929*. Cambridge: Cambridge University Press, 1985. Stimulating account of early Bolshevik efforts at agitation, propaganda and political education.

———. *Civil War in South Russia, 1918–20*. 2 vols. Berkeley: University of California Press, 1971–77. One of the best accounts of the civil war, and indispensable for the study of the South Russian campaigns and Denikin.

Leggett, George. *The Cheka: Lenin's Political Police. The All-Russian Extraordinary Commission for Combating Counter-Revolution and Sabotage*. Oxford and New York: Oxford University Press, 1981. Origins and development of the secret police, with emphasis upon Lenin's role, but also the involvement of others such as the Left SRs.

Lincoln, W. Bruce. *Red Victory: A History of the Russian Civil War*. New York: Simon and Schuster, 1989. Very good and readable history of the civil war.

Malle, Silvana. *The Economic Organization of War Communism, 1918–1921*. Cambridge: Cambridge University Press, 1985. Examines the economic policies of the Soviet regime under War Communism; excellent.

Mally, Lynn. *The Culture of the Future: The Proletkult Movement in Revolutionary Russia 1917–1922*. Berkeley: University of California Press, 1990. Very good account of the most important of the visionary movements that intended to create a new society through cultural transformation.

Mawdsley, Evan. *The Russian Civil War*. Boston and London: Allen and Unwin, 1987. Very good history of the civil war, especially strong on the military aspects.

McAuley, Mary. *Bread and Justice: State and Society in Petrograd, 1917–1922*. Oxford: Clarendon, 1991. A study of the interrelation of social and political factors during early Bolshevik rule and how they shaped the Soviet state.

Pereira, N.G.O. *White Siberia: The Politics of Civil War*. Montreal: McGill-Queens University Press, 1996. The civil war in Siberia, with emphasis on the White governments.

Pipes, Richard. *The Formation of the Soviet Union: Communism and Nationalism, 1917–1923*. rev. ed. Cambridge, MA: Harvard University Press, 1964. Classic account of the nationality question and the formation of the Soviet Union.

Radkey, Oliver H. *The Unknown Civil War in Soviet Russia. A Study of the Green Movement in the Tambov Region, 1920–1921*. Stanford, CA: Hoover Institution Press, 1976. Explores the Tambov, or Antonov, rebellion, and the phenomenon of peasant insurrection.

Remington, Thomas F. *Building Socialism in Bolshevik Russia: Ideology and Industrial Organization 1917–1921*. Pittsburgh, PA: University of Pittsburgh Press, 1984. Excellent study of War Communism and the interplay of ideology and practicality in early Soviet economic policies.

Rigby, T. H. *Lenin's Government: Sovnarkom 1917–1922*. London: Cambridge University Press, 1979. A careful study of how the early Soviet government developed and functioned in the context of civil war and war communism.

Sakwa, Richard. *Soviet Communists in Power: A Study of Moscow During the Civil War, 1918–1921*. New York: St. Martin's Press, 1988. Contributes significantly to understanding of the development of Bolshevik policies during the civil war.

Schapiro, Leonard. *The Origin of the Communist Autocracy. Political Opposition in the Soviet State: First Phase, 1917–1922*. Cambridge, MA: Harvard University Press, 1955. An early, but still valuable, account of the politics of early Soviet Russia.

Smele, Jonathan. *Civil War in Siberia*. Cambridge and New York: Cambridge University Press, 1996. Exhaustive, detailed, account of the civil war in Siberia.

Smith, Jeremy. *The Bolsheviks and the National Question, 1917–1923*. New York: St. Martin's Press, 1999. Perceptive discussion of the development of a Bolshevik policy on the explosive nationality question, and how that led to the formation of the USSR.

Swain, Geoff. *The Origins of the Russian Civil War*. London: Longman, 1996. Traces the origins of the civil war back to the second half of 1917, but focuses on 1918; excellent for discussion of the complexity of the opposition to the Bolsheviks, especially the often overlooked role of moderate socialists.

Von Hagen, Mark. *Soldiers in the Proletarian Dictatorship: The Red Army and the Soviet Socialist State, 1917–1930.* Ithaca, NY and London: Cornell University Press, 1990. Excellent study on the Red Army and its relationship to the building of the new state.

FOREIGN RELATIONS AND INTERVENTION

Debo, Richard K. *Revolution and Survival: The Foreign Policy of Soviet Russia, 1917–1918.* Toronto: University of Toronto Press, 1970; and *Survival and Consolidation: The Foreign Policy of Soviet Russia, 1918–1921.* Montreal: McGill-Queen's University Press, 1992. The best account of Soviet foreign policy of this period.

Foglesong, David S. *America's Secret War Against Bolshevism: U.S. Intervention in the Russian Civil War, 1917–1920.* Chapel Hill: University of North Carolina Press, 1995. A new and insightful account of American intervention.

Kennan, George Frost. *Soviet-American Relations, 1917–20.* 2 vols. Princeton, NJ: Princeton University Press, 1956, 1958. The classic account of early Soviet-American relations and intervention; a wealth of detail not readily available elsewhere.

McDermott, Kevin, and Jeremy Agnew. *The Comintern: A History of International Communism from Lenin to Stalin.* New York: St. Martin's Press, 1997. A good recent account of the development and functioning of the Comintern.

Thompson, John A. *Russia, Bolshevism, and the Versailles Peace.* Princeton, NJ: Princeton University Press, 1966. Russia's role, and the Bolshevik question, at the peace conference.

Ullman, Richard H. *Anglo-Soviet Relations, 1917–1921.* 3 vols. Princeton, NJ: Princeton University Press, 1956–58. Best work on Soviet-British relations of the era; very detailed.

Unterberger, Betty. *America's Siberian Expedition, 1918–1920.* Durham, NC: Duke University Press, 1956. Fine work on American intervention in Siberia.

Wade, Rex A. *The Russian Search for Peace, February–October 1917.* Stanford, CA: Stanford University Press, 1969. Study of the Russian effort to get out of the war in 1917, and the impact of that on Russian politics.

Warth, Robert D. *The Allies and the Russian Revolution: From the Fall of the Monarchy to the Peace of Brest-Litovsk.* Durham, NC: Duke University Press, 1954. Good account of the Allied governments' responses to the Russian Revolution.

White, John A. *The Siberian Intervention.* Princeton, NJ: Princeton University Press, 1956. Fine work on Allied intervention in Siberia.

Index

About the Author

REX A. WADE is Professor of Russian history at George Mason University. He is the author of several books on Russian history, including *The Russian Revolution, 1917* (2000), *Red Guards and Workers' Militias in the Russian Revolution* (1984), *The Russian Search for Peace, February-October 1917* (1969), and *Documents of Soviet History* (1991–1995). He is also the author of numerous articles and essays on Russian and Ukrainian history.